THOMSON
COURSE TECHNOLOGY
Professional ■ Technical ■ Reference

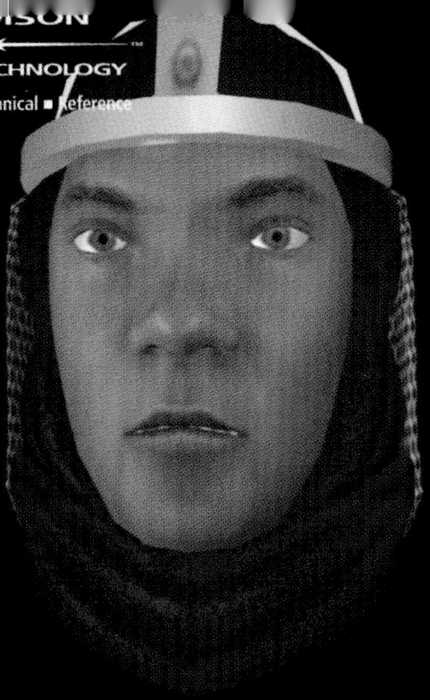

Character Emotion

in 2D and 3D Animation

Les Pardew

ISBN-10: 1-59863-381-3

ISBN-13: 978-1-59863-381-8

Library of Congress Catalog Card Number: 2006940095

Printed in the United States of America

08 09 10 11 12 BU 10 9 8 7 6 5 4 3 2 1

Publisher and General Manager, Thomson Course Technology PTR:
Stacy L. Hiquet

Associate Director of Marketing:
Sarah O'Donnell

Manager of Editorial Services:
Heather Talbot

Marketing Manager:
Jordan Casey

Acquisitions Editor:
Megan Belanger

Marketing Assistant:
Adena Flitt

Project Editor:
Jenny Davidson

Technical Reviewer:
Kelly Murdock

PTR Editorial Services Coordinator:
Erin Johnson

Interior Layout Tech:
Bill Hartman

Cover Designer:
Mike Tanamachi

CD-ROM Producer:
Brandon Penticuff

Indexer:
Katherine Stimson

Proofreader:
Sara Gullion

THOMSON
COURSE TECHNOLOGY™
Professional ■ Technical ■ Reference

Thomson Course Technology PTR, a division of Thomson Learning Inc.
25 Thomson Place ■ Boston, MA 02210 ■ http://www.courseptr.com

ACKNOWLEDGMENTS

I want to acknowledge and thank all of the many people who have helped me to create this book. My deepest thanks go to my family and especially to my wife who has put up with living with an artist and all of the ups and downs that brings. I also want to thank the many mentors who taught me about art. They may never know how much they have influenced my life. I also want to thank my editors Jenny Davidson, Megan Belanger, and Stacy Hiquet without whose help this book would be impossible.

ABOUT THE AUTHOR

Les Pardew is a videogame and entertainment industry veteran with over 22 years of entertainment industry experience. His work in the industry includes more than 120 videogame titles, 12 books, and numerous illustrations for magazines, books, and film. He began his career in film animation and later moved to videogames where he has found a permanent home. He currently serves as president of Alpine Studios, which he founded with Ross Wolfley in the fall of 2000.

Les is a prolific artist who loves to work on the computer and with traditional media. On the computer he is an accomplished 3D artist, creating and animating characters for many videogames. In traditional media, his first love is drawing followed closely by oil painting. His favorite subject is people. He can often be seen drawing a portrait or designing a character for a game in his sketchbook.

CONTENTS

Introduction vi

Chapter 1: Emotion in Life 1
- Seeing Emotion 2
  - Get a Mirror 2
  - Actor 3
  - Observation 4
- Human Emotion 4
  - Contrasting Emotions 6
- Above and Beyond 8
- 2D and 3D Animation 8
  - Software 8
  - Getting Started 11

Chapter 2: Body Language 13
- The Most Important Language 14
  - Acting 14
  - Fluency 14
- Animating Body Language 15
  - Figure Artist 17
- The Emotional Body 24
  - Anger 24
  - Surprise 25
  - Happy (Joy) 25
  - Sad (Dejected) 26
  - Authoritarian (I'm the Boss) 26
  - Only a Sampling 27

Chapter 3: Emotional Transitions 29
- Woody 30
- States and Reactions 30
- Animating Reactions 30
  - Anticipation 31
  - Building 31
  - Key Reaction 32
  - Let Down 32
- Animating Emotional States 33
  - Surprise 34
  - Fear 39
  - Anger 42

Chapter 4: Exaggeration in Animating Emotions 47
- How Emotions Are Exaggerated 48
  - Contrast 48
  - Purpose 48
  - Types of Exaggeration 48
- Multiple Exaggerations 63

Chapter 5: Facial Expressions 65
- Expressions in Real Life 66
- Understanding the Human Head 67
  - Bones of the Head 68
  - Muscles of the Head 69
- Animating the Head in 3D 72
  - Building 3D Heads That Animate 72
  - Adding Influence 75

Chapter 6: Emotion and Timing 115
- Types of Timing 116
  - Internal Timing 116
  - External Timing 123
  - Story Timing 128
- Timing and Emotions 130

Chapter 7: Emotions, Story, and Environments 133
- Characters and Settings 134
  - Perspective 134
  - Contrast 135
  - Style 136
  - Lighting 137
- Dramatic Effect 137
  - Humor 138
  - Suspense 138
  - Sentiment 138
  - Surprise 139
  - Fear 139
  - Anger 139
  - Intrigue 140
  - Interest 140
- Dramatic Techniques 140
  - Timing 141
  - Camera Movement 141
  - Expression 142
  - Lighting 142
  - Sound Effects 142
  - Dialogue 143
  - Music 143
  - Drama in Your Production 143
- Creating a 3D Set 144

Chapter 8: Bringing It All Together 187
- The Audience 188
  - Defining Your Audience 190
- Total Production 191
  - Story 192
  - Animation 192
  - Music 192
  - Characters 193
  - Sound Effects 193
  - Sets 193
  - Voice 194
  - Production 194
- Bringing It Together 194

Appendix A: Maya Tutorial 197

Appendix B: Image Gallery 221

Index 244

INTRODUCTION

If you picked up this book, you are probably looking for a way to bring more emotion to your animated characters. Emotion in animation is much more than just depicting emotion in a character. In this book, character emotion is covered as well as other aspects of animation, such as environments and conveying emotion to the audience. My hope in writing this book is to give you an overall look at how to develop emotion in your animation from animating emotions in your characters all the way to developing emotion through the entire show.

Many years ago when I was beginning my animation career, I had an opportunity to animate Mickey Mouse for a Disney computer game. Up until that point I had created animation for videos, film, and games but never had a challenge like animating Mickey. It became evident very quickly to me that Disney cared a great deal about how Mickey animated. After my first several attempts were rejected, I received some very specific guidelines on how he was to look. One of the main things my animation was missing was emotion. My animation moved smoothly and was correct in many ways, but it lacked life because it didn't show any emotional qualities. I had to start over again, but eventually I was successful in getting Mickey to walk and move with feeling.

From the experience of animating Mickey, I began to see that animation is more than technical knowledge; it is the ability to express emotions to the audience. I began to experiment with my characters and observe emotion in real life. I think every animator needs to go through the same process.

Getting a character or scene to have emotion means more than just animating smooth animation. It means that you understand and develop movements and environments that are expressive. You need to create something that carries the emotion to your audience. In writing this book, I have included many concepts and ideas that I have learned over the years to bring greater emotion to my work.

I don't know if these concepts are taught in schools because I had to learn most of them on the job.

Most of what I have gained about emotion in animation has come from observation. There is no school quite as good as watching how people move in real life. Although much of animation is exaggerated, it finds its basis in the day-to-day reality that is our own existence. By drawing on the emotions we see in life, the animator is enabled to show animation that people can identify with because they recognize how it feels.

There is really no way that I can show you every emotion and give you detailed instructions on how to animate all those emotions. What I have attempted to do in this book is to explain how to understand emotion animation in general and give you some tools for developing an understanding of how to animate emotion. From there my hope is that you will be able to take the things you learn from this book and further your study of emotion by drawing from the emotions that surround you. By careful observation, you should be able to learn how to develop any emotion in animation.

In addition to character emotion, I also include some chapters about developing emotion in environments and the overall story. For emotion to truly be effective, it must touch the audience. If every aspect of the scene contributes to the emotional message, the animator will be many times more effective in communicating the real feeling or message of the animated sequence.

Thanks for picking up this book. I hope it helps you in your animation. Good luck!

Les Pardew

CHAPTER 1

© istockphoto.com/ Sharon Dominick

Emotion in Life

Life is full of emotion. People experience thousands of emotions every day. Some emotions are blatant, such as an angry gesture from a passing motorist on the highway, while others are subtle, such as the slight lifting of an eyebrow at an interesting discovery in an animation book. Your life is a constant stream of emotions that can be read, from the way you stand, how you move, what you say, to the subtle movements of your face.

You learn to read emotion at a very young age. Children pick up on the emotion of their parents. If mom and dad are happy, the child will feel more at ease. If they are upset or angry, the child will pick up on it and feel uncomfortable.

As you grow older, your ability to interpret emotions in others becomes more acute. For example, students learn how to judge the moods of their teacher; salespersons learn to study the interest of potential buyers; executives learn to read the intent of their peers; and animators learn to express emotions in their animated drawings. Some people are better at detecting emotions than others. You need to be one of the best at detecting emotions in others.

In animation, one of your biggest challenges will be to express emotion in your characters in a convincing manner. To express emotion you first have to understand emotion. You need to be able to recognize the myriad ways that emotion is portrayed. Things like an angry gesture are easy to understand, but you have to know how to make a person look confused or pensive or even wistful. What is a contemplative stance? How do you animate bewilderment? What does a person look like when they are apathetic or despondent?

In this chapter you will first learn how to see emotion in your everyday life so that you can then apply what you see to your animated characters. Animation, like acting, is based on life. Life is the foundation, even if the animation is exaggerated. By first learning how to see emotion, you will then be better equipped to portray emotion in your animation.

Seeing Emotion

Emotion is so much a part of our lives that we tend to recognize it on a subconscious rather than on a conscious level. As an animator you will need to focus your attention on recognizing the thousands of subtle changes that indicate specific emotions. These changes are noticeable in just about every aspect of our bodies. Emotion in animation is much more than learning a few facial expressions; you have to look at the body as a whole, including the face.

Not everybody expresses his emotions in the same way. Some people are very reserved, showing very subtle changes in emotional reaction. Others like the young man in Figure 1.1 have extreme emotional reactions.

Figure 1.1 The young man has an extreme emotional reaction. © istockphoto.com/ Nicholas Monu

As you can see, his emotional reaction is extreme and he is easy to recognize as someone who is both surprised and excited at the same time. Even though the reaction is extreme, you should note some characteristics of the emotion. For example, the wide-open mouth, the raised eyebrows, and the popping eyeballs all are characteristic of this type of emotion. You can use each of these to varying degrees to create varying amounts of excited surprise in your animated characters. If you want, you can take your animation to an even greater extreme than what is possible in real life, like exaggerating the popping eyeballs or the opening of the character's mouth.

Before you start to draw, you should practice the emotion yourself. Some tips for practicing are listed next.

Get a Mirror

You are your best source for experimenting with different emotions. You are the only person who can understand the emotions that you feel. You may be able to see emotions in others, but you can feel your own. This is where a mirror becomes an essential tool for animators. Place it on your desk and look into it often. It has nothing to do with vanity. You are not admiring yourself. You are learning from yourself.

Once you have the mirror in place, try a few facial expressions and see what happens to your face with each one. Take notes if you have to so you can remember the characteristics of each emotion. The idea here is for you to gain familiarity with the range of expression that you can achieve with your own face.

Often an animator's best friend is a mirror. It is standard equipment for every animation studio that I know of.

EXERCISE

With a mirror in front of you, try making some extreme facial expressions and sketch the results. See how large you can make your eyes and how far you can open your mouth. Watch how your face changes when you smile or frown. Notice how your eyes change with each expression. Watch your brow.

As you experiment, you should begin to see that even the smallest changes can have completely different meanings. For example, try lifting your brow when you smile. Next, try lowering your brow when you smile. Even though both expressions are smiling expressions they will seem entirely different in meaning to the observer.

Expression is more than just facial changes. It usually incorporates the entire body. Step back from the mirror so that you can see your entire body in it. Try standing in a happy stance. Next, try standing in a sad stance. What happens when you are excited? What about if you are scared?

While it may be a little difficult to sketch while you are posing, you can make quick sketches in your sketchpad capturing the important changes in posture for each emotion.

Actor

Often in the middle of working, animators will get up from their desk and go through the action they are attempting to animate. To the casual observer, the scene must seem a little odd but there is real purpose in the animator experiencing the motion and seeing it in a mirror. If you are ever struggling with a movement or emotion, work on acting it out yourself. This will help you to not only see what the motion should be but also to experience it. The experience will tell you if the motion seems awkward or natural. It will also help you to feel and experience what you want to put your animated character through.

Animators are actors. They act through their drawings rather than on stage. You may not think of yourself as a performer but if you want to be an animator, you need to be one. In fact, it could be argued that good animators know more about acting than actors do. You have to study acting in every detail. Nothing can be left to chance because you have to draw each action and emotion. While you may not be able to perform on stage, the characters created can have every aspect of a premier performance.

The advantage of understanding acting gives you, the animator, a greater range of experience in developing personality and emotion in your characters. Animators should take acting classes or even work in amateur performing groups, if there are any available. More than anything, however, you need to study life.

Observation

The foundation for acting is in life. The best, most natural actions come not on the stage but in the daily affairs of life when people are dealing with real emotions rather than made up ones. A great actor mimics real emotions. In life the characters are not acting but they are expressing real emotion. Therefore, to see real emotion you need to be observant of all of the emotion that surrounds us each day.

Keenly observing others may seem a little uncomfortable at first because in society we are often taught to ignore others' outbursts. The reasons for this are many but the biggest one is that seeing others' emotions often touches our own, causing us to feel to some degree the pain or hurt of the other person. This connection can be draining so to protect ourselves from emotion overload, we learn to only share with a select few. Because of this reluctance to keenly observe others, most people go through life never really seeing or understanding how emotion is expressed.

Because ignoring life will never help you depict it, you don't have the luxury of passing by the emotions of others. Instead you have to be open to any and all emotions, taking mental notes or sketching them as they occur. To help you get started, this next section of the chapter will provide some examples of emotions and give you the chance to study them.

Human Emotion

In this section of the chapter we will be examining some photographs of real people expressing a variety of emotions. Study each photograph looking for the specific traits of the emotion. Sketch a few of them to get more familiar. While we can't go through every emotion, we can get you started in learning how to analyze emotional reactions in people. From there you should be able to find ample examples in your own surroundings for the vast array of human feeling.

Frustration

We show frustration in many ways. Here is an example of someone showing extreme frustration in Figure 1.2. You can see it in her facial expression and also in her stance.

There are many signs of this woman's frustration. Her eyes are closed tightly. Her mouth has the lips parted and pushed forward. Her brows are scrunched together and forward. Her head is pushed forward with her neck extended. Her arms are raised to the sides of her head as if she is ready to pull her hair out. Her back is bowed as if she is coiled to explode.

A photograph can only show a specific moment in time and not the full actions that a person goes through to express an emotion. This picture shows a moment of frustration. The full animation will have to be imagined. Can you see her throwing her hands forward and lifting her head in a scream with neck clenched?

Figure 1.2 This woman is having a hard day and showing it in both her expression and actions.
© istockphoto.com/ Sharon Dominick

Carefree

Now let's look at the other extreme. Figure 1.3 shows a picture of a carefree young lady in an outdoor setting.

This photograph shows a person who is having a good, carefree day. She is in an open posture with arms extended and relaxed. Her body is loose with no tension showing in the shoulders and neck area. Her hands are also open and relaxed. Her face is relaxed with a dreamy smile as if she is enjoying the moment immensely.

Contrasting the two previous photographs can show the extreme difference between these two very different emotions.

Figure 1.3 The relaxed stance and open smile show the woman in this picture is stress free.
© istockphoto.com/ Valentin Casarsa

Daydreaming

For our next example, take a look at Figure 1.4.

The girl in the picture appears to be daydreaming. From the look of the picture it is a pleasant dream because she doesn't seem to be tense but rather relaxed and contemplative. The aspects of the picture that give her the daydreamy look are the way she is pursing her lips and the way her eyes are rolled up. The raised eyebrows also help suggest her mood.

Figure 1.4 Why does the person in this picture look like she is daydreaming? © istockphoto.com/ Lucas Cornwell

Pain

For the next example let's take a look at someone who is obviously in pain, as shown in Figure 1.5.

Pain is another powerful emotion. In the photograph, the girl is in obvious pain. The pain is written in her expression and her stance. Her hands are placed around her face. Her head is tilted slightly back with her brows pinched together and her eyes closed. In addition her mouth is open and in a grimace.

Figure 1.5 Why does this girl look like she is in pain?
© istockphoto.com/ Fred Goldstein

Contrasting Emotions

Another good way to study emotions is to contrast similar emotions and look for significant differences. These differences may be as small as a clenched fist or a raised eyebrow. The important thing to learn is how to spot the differences so that you can put them in your own animation.

Let's look at something that is emotionally a little closer together than the previous examples. Figures 1.6 and 1.7 are similar in that the person in each photo is sitting with one or more hands raised to the face.

Okay, this one is a little subtler. Obviously from the setting you can tell that Figure 1.6 takes place in what appears to be a bedroom and Figure 1.7 on the sidelines of a soccer game. Both people in these photographs seem to be upset but the nature of why they are upset is different and so are their reactions.

The soccer player seems angry at being benched, while the other guy seems to be more introspective. They may both be angry but the signs show that the anger for the soccer player is directed outward and the anger for the other guy is inward. Note, for example, the clenched fists and direct stare of the soccer player. His posture even while sitting is squared off and ready for action.

On the other hand, our other guy only has one hand raised while the other is resting on his thigh. His posture is more relaxed.

The key difference in the two, however, is in the eyes. The soccer player has his eyes open and looking straight ahead, while the other guy's eyes are half-closed as if he isn't really looking at anything. This is the type of subtle difference that can completely change the feeling of an animated character.

Figure 1.6 The person in the photograph appears to be unhappy. Why? © istockphoto.com/ Renee Lee

Figure 1.7 This person is also unhappy but there is a difference. What is it? © istockphoto.com/ nikada33

Take a look at the following photographs in Figures 1.8, 1.9, and 1.10 and see if you can find the characteristics that define each emotion.

What were you able to come up with? Did you catch the way the caller in the first picture was holding his mouth? What did that tell you about what he was thinking?

The second photo was filled with action. He seems to be excited. What would you need to change in the character to make him appear angry?

In the third picture the person is holding his head but it doesn't appear to be a headache because there is no tension in his brow. He seems to have just remembered something that he forgot.

Each of the people in these photographs is telling us a part of a story by their actions. In animation you will be doing the same with your characters as they move about the screen. You can enhance your animation by telling the audience the right story or you can detract from the story by confusing the audience with mixed messages from your character's actions.

A good animator understands how every subtle element of the character's action communicates a message to the audience. Instead of just having the character perform generic lifeless tasks on the screen, the good animator will use actions and movements that are expressive and clear to the audience.

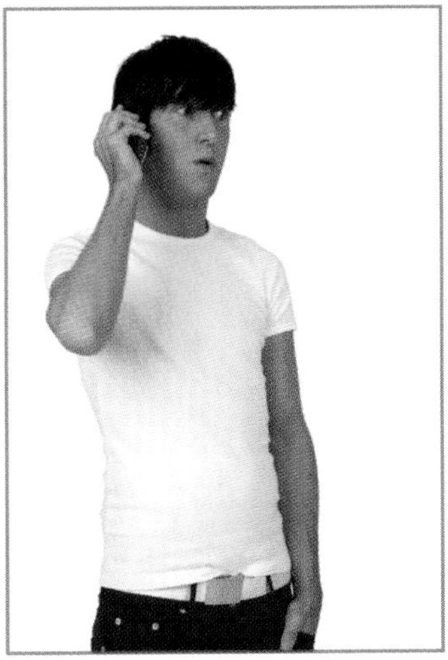

Figure 1.8 You can almost tell what this person is hearing over the phone. © istockphoto.com/ Mikhail Lavrenov

Figure 1.9 This person is showing great excitement. © istockphoto.com/ Bonnie Schupp

Figure 1.10 Does this person have a headache or is something else wrong? © istockphoto.com/ Peter Albrektsen

Above and Beyond

Now that you have identified some elements of individual emotions, it is time to take that experience into the field and use it with your character animation. In this Above and Beyond exercise you need to take one of your characters and draw one of the emotions you see in the photographs in this chapter. See if you can get your character to duplicate the emotion as closely as possible.

At this point you don't want to exaggerate the emotion. It is more important for you to capture the emotion. Once you have a good feel for a particular emotion, you will be better able to exaggerate it because you will understand the important signs of that emotion.

2D and 3D Animation

This book will deal with depicting emotion in both 2D animation and 3D animation. While many of the techniques for creating 2D and 3D animation differ, emotion doesn't really change. What changes are the methods used to create the emotion. This book will focus on not only emotion but also give examples of how to develop that emotion using a variety of 2D and 3D techniques.

Software

Because so much of animation is done on the computer today, many of the examples and techniques shown in this book will use specialized software for examples and exercises. The CD includes links to trial versions of the software used in this book so you can experiment and follow along with the exercises and examples. The software is primarily trial versions to give you an idea of how they work. Later if you decide to continue your study of emotion in animation you may choose to purchase the software. Following is a quick overview of the software used in this book.

Poser

Poser is a 3D animation tool used by many artists for creating complex scenes with animated figures. Poser comes with a huge variety of tools for creating full body animation, including facial animation. It is a very powerful program and not that hard to understand once you get familiar with it. I will go through the basics with you so you can come up to speed quickly. Figure 1.11 shows the Poser interface screen.

Poser is a great program for exploring 3D character animation without having to create the 3D model. Poser comes with several professionally created 3D models and includes a large wardrobe of costumes and props that you can add to your animation. I am sure you will enjoy working with it.

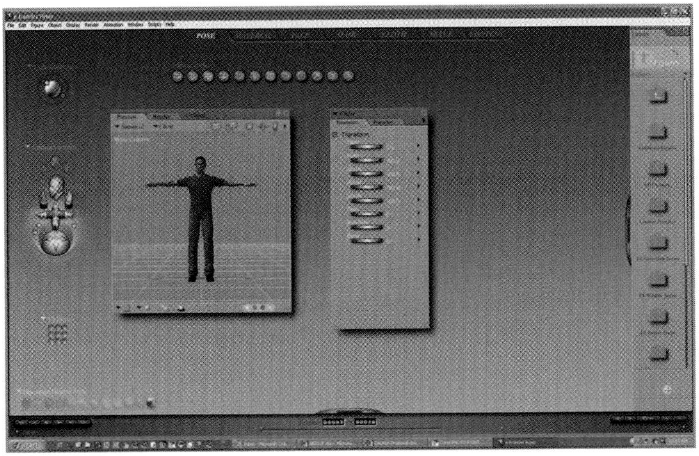

Figure 1.11 This is the Poser 7 Interface screen.

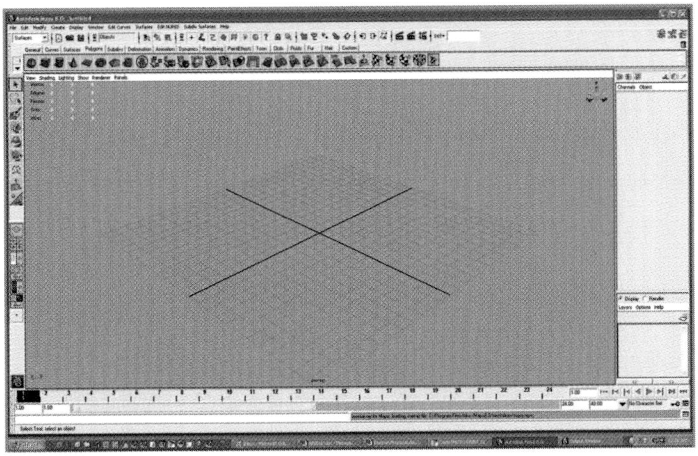

Figure 1.12 This is the Maya 8 Interface screen.

Maya PLE

Maya is a full feature 3D program used for development of professional-quality graphics in motion pictures and video games. It is one of the most powerful 3D programs available on the market today. A link to the full feature personal learning edition is included on the CD accompanying this book. The personal learning edition does not have a trial period but rather lets the user work with the software for as long as needed for personal learning but their files are incompatible with the commercial version. It adds a watermark to the images to indicate that they are for personal use only. Figure 1.12 shows the Maya interface.

Learning to develop emotion in 3D characters requires that you learn how to create the characters so they can be animated for emotion. This book will cover how to set up your models so they can be animated with emotion.

Corel Painter

Corel Painter is a very powerful 2D painting program that focuses on traditional media. In other words, it simulates working with traditional media like pencil, chalk, watercolor, oil paint, and many others. It also has a very useful animation feature that simulates tracing paper levels and allows you to see levels of animation from frame to frame. I am sure you will enjoy this program and find it useful for a number of tasks beyond just animation. Figure 1.13 shows the Painter interface.

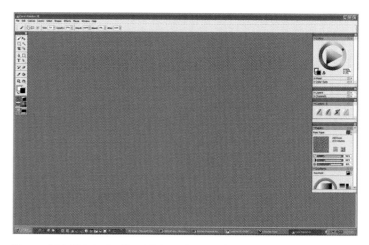

Figure 1.13 This is the Corel Painter 9.5 Interface screen.

FlipBook

FlipBook is a very useful 2D animation program used for creating 2D animations on the computer. With FlipBook you will be able to create your own 2D animated movies. It includes a number of features that make it very useful, like the ability to have multiple levels of animation, X sheets, ink and paint, and camera movements. Figure 1.14 shows the Flipbook interface.

There are of course, many other software programs that animators can use but we don't have space here to cover all of them. These programs should give you a very good start in creating your own wonderfully emotional animations.

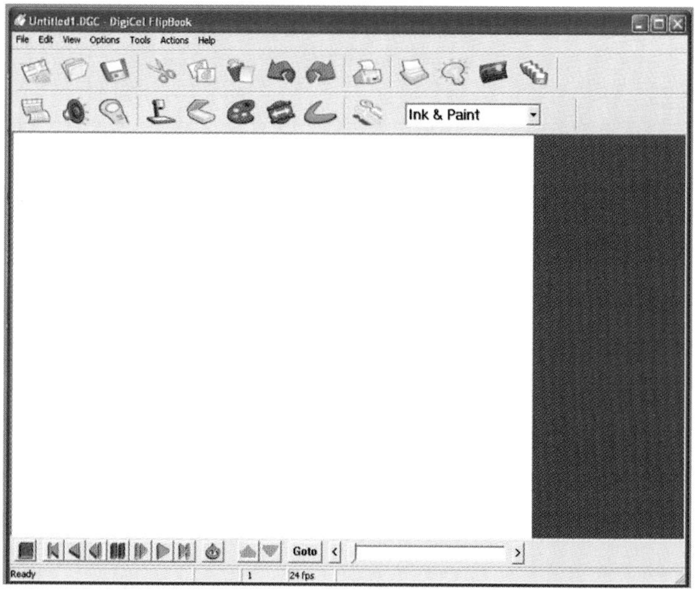

Figure 1.14 This is the Flipbook 4.5 Interface screen.

Getting Started

This book will cover a number of aspects of animation including developing emotion in animation. It is designed to be informative and useful to you the reader. To get the most out of the book, you will need to follow the exercise instructions and also follow along with the many project activities in the book. I have found that one of the best ways to learn a concept in animation is to practice it. Therefore, I have included several step-by-step projects in the book for you to use to help you learn about creating emotion in your characters.

Now if you are ready, let's move on to Chapter 2, where we will take a closer look at body language and how it is one of the most powerful communicators of a person's emotions in all of animation.

CHAPTER 2

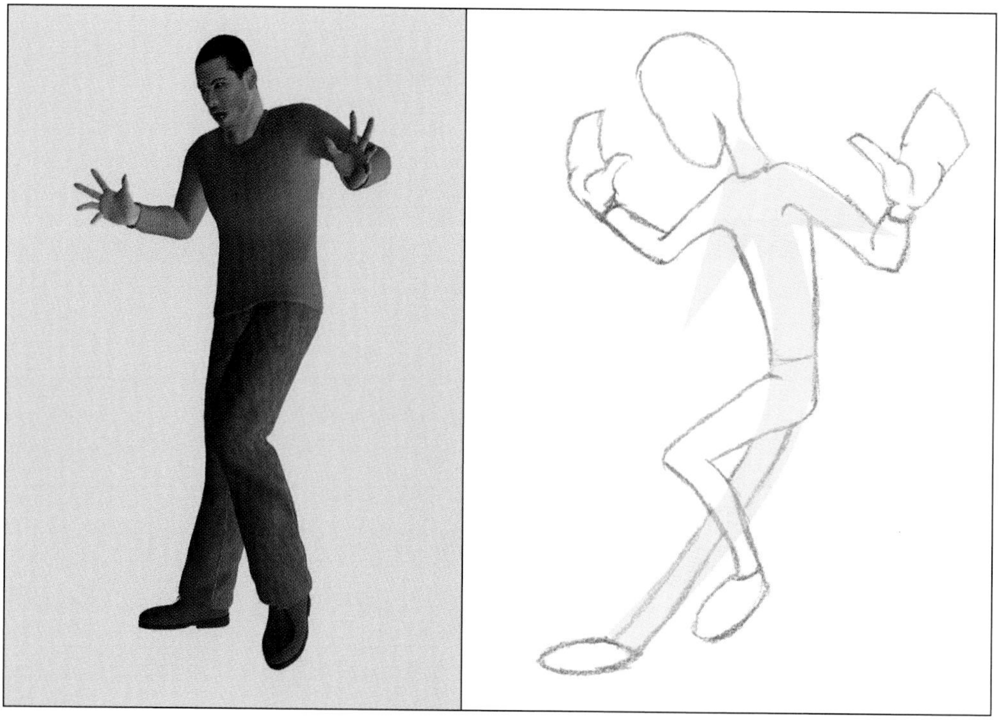

Body Language

Body language is the nonverbal communication of our body. It includes things like hand gestures, posture, facial expressions, and motion patterns. We use body language in our communication every day. In fact, you are probably using it right now even if you don't realize it by the way you are sitting or standing while you are reading this book.

Body language is the first language we learn as a child. Most children can tell if mommy is happy or sad even before they learn the meaning of those words. As we grow older, we refine our skills in body language. We learn how to tell if someone is bored or excited. We learn how to tell when someone is listening to us or ignoring us. We learn how to tell if someone likes us or dislikes us.

The Most Important Language

Even if you don't realize it, you probably use body language more in your day-to-day life than you do verbal or written communication. For example, if you are meeting someone for the first time, you will probably gather more information about that person through body language than you will through conversation. You will no doubt notice whether or not the person is interested in you by the way he looks at you and the way he stands.

Have you ever met someone and immediately liked or disliked him for some reason? The reason for your like or dislike was probably due to how the person acted more than what he said or didn't say. You could probably tell if he was genuine or false. There might have been something about him that just made you feel creepy. Even if you didn't consciously recognize the subtle clues that told you whether to trust this person, you formed an opinion about him because of the body language he was using.

Acting

In many ways, acting is the study of body language. The performer has to do much more than memorize lines. The actor has to convey the message of the part through the body language he employs. Seldom is an actor said to be a good actor or a bad actor because he missed a line. Usually the body language distinguishes a great actor from a poor actor. If you think about some of the greatest performances you have witnessed, there is a good chance that it was the *way* the actor acted the part more than the words said that made the performance wonderful. Like the actor on stage, you need to have a great understanding of body language.

As an animator, you are an actor. Rather than performing live or in front of a camera, you perform through drawings. Your characters do the performance, but you are the one who creates that performance one frame at a time.

Animators arguably use body language more in their work than any other performer. Many animated shows like Disney's "Fantasia" have little or no dialogue. Some animated productions are completely enacted through character actions. In these types of productions where everything relies on the actions of the characters, you have to be fluent in body language.

Fluency

Because body language is so important to animation, it goes hand in hand that you have to understand body language on a conscious level. Most people use body language without thinking about it. If you have ever seen someone waving his arms while talking or tapping his feet while waiting, you have witnessed body language. It is so much a way of life that we don't think about how we are using it similarly to how we seldom think about verb conjugation when we are speaking. Nevertheless, just like the writer who has to understand grammar rules to communicate, you, the animator, have to understand how body language works. If you want to become an animator, body language has to become your language. You have to become as fluent with body language as you are with spoken language.

Animating Body Language

In the first chapter of this book, you should have started looking for emotions in the people around you. Hopefully you have several pages of sketches of people expressing emotions in their day-to-day lives. In this chapter, you will begin to translate your study of emotion into your animations. We will be starting with large movements and working our way down to smaller and more subtle ones. Before we get started, we need a tool to work with to help give you an organized way to develop your animation skills.

One of the best tools for exploring body language that I have found is a software program called Poser from eFrontier, shown in Figure 2.1.

Figure 2.1 The Poser interface.

A link to a demo version of the software is included on the CD with this book so you can use it right away.

eFrontier has another software package, Figure Artist (shown in Figure 2.2), that was created specifically for artists to use for virtual figure models.

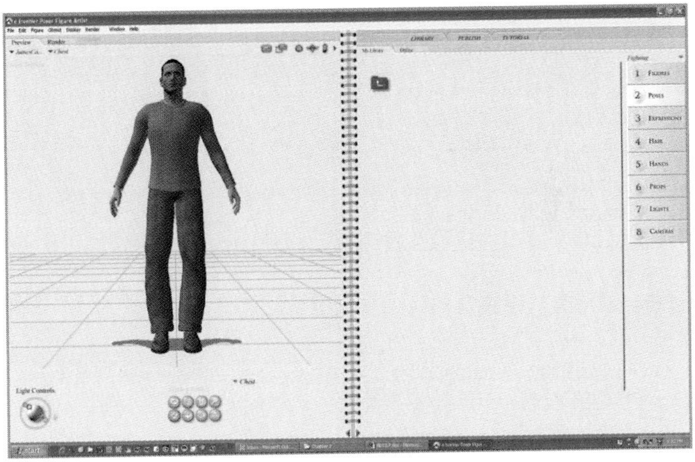

Figure 2.2 The Figure Artist interface.

A link to a demo version of that software is also included on the CD.

The main difference between the two programs is the purpose for which they are used. Figure Artist is specifically designed for virtual model reference. Poser, on the other hand, is a more powerful application designed for posing and animating human characters. Either program is useful for studying body language, but for some of the more advanced aspects of animation, Poser is the better choice. Both programs allow you to load, edit, and save poses and animations. They also come with a library of poses you can use right away.

> **NOTE**
>
> The advantage these two programs give you is that they come with well-constructed 3D models that are already set up for animation. Later in the book, I will show you how to build and set up characters for animation similar to the characters in Figure Artist and Poser. For now, all you need to worry about is how to animate the characters that come with the program.

Figure 2.3 is a sample of one of the models found in both Poser and Figure Artist. Can you tell anything about the model by his pose?

The model is standing in a thoughtful pose. The arm across his chest is a signal to leave him alone while he is thinking. The hand on his chin is an indication that he is deep in thought. Now let's look at another picture of our model in Figure 2.4.

This pose goes beyond confident and into the realm of super confident. The model's feet are very far apart. His arms are open and ready for action. He is looking straight ahead as if to say he is ready for anything.

These two examples show some of the possibilities of working with a program like Poser or Figure Artist. In this next section, I will go over the basics of how to use Figure Artist.

Figure 2.3 The model is in a thoughtful pose.

Figure 2.4 Here the model is standing in a confident super hero pose.

Figure Artist

Let us begin with Figure Artist because it is similar to Poser but not as complex. Your first step is to find and install the demo version of Figure Artist on your computer. You don't need a super new computer to run Figure Artist; however, you need to be running either Windows 2000, Windows XP, or Vista for PC computers and Mac OS X 10.2 or later for Macintosh computers. You will also need to have 256 to 512 MB system memory and about 500 MB to 2 GB of free hard drive space. Graphics programs on computers are memory hogs and take a lot of system memory.

Install the Figure Artist trial version. Once you are ready, bring up the software and we will begin.

Figure 2.5 show the different parts of the Figure Artist user interface. I won't be going into every aspect of the software because you can look in the online help to see the reference manual and tutorials. Instead, I will give you a brief overview and get you started with the program.

The screen is divided into two major parts. The left-hand side of the screen is your document area or stage and the right-hand side contains rooms. The document area is where you set up poses and animation. The rooms give you access to figures, objects, accessories, props, and other elements that you can include in your scene.

The program will launch with a figure model, James, already loaded. James is the figure that we will be working with for now.

There are other figure models in the library that you can explore and work with also.

If you look toward the bottom of the screen on the left-hand side, you will notice some tools that can be used for animating the figure model in the work area. These tools are used for posing the figure, setting up the scene, and changing the lighting, and are similar in both Poser and Figure Artist.

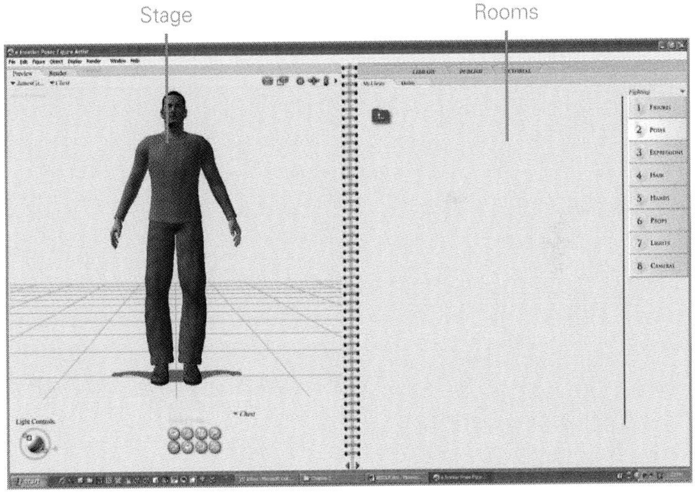

Figure 2.5 The Figure Artist screen is divided into two parts.

Tools

The tool on the lower left of the screen is the Lighting control, shown in Figure 2.6. It can be used to change the intensity and placement of the lights in the scene.

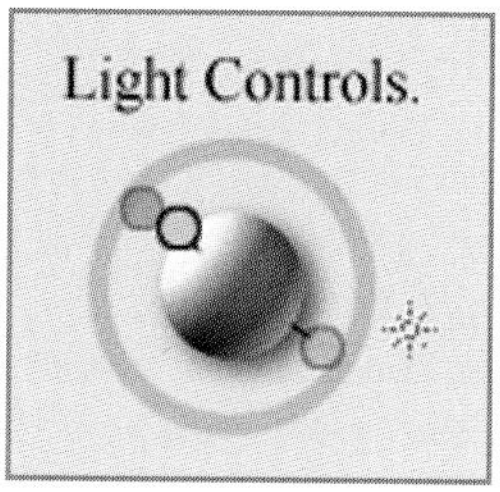

Figure 2.6 The light controls are used for changing the lighting in the scene.

The set of icons in the lower center of the left side are manipulation tools and are shown in Figure 2.7. They are used for scaling, rotating, and moving elements on stage.

Figure 2.7 The editing tools are used for editing elements on stage.

The dials on the right side of the left half of the screen are the parameter dials, shown in Figure 2.8. These dials are used for fine adjustments of the model. You can see the name of each dial if you rest the cursor over it.

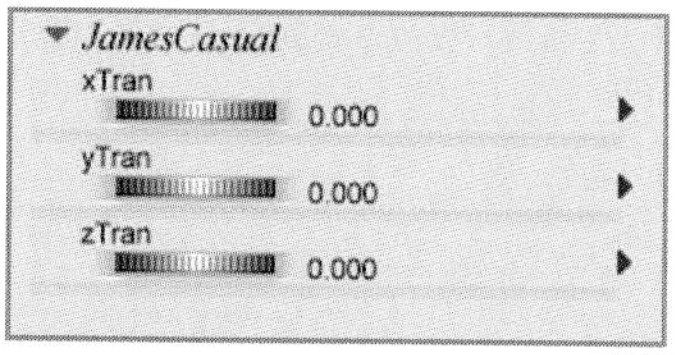

Figure 2.8 The parameter dials are used for fine adjustments.

Using the Tools

Okay, now that you understand a little about the tools, let's try using them. In the drop-down menu just above the parameter dials, select James Casual. James Casual is the name of the model we are using. When you select it from the drop-down menu, you are selecting the entire model rather than just one part of it.

When you select James Casual, you will notice that the parameter dials change. Every selection has its own set of dials. In this case, you are selecting the entire model. This means that any adjustments of parameters will affect the entire model rather than just one part of the model. Make sure the bottom-left edit tool, ztran, is selected. It is the one that looks like a plus sign with an arrow on each end. Go down to the bottom dial labeled "ztrans." This dial controls the model in the z direction. If you click on the dial and move the cursor to the left or right, you will see the model move toward you and away from you. Move your model away from you until it is about the size shown in Figure 2.9.

The other two dials will move the model from side to side and up and down on the stage.

You may notice a set of coordinates next to each dial. These coordinates indicate where the model is in relation to its default position. When you moved the model back, the number next to ztran changed. If you want to move your model a specific distance, you can type the number directly into the coordinate system.

The Rotate Edit tool is located just above the Move tool. Select the Rotate tool. Notice that the dials change when you change the tool. Each edit tool will have its own set of dials, depending on what you have selected on the model. Some parts of the model like the shoulder joints only rotate and do not move.

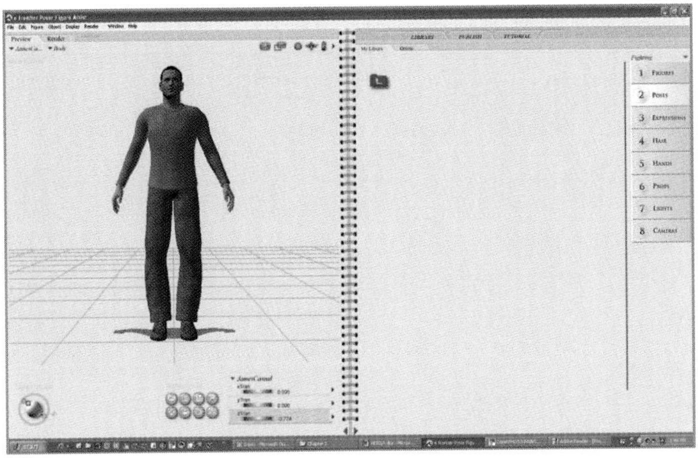

Figure 2.9 Move the model into the stage a little so it is smaller.

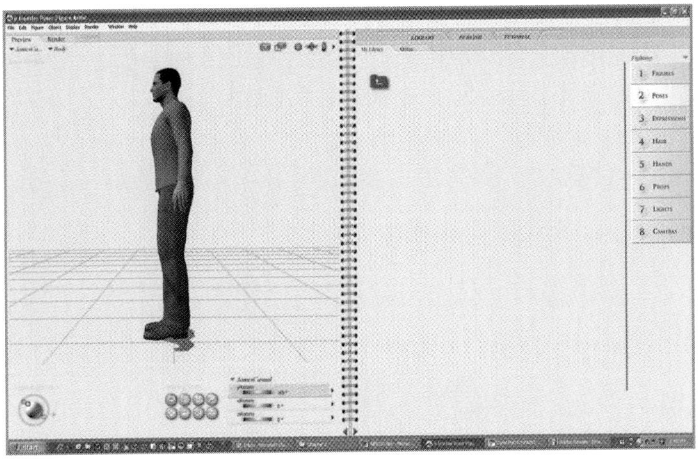

Figure 2.10 Rotate the model to the side.

Try rotating the model so you are seeing him from the side, as shown in Figure 2.10. With the Rotate tool, you are changing the position of the model. You can also change the view by selecting the camera instead of the model. If you rotate or translate the camera, you are moving around the model rather than moving the model. This is an important distinction. When you move the model, you are moving it in 3D space. When you move a camera, you are changing the view and the model does not move in 3D space.

Okay, now that you know how to move your model around, let's take a look at how to move parts of your model. Go to the main menu and select File, New to reset the model to its original position.

You can select the parts of the body you want to move right from the model. Move your cursor over the model. You will notice that parts of the model are outlined as you scroll over them. There are two ways to select parts of the model's body. One is to select the body part from the list like you did when you selected James Casual. The other way is to click on the body part on the model. When selecting parts of the body, I prefer to just click on the body part. The program will only let you choose one body part at a time.

Let's try moving the model's arm. Select the model's left arm around the bicep. You will notice that the parameter dials change to Twist, Front-Back, and Bend. We will be using the Bend parameter to raise the arm. Use the dial and raise the model's left arm, as shown in Figure 2.11.

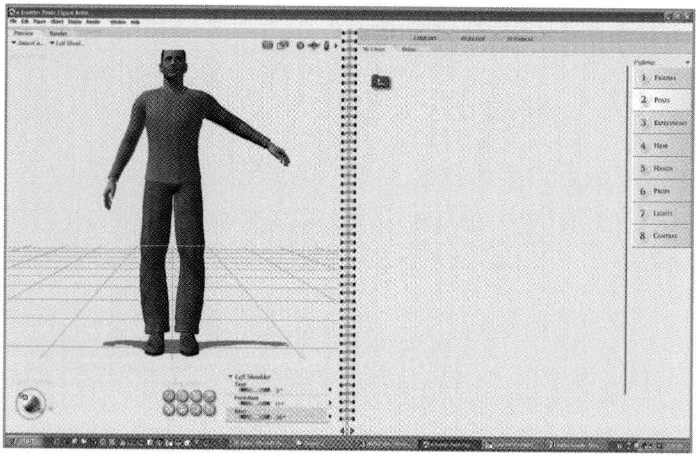

Figure 2.11 Raise the model's arm using the Bend dial.

See, that was fairly easy. You can play around with the model and move different legs and arms if you like. Just select a limb and use the dials.

Using a Library

Figure Artist comes with a selection of poses in several libraries. Often if I am looking for a specific pose, I will browse their libraries and find a pose that is close to what I need. I find it easier to start with a pose that is close to what I want rather than always starting from the new scene spread pose. If you look at Figure 2.12, you will see that there are several folders here, one for each of the preloaded models. You can find these folders by clicking on the up arrow folder.

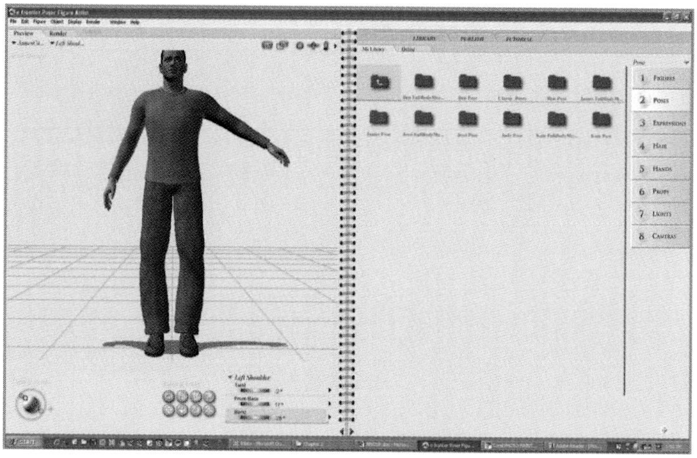

Figure 2.12 There is a folder of poses for each model.

We are using the James model, so select it and then select the folder titled "standing" to select the preloaded standing poses. The folder will open up to look like Figure 2.13, with each type of pose shown in miniature.

I selected "stand 03" by double-clicking it, as shown in Figure 2.14. The model assumes the chosen pose.

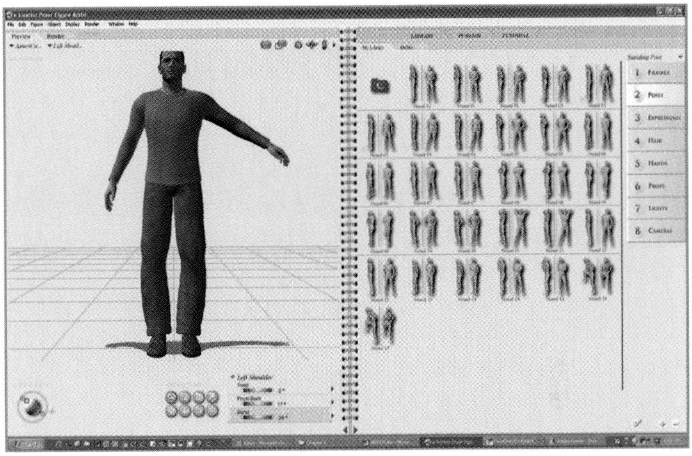

Figure 2.13 Select the standing pose folder.

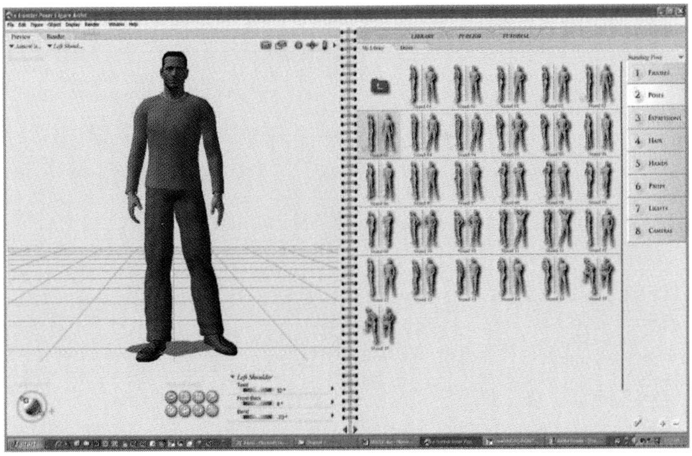

Figure 2.14 The chosen pose is applied to the model.

STEP-BY-STEP

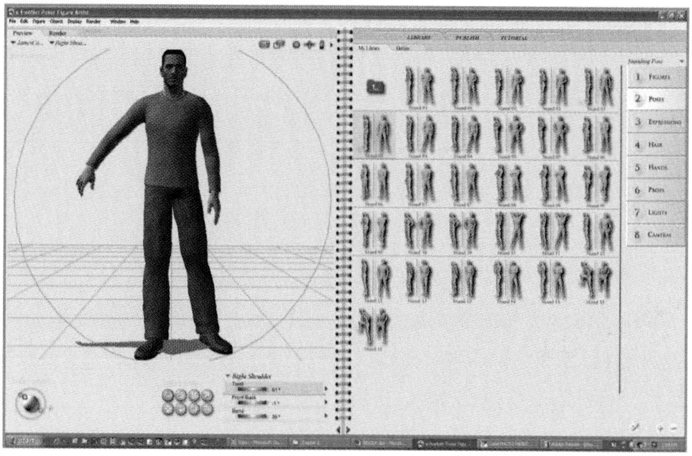

Figure 2.15 Raise the arm.

This is a good pose to start from because it is more of a natural stance. What I want to do is change the pose so his right hand is resting on his hip. Follow these steps:

1

Select the character's right arm and raise it, as shown in Figure 2.15.

2

Twist the forearm so the palm of the hand is facing back.

3

Select the forearm and bend, as shown in Figure 2.16.

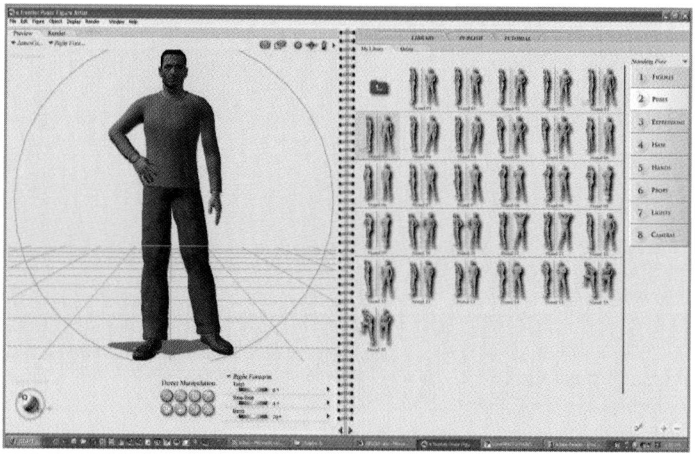

Figure 2.16 Bend the arm at the elbow.

STEP-BY-STEP

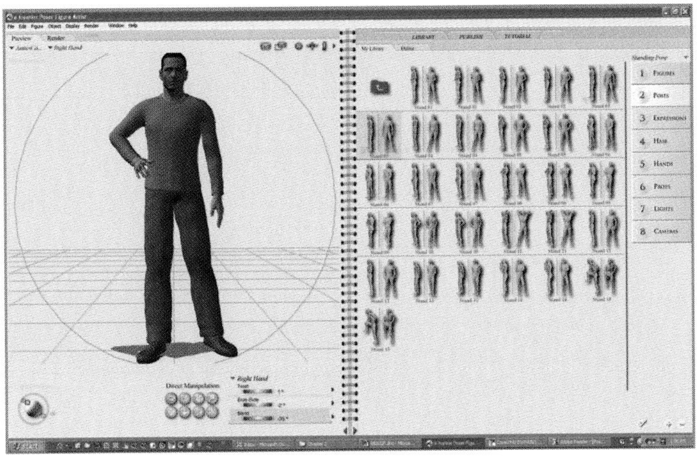

Figure 2.17 Bend the hand up so it can rest on the hip.

4

Select the palm of the hand and bend it up, as shown in Figure 2.17.

5

Place the hand on the character's hip by twisting the upper arm and also bending it until it is in position. Adjust the shoulders as well to make the pose look more natural, as shown in Figure 2.18.

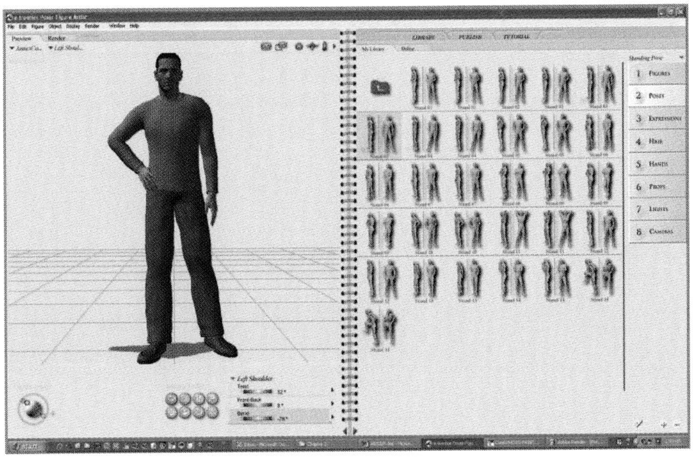

Figure 2.18 Now the model is standing with one hand on his hip.

Okay, these examples are very simple, but I think you can see that this software is great for experimenting with different poses. With it you can work on just about any pose you want and refine it until it is exactly how you want it. Each pose you create can be a reference for developing your key frames. Key frames are key positions during an animation that are at the extremes of a movement. The nice aspect of exploring key frames using Figure Artist is that once you have the model in the exact right position, you can view him from any angle.

The Emotional Body

Our emotions are often expressed through our body language. Close observation will show that there are unique characteristics to almost any emotion. When we react to an emotion, our reaction takes on these characteristics. While not every reaction will be the same, there will be similarities. As you explore the characteristics of each emotional reaction, you will start to notice that there is a flow or overall directional movement. This is very important to notice because the major flow of the body is the most likely aspect of body language for exaggeration, which we will get into in Chapter 4.

Let's take a quick look at a few of the more common emotions and how you might try to depict them in your animation.

Anger

One of the most powerful emotions that an animator has to depict in a character is anger, as shown in Figure 2.19. Anger is also one of the easiest emotions for the audience to interpret.

Anger is indicated by a stiff gesture, with many muscles straining against one another. The stance often looks like two upward pointing arrows, one over the other, as shown in Figure 2.20.

Some general characteristics of anger are as follows:

- The joints in the legs and arms are locked, and the muscles of the limbs strain against one another.
- The feet are firmly planted on the ground, and the hands are tightly clenched.
- The head is often lowered forward, with the shoulders raised.

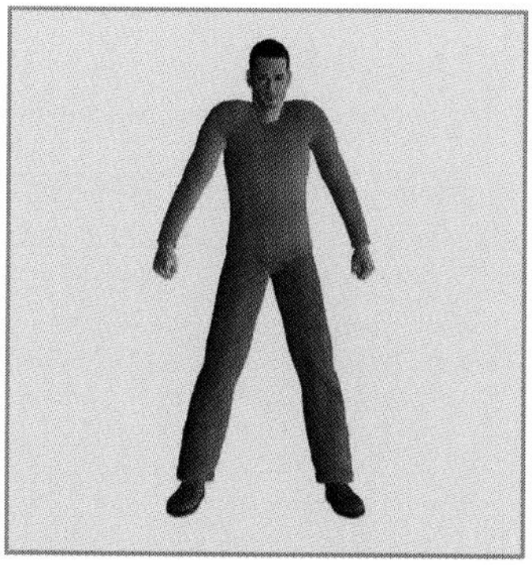

Figure 2.19 Anger is shown by tension in the limbs.

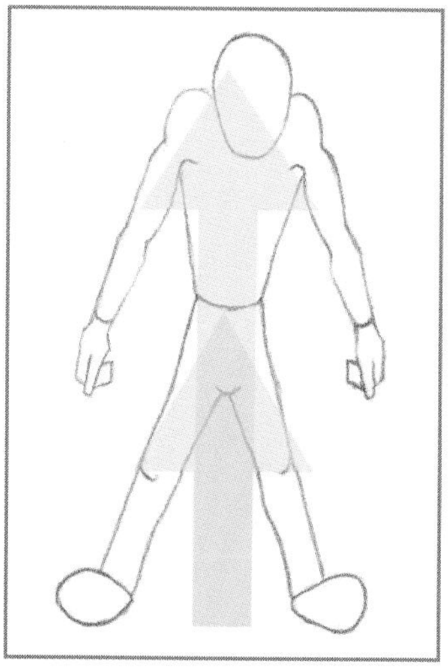

Figure 2.20 Anger often has a double arrow directional movement.

Surprise

Surprise, as shown in Figure 2.21, is a common emotion in animation. It is used often because it involves a lot of drama and has an impact on the audience.

Figure 2.21 Surprise is seen often in animated productions.

Figure 2.22 A strong curve is often found in a surprised reaction.

Surprise is an open gesture that recedes from the object of the surprise. It is characterized by a very strong curve in the character, as shown in Figure 2.22.

Some general characteristics of surprise are as follows:

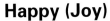

- When a person is in the midst of recoil from a surprise, the hands are opened with the palms forward and the fingers and thumb bent back.
- The arms and sometimes one of the legs are cocked.
- There is a strong action line that curves dramatically from the foot through the body to the head.
- The eyes are usually locked on the object of surprise.

Happy (Joy)

Joy is a happy expression of gleeful contentment, as shown in Figure 2.23. It is a strong contrasting emotion from anger and dejection.

Animators often exaggerate happy emotions to emphasize the character's feelings to the audience. It is a sweeping gesture that pulls the eye upward from the feet to the head, as shown in Figure 2.24.

Figure 2.23 Animators often exaggerate happiness.

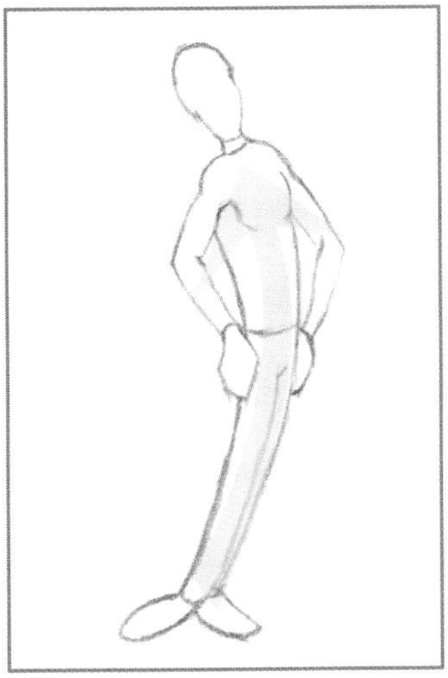

Figure 2.24 Happiness is often a sweeping uplifting gesture.

Some general characteristics of happiness or joy are as follows:

- The arms often form a diamond shape, with the elbows spread wide.
- The hands are either laid flat against the body or clasped.
- Sometimes, the arms are brought in, and the hands are clasped just below the chin. However, this could be confused with the action of pleading.
- The feet and legs are usually close together.
- The head is almost always at an angle following the arch of the body.

Sad (Dejected)

Sadness, as shown in Figure 2.25, is another powerful emotion. It resonates with the audience because it is a common emotion that promotes sympathy for the sad character.

The general action line of a sad character is hooked, or bent at the top, with the head down-turned, as shown in Figure 2.26.

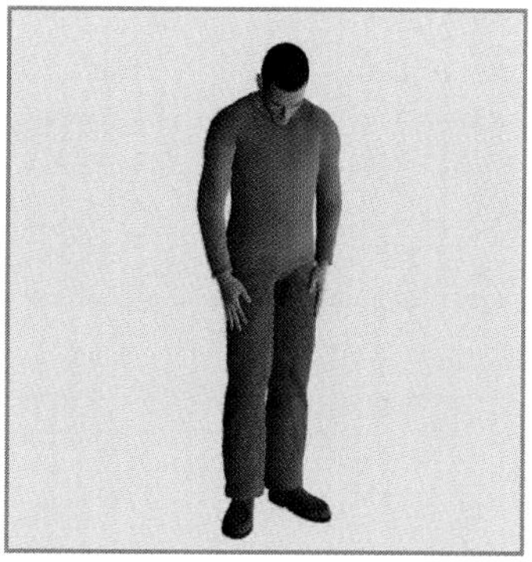

Figure 2.25 The head turned down often shows sadness.

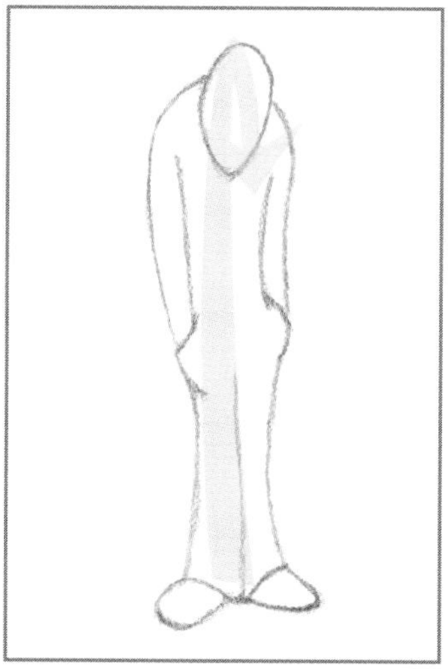

Figure 2.26 The final movement of the curve in a sad person is downward.

Some general characteristics of sadness are as follows:

- Drooping shoulders characterize sadness.
- The arms and legs are held close to the body as if the character wants to recede into itself.
- The head is downcast.

Authoritarian (I'm the Boss)

You will often want to show that a character is in charge by putting him in an authoritarian posture, as shown in Figure 2.27. This type of stance is filled with pride and arrogance.

The arrogant character has a very strutting posture with strong lines leading to the person's head in a "look at me, I am important" pose, as shown in Figure 2.28.

Some general characteristics of an authoritarian or arrogant character are as follows:

- Strong directional motion toward the character's head.
- Chest puffed out with the hips tilted forward.
- Head slightly tilted back so the character is looking down his nose.

Figure 2.27 This character seems very arrogant.

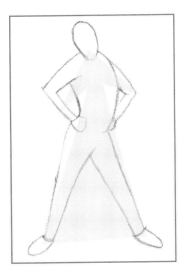

Figure 2.28 The spread feet of the character give a strong directional motion.

Only a Sampling

These are just a few of the many emotions. This book is not long enough to list every emotion and its general characteristics. In order to cover the ones discussed here, I have had to generalize a great deal. The preceding examples are meant as an example only and are certainly not the only way that a particular emotion is expressed. We have so many ways to express emotions that there are no hard and fast rules. Again, your best aid in understanding emotions is to observe natural reactions in real life.

In the next chapter we will take a closer look at the full range of action in an emotional reaction.

CHAPTER 3

Emotional Transitions

In the first two chapters of this book, we covered a number of aspects of showing emotion. Thus far we have isolated a moment in time, which would be fine if this book was about illustration, but animation is about movement. In this chapter, we will explore the range of motion that describes an emotional transition. For example, if you are going to animate a character being surprised, you can't just show a surprised expression, you have to lead into and out of the surprised expression so that the animation blends with the other movements.

Woody

In this chapter I will provide you with several examples of how to animate emotional transitions. At this point I only want you to look at the large body movements and not at facial expressions. We will cover facial expressions in Chapter 5. Because of this I will be using a simple character for animation examples. Let me introduce him to you. His name is Woody, and he is shown in Figure 3.1.

Figure 3.1 We will use Woody for the animation examples in this chapter.

Woody is a virtual wooden mannequin model found in both Figure Artist and Poser. He is much like the wooden mannequins you can find in many art supply stores. He is ideal for examples in this chapter because as you can see, his face has no features.

States and Reactions

Emotions in animation are shown in basically two ways: emotional reactions and emotional states. An emotional reaction is a short display of emotion, whereas an emotional state can last for a long period of time. Some emotions like happy, sad, shy, and content are more likely to be emotional states. Emotions like surprise, shock, stun, and chagrin are more likely to be reactions.

In this chapter we will be dealing with transitions between emotions. These transitions are the points where the character is moving from one emotion to another. It really doesn't matter if the character is changing from one emotional state to another or going from an emotional state to an emotional reaction—the same rules of animation apply.

Changes between emotional states can be slow and gradual or they can be abrupt, whereas emotional reactions are almost always abrupt.

Animating Reactions

An emotional reaction, no matter what it is, can be broken into several component parts, as shown in Figure 3.2. These parts are anticipation, building, key reaction, and let down.

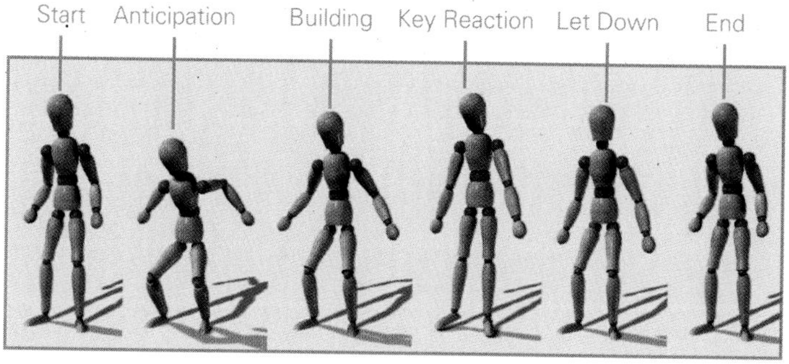

Figure 3.2 Every reaction has to flow through several component parts.

Anticipation

Anticipation is usually the quickest part of an animation. It is usually a slight counter motion that is used to emphasize the major action. Basically the character needs to prepare the audience for the movement by doing a slight counter movement first. The counter movement is a very brief movement in the opposite direction from the main movement of the reaction.

Anticipation lets the audience know that something is about to happen. It is only a small movement but maybe one of the most important aspects of a reaction. It is like contrast in a picture; it makes the major movement more pronounced when there is a small counter movement just prior to the first reaction.

Below in Figure 3.3 is an example of the windup for a punch, which is much like the anticipation phase of a reaction animation.

Figure 3.3 Anticipation is the slight counter movement just before the main action.

Building

In the building step of animating an emotional reaction, the character is transitioning from one emotional state to another. This transition is also a short animation like the anticipation phase. Its length depends on the type of reaction and the intensity of the reaction. For example, surprise is usually a fast reaction, while confusion is slower. In a fast reaction, the building phase may only be a couple of frames. A slower reaction may take a couple dozen frames.

The building phase of a reaction starts at the end of the anticipation phase and goes until the key reaction. It is the most dynamic of all of the movements in the reaction because it is traveling from the character's current emotional state to a new one. Because it is the most dynamic of the motions in a reaction, it needs to be well plotted in both distance and timing.

A good way to make sure the animation looks right is to plot the course of the movement of the character's head, as shown in Figure 3.4.

All movements from anticipation to the key reaction should be in arcs, meaning that you should be able to draw an arc that follows the path of the motion, as shown in Figure 3.5.

Figure 3.4 Plot the movement of the character.

Figure 3.5 All motion should follow an arc.

The human body is an organic system that moves based on pivoting joints. There are no completely straight movements. If your animation runs in a straight line during the building stage of a reaction, it will appear stilted or mechanical.

Key Reaction

The key reaction phase of an emotional reaction is probably the most important phase of all. It is the defining aspect of the reaction that should stay in the mind of the audience well after the reaction is over.

The key reaction, as shown in Figure 3.6, is the period of time that the character is fully engaged in the emotional reaction. All other phases of the reaction are building to or receding from this key moment. Technically it is just one frame but because it is so important, animators will often hold the phase for several frames to emphasize the emotion in the audience's mind.

Figure 3.6 The key reaction is the most important phase of an emotional reaction.

To emphasize emotion, animators will often exaggerate the key reaction phase by over shooting what it might naturally appear like in the real world. For example, you might expect a character in a surprised reaction to have his mouth open. To exaggerate the reaction, you could extend the mouth opening far beyond what is humanly possible. If the reaction is embarrassment, the character might recede into itself far beyond what a normal human might be able to do. Emphasizing the emotion by exaggerating it is a great technique because it is showing a feeling that the audience can identify with. If you are going to exaggerate any part of the reaction, the key reaction phase is ideal. We will cover exaggeration more in Chapter 4.

Let Down

The let down phase, as shown in Figure 3.7, is the stage of the reaction that transitions from the high emotional state of the key reaction to a more constant emotional state or to another emotion. That is not to say that the character isn't still experiencing the same emotion—just not as intense. Whereas the key reaction is an exclamation point, the let down phase is a period. During the let down phase, you should keep several things in mind, such as the following:

- The let down should pull the emotional state back to something that is sustainable.
- Look to the future to see the next change of emotion so the let down can move the character toward that state.
- Constant high emotion can be overwhelming to the audience. The let down gives the audience a rest, letting them prepare for the next intense moment.
- The let down is the longest phase of an emotional reaction, sometimes longer than all of the other phases put together.

Figure 3.7 The let down phase relaxes from the high emotion of the key reaction.

Animating Emotional States

When animating an emotional state, you are not just dealing with one short moment of emotion; rather, you are dealing with a state of being for the character. This means that the character may perform a number of tasks in a scene while in the emotional state. For example, if the character is bashful, the bashfulness is not a single emotional moment but rather something you have to incorporate into all of the movements and actions of the character. A bashful character will move differently than a confident character. The bashful character will hang his head and seek not to be the center of attention, while the confident character will be comfortable with his surroundings and not be afraid of attention. As you can see, the expression of these emotional states is conveyed over time and must be part of the overall animation of the character.

The fundamental difference between animating an emotional reaction and animating an emotional state is that when you animate a reaction, you are actually animating the emotion. On the other hand, when you animate an emotional state, you are incorporating the emotion into all of the animations of the character in which that character is feeling the specific emotion.

In life people experience a wide range of emotions every day. You are probably experiencing some right now as you read this book. Take some time and think about the emotions that you felt today. Write a list. If you keep track of your emotional states, you will find that you probably go through several during the course of a single day. Now if you go through several emotional states in a day, it stands to reason that your characters in an animated production will go through several as well.

Beginning animators often don't consider emotion to the full extent that they should when animating their characters. Animating a character without incorporating an emotional state is kind of like cooking without seasonings. The animation lacks spice. If you leave emotion out of your animation, you are leaving one of your greatest tools unused.

A good practice of an experienced animator is to use emotion to help develop the personality of the character. When you are planning your animation, use the notes area on the X sheets to indicate your character's emotional state. An X sheet is the document that animators use to organize all frames in an animation. If the state changes, indicate that in the notes. This will help you to keep track of your character's emotions and add the spice that will make your character lifelike. Figure 3.8 shows the Action column on the X sheet.

Now that we have gone over how to animate emotional reactions and emotional states, let's move on to animating some.

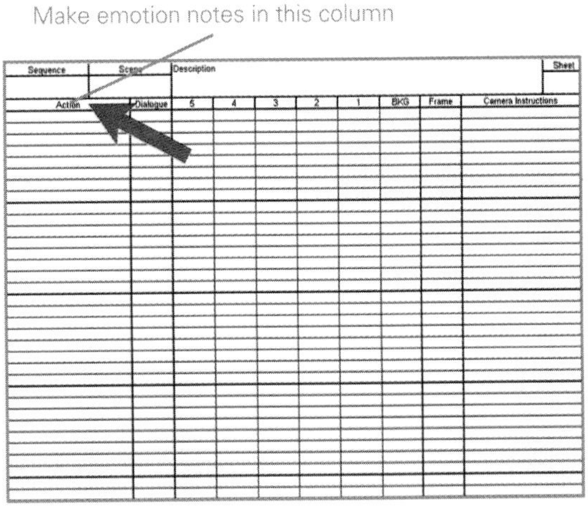

Make emotion notes in this column
Sequence
Scene
Description
Sheet
Action
Dialogue
5
4
3
2
1
BKG
Frame
Camera Instructions

Figure 3.8
Keep track of the emotional state of the character in the Action column on the X sheet.

Surprise

Surprise is almost always an emotional reaction. It is also a transition emotion. A character that is surprised usually will transition into an emotion that is spawned by whatever the object of the surprise encompasses. For example, at a surprise birthday party, the character will be surprised for a few moments and then go into a happy emotion like glee or joy. If on the other hand the character is surprised by a tragic event, sadness and despair may follow. A scary surprise will be followed by fear.

While surprise is a short-lived emotion, it is a very dynamic emotional reaction and is used often in animated shows because of its emotional impact. Surprise is a universal emotion that is common in our lives. We have all been surprised so we all can understand a character who is surprised.

There are several things to remember when animating a surprise reaction.

- Surprise works best if there is a strong anticipation phase.
- Make the reaction fast. A long surprise isn't really a surprise, is it?
- Emphasize the key reaction with a pause or a vibration.
- Make the let down phase the longest of all phases in the reaction.

We will be using Poser for this demonstration of a surprise reaction because of its built-in animation capability and the fact that you won't need to create a model. Instead, you can just focus your attention on animation. Poser is very similar to Figure Artist, so it shouldn't be too hard for you to get used to how it works.

In Poser the animation controls are on the bottom of the page, shown here in Figure 3.9. The controls on the left side of the screen are for playing the animation and are similar to the controls found on a VCR. The controls in the middle of the screen are for changing the current frame. The arrow can be moved along the timeline to change the frame, or the current frame can be changed by changing the number in the frame counter on the left. The frame counter on the right shows the total number of frames in the animation.

The controls on the right side of the screen are for creating key frames. The button with the plus symbol on it is used for setting a key frame. The button with the minus sign is used for removing a key frame. The button with the key on it, or keyframe button, is used when you want to edit a key frame that you have already set.

Now that you know a little about the animation controls, let's get started animating.

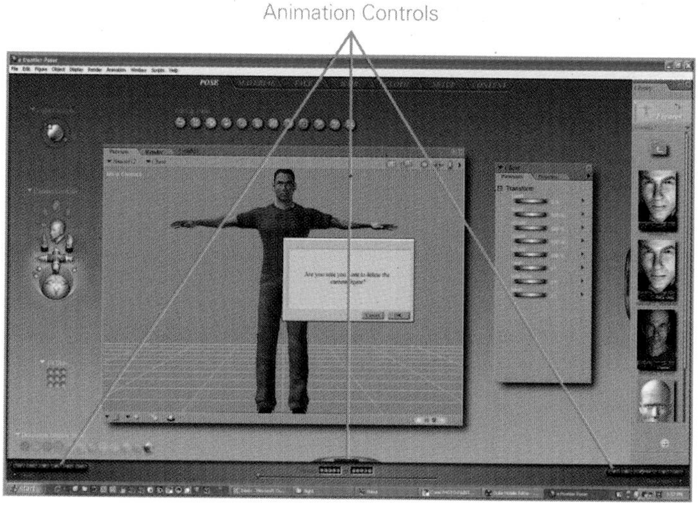

Figure 3.9 The animation controls are on the bottom of the interface.

STEP-BY-STEP

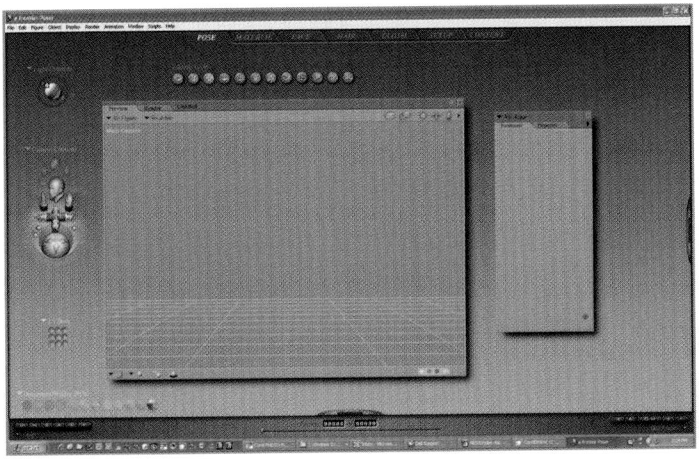

Figure 3.10 Delete the default figure.

1

Open Poser and change the default figure to the Woody mannequin model. To do this, you need to delete the current default figure by going to the Figure menu and choosing Delete Figure. A window will appear, as shown in Figure 3.10. Click Okay to delete the default figure.

2

Next, select the Woody mannequin model from the figure library, as shown in Figure 3.11. It is in the Additional Figures folder.

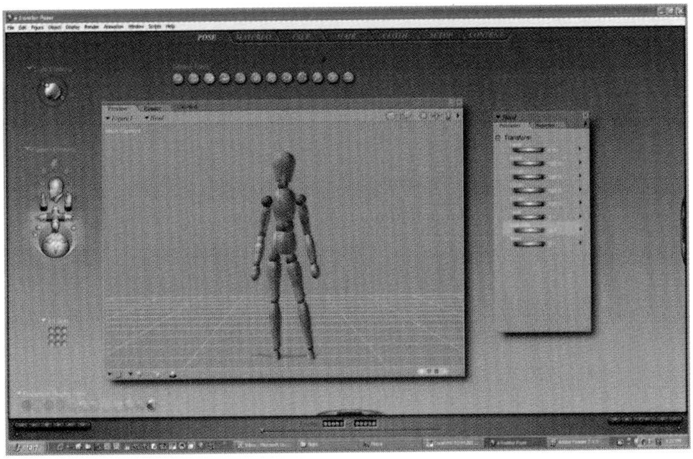

Figure 3.11 Load the mannequin model.

3

The model is now ready to animate. Poser uses key frame animation. All you need to do is pose the figure in the different phases of animation and the program will automatically create the in-between motions. First you need to pose the figure in the start phase, as shown in Figure 3.12 by rotating the joints and moving the figure.

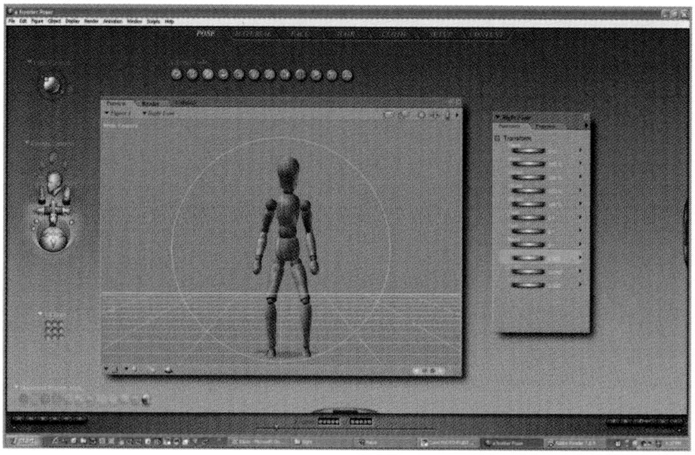

Figure 3.12 Pose the figure in a start pose.

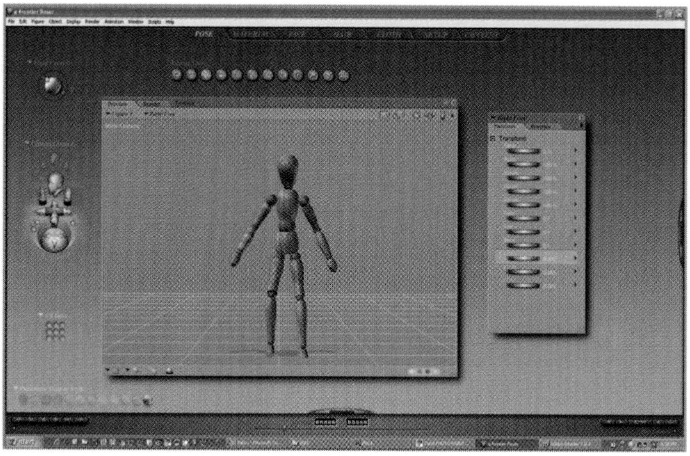

Figure 3.13 Set a key frame for the anticipation frame.

4

Once you have the model in a natural pose, you need to set a key so the program will remember the position of the model at this frame. Click the key frame button.

5

Go to frame 4 and change the pose of the figure to an anticipation pose, as shown in Figure 3.13.

6

Now go to frame 6 and create a pose for the building phase. This is an important step because the program will interpret the motion in a straight line for the in-between motions. You want the motion to arc or swing rather than move in a straight line. The building phase needs to be at the apex of the arc for the hands, as shown in Figure 3.14. The character will also be taking a step to the side for a wider stance, so in the building key I lifted the character's right foot for the step.

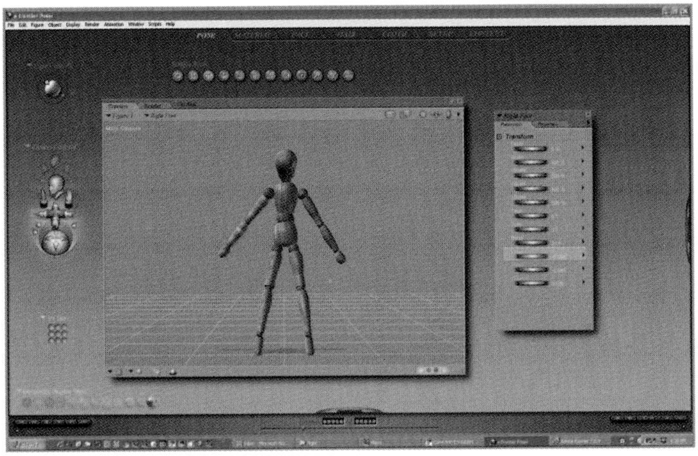

Figure 3.14 Place the building key at the apex of the motion arc.

7

Now it is time to move to frame 8 and create the key reaction frame, as shown in Figure 3.15. You will want the animation to pause for three frames at this point to emphasize the phase so once you set the first key, move to frame 11 and set a second key there also.

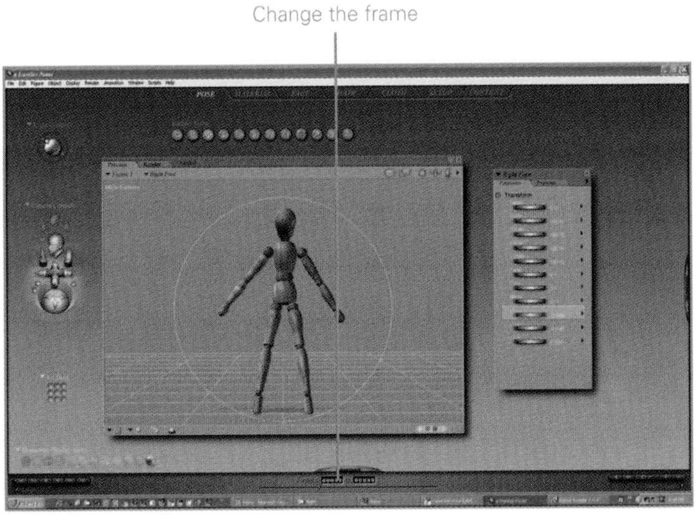

Figure 3.15 Create the key reaction key frame.

8

After the key reaction frame, you need to create a let down key frame at frame 18, as shown in Figure 3.16. Here the character is catching his balance from the surprise reaction. He steps back with his right foot.

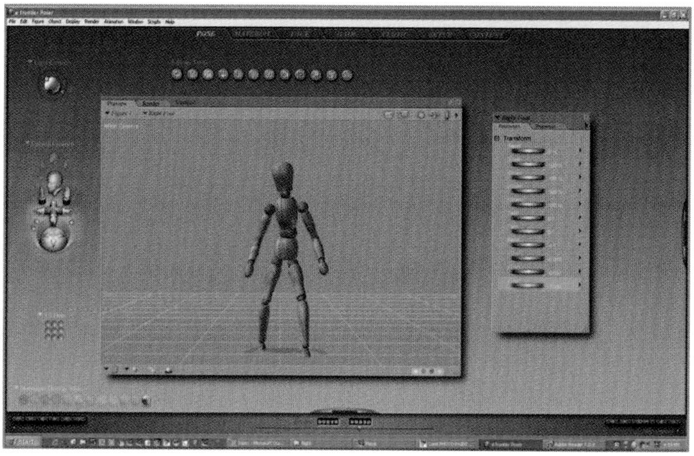

Figure 3.16 In the let down key frame, the character is catching his balance after the reaction.

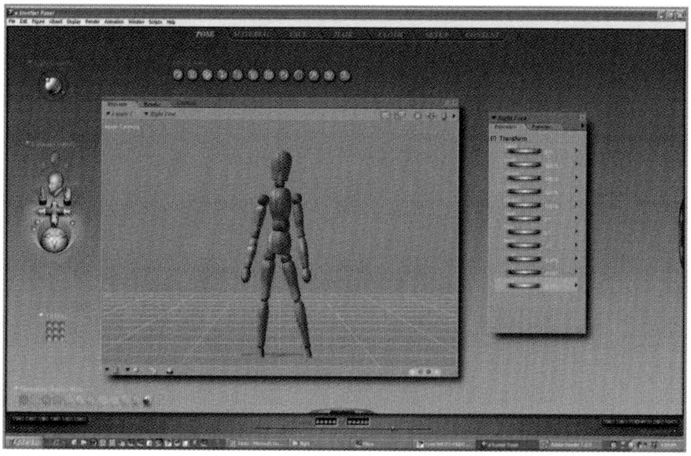

Figure 3.17 The last frame is similar to the first frame.

9

The last key for this demonstration is the standing frame similar to the first frame in the animation, as shown in Figure 3.17.

You've completed your first emotional transition animation. Did you notice that the key frames followed the phases outlined in the first part of the chapter?

Fear

Fear is usually an emotional state. It may begin with a scare and continue with the character showing traits like shaking or tentative actions. When a character is scared, he should show reluctance in his movements. He might close in on himself, holding arms and legs close to his body. In severe cases, the character might turn and flee from the source of his fear.

We show fear in a number of ways, and there is no specific action that is universally thought of as a fearful pose. The following example is just one way to show a fearful emotion. Once you have completed this exercise, try creating a few variations. You may be surprised with the variety of ways that you can show fear.

STEP-BY-STEP

1

You can use the same animation that you used to create a surprised reaction, just increase the number of frames to 60 in the frame counter. Just click on the counter and change the number to 60. Move the arrow to frame 24 and you are ready to begin your next animation.

2

You will want the standing pose to pause for just a moment, so move the frame counter to 28 and set a key at that frame.

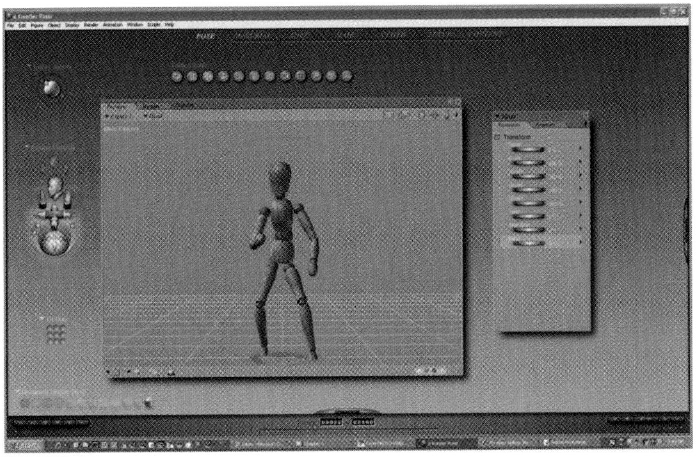

Figure 3.18 Create an anticipation frame at frame 32.

3

Move to frame 32 and change the pose to an anticipation pose, as shown in Figure 3.18.

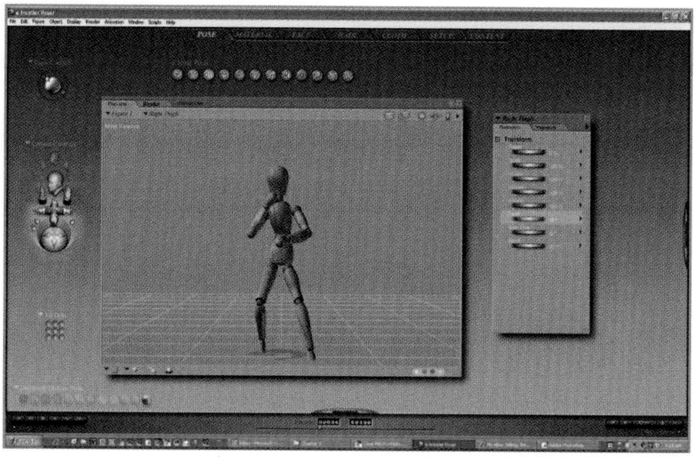

Figure 3.19 The character begins to crouch, ready to run away.

4

In the building frame, the figure is backing away with the hand moving toward the face and beginning a crouch to be ready to run, as shown in Figure 3.19. Set the building frame at 36.

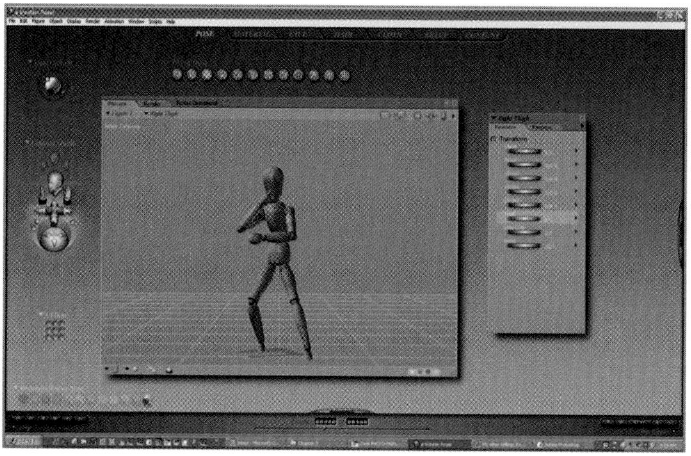

Figure 3.20 Set the key reaction frame at frame 40.

5

The key reaction frame is at frame 40. Here the figure is crouching with one hand up for protection and the other raised to his face (see Figure 3.20).

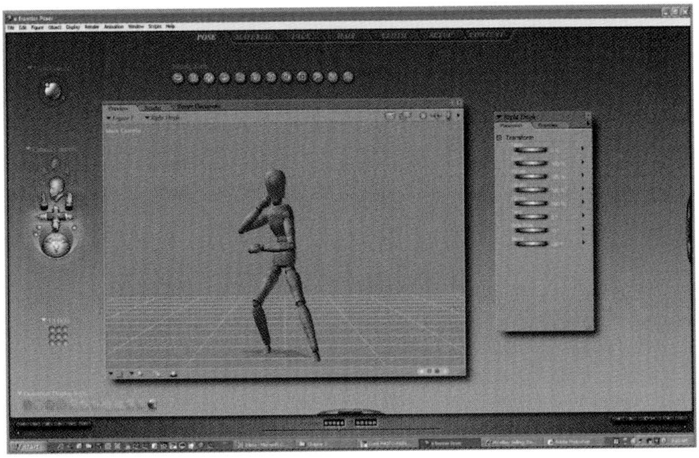

Figure 3.21 Have the character look around at the key reaction phase.

6

Instead of immediately going to the let down phase, have the figure look around a little to make sure everything is okay. Set a key frame with the character looking to its right at frame 44, as shown in Figure 3.21 and a look left key at frame 52, as shown in Figure 3.22.

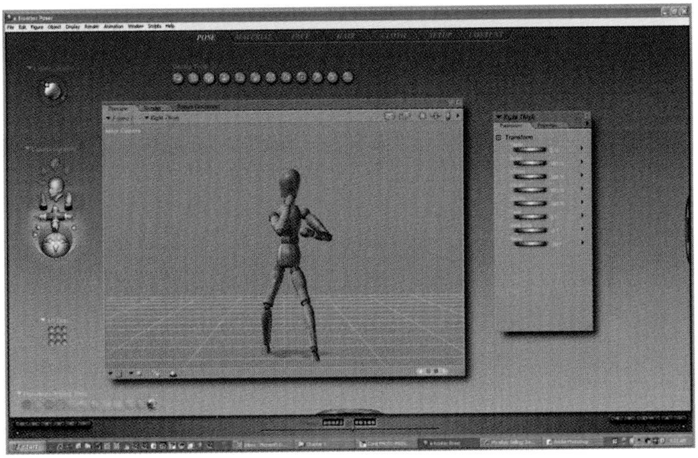

Figure 3.22 The look left takes more frames because the character has farther to travel.

7

With relief the character relaxes in the let down phase on his way back to the standing pose. Set the let down key at frame 56 with the character lowering his arms and beginning to straighten back up, as shown in Figure 3.23.

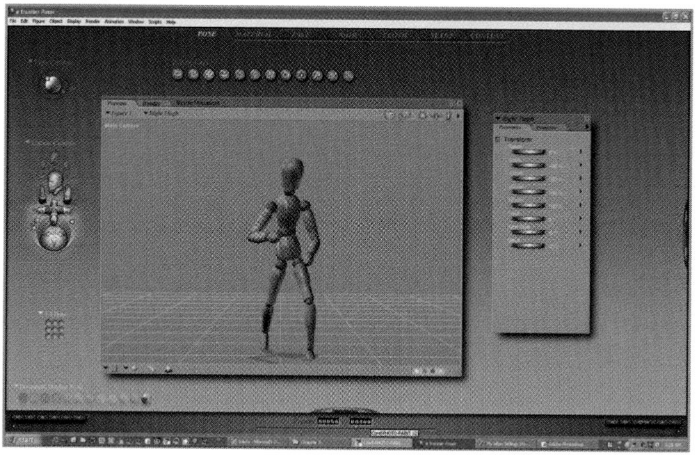

Figure 3.23 The character begins to relax at frame 56.

8

The last frame is frame 60 where the character goes back to a standing pose like in the beginning. Having the character return to a default pose is useful when multiple animations are needed from the character like in video games. If all the animations start from the same pose they will blend better during the game.

Now you have two emotional reactions, one after the other, in an animation sequence. Play the animation to see how you did by pressing the play arrow in the play controls. If you see anything that doesn't look accurate, you can go back and edit the key frames until the animation looks right.

Anger

Anger is another strong emotion that is also an emotional state. Anger is usually shown in a character by clenching of the jaw and hands making fists. Everything about the character should be tense, including the muscles of the arms and legs. Movements will be stiff and clipped, usually short and fast.

When a person is angry, he is sometimes irrational, so his movements will tend to be that way too. Sometimes the person will wave his hands or shake a fist.

Sometimes he will kick things or pound things with his hands. All of these actions are part of anger and can be included in your animations to emphasize the emotion.

Like fear, there is no specific sequence of movements that typify anger. People show anger in a number of ways. Some people will be very vocal and loud in their displays of emotion, waving arms with extreme gestures. Other people will be very minimal in their reactions, showing small signs like clenched fists or a stiff walk. In the example that we will be showing here, the character stiffens and points at the object of his anger. This is just one way to show anger. Once you have completed this exercise, be creative and try a few reactions of your own making. Maybe you can animate how you react when you get angry.

STEP-BY-STEP

1

Start the angry animation at the end of the fear animation that you already created. Change the total number of frames counter to 100 so you will have 40 frames of animation to work with.

2

Go to frame 64 for the anticipation key. Here the character takes a deep breath coming to his full height, as shown in Figure 3.24.

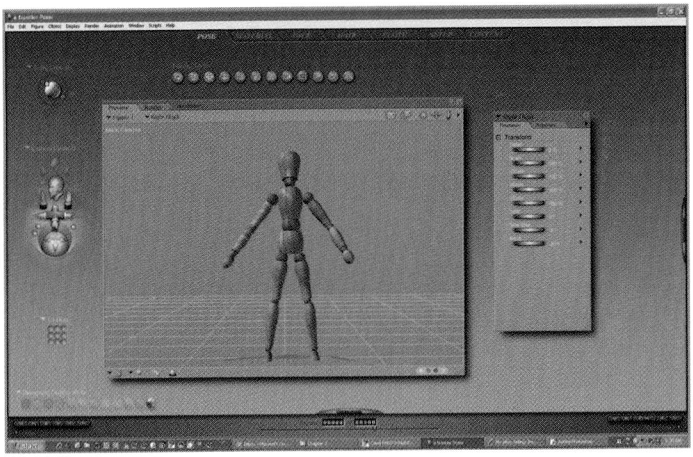

Figure 3.24 The anticipation key has the character standing to his full height.

3

In the building key on frame 68, the character begins to raise his arm on his way to a stiff standing pose, as shown in Figure 3.25. He also takes a step to the side to get a wider base.

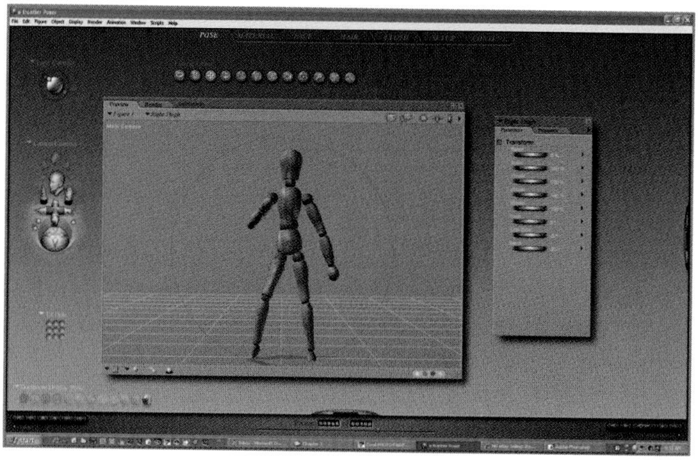

Figure 3.25 The character builds to an angry pose.

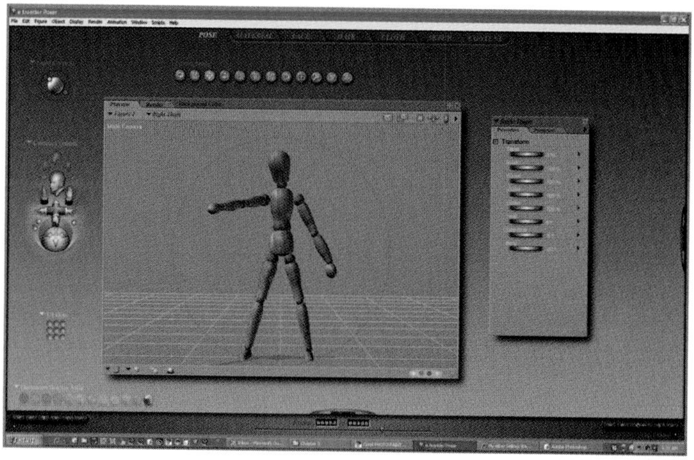

Figure 3.26 The character shows a dramatic angry key reaction pose.

4

The key reaction frame is set as frame 72 with the character's arm pointing sharply and the off hand clenched in a fist. The whole pose is stiff and dramatic, as shown in Figure 3.26.

5

Pause the pose about five frames for dramatic effect, setting a key at frame 77.

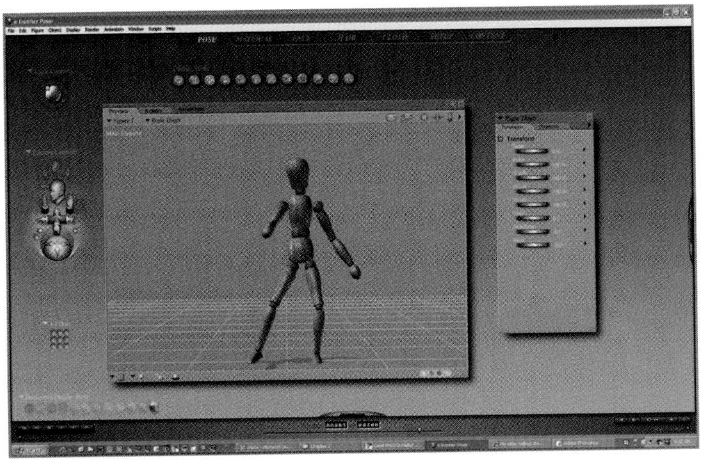

Figure 3.27 Set the key reaction frame at frame 40.

6

The let down phase will be a little longer for an angry emotion because anger is not an easy emotion to come out of. Set the let down key at frame 87, using a full ten frames. Pose the figure so he is relaxing from the stiff angry pose to a more casual standing pose, as shown in Figure 3.27.

7

The final frame can be set somewhere around frame 97, with the character returning to the basic standing pose.

You've now practiced creating an emotional transition with the three examples from this chapter. There are many ways to animate emotions. Hopefully these examples will provide you with a foundation from which to hone your skills.

We used a 3D animation program and a simple model for these examples so you were able to focus on the movement without worrying about the character. Some teachers prefer to have the student learn animation in 2D first before advancing to 3D, but I feel it is better to understand motion in 3D space first before you work in 2D. That way when you start developing 2D drawings, you will already be familiar with how the character should move within the world. Often the beginning animator struggles with drawing, so by supplying a 3D model he can just work on the study of motion without having to worry about his drawing skills.

Now that you are a little more comfortable with Poser as an animation tool, try to develop a number of emotional reactions based on the formulas in this book. As you develop these animations, play them back several times to see how they look. If you can, have a few friends look at your animations to see if they recognize the emotion you are trying to animate. There is nothing like good audience feedback to help you understand how to develop your animation.

I hope you enjoyed this chapter. In the next chapter we take a look at exaggeration in animation.

CHAPTER 4

Exaggeration in Animating Emotions

One of the most common techniques for emphasizing emotions is to exaggerate certain aspects of the emotional reaction. Exaggeration helps to convey to the viewer that the character is experiencing an emotion. For example, exaggerating the dropping shoulders of a character who is depressed brings added feeling to the downcast nature of the character. Often without exaggeration the audience may miss the emotion entirely.

Emotion is something that isn't often recognizable in life. In real life, people tend to hide their emotions in public to avoid embarrassment. They may also mask what they are really feeling with another emotion like humor or sarcasm. While we are all familiar with how we feel, we may not be as adept in seeing emotions in those around us. In animation, however, the emotion needs to be clear to the viewer in most instances.

In this chapter, we will take a closer look at how exaggeration of emotions can help to emphasize them to your audience. We will take a look at how to exaggerate and also when to exaggerate to get the best effect. We will finish up with some examples of 2D and 3D exaggerations for you to practice some of the concepts in this chapter.

How Emotions Are Exaggerated

In animation there probably isn't anything that can't be exaggerated. The animator has complete freedom because he can draw a character or scene any way he chooses. This freedom can be a blessing for the animator, but it can also be a curse. Too much exaggeration can create feelings of disconnect with the audience because they will not understand or sympathize with the characters or situations in the animation. The animator needs to run a balance between exaggeration and reality to keep the production within the boundaries of believability for the audience.

For exaggeration to be an effective tool for the animator, it needs to have contrast and purpose. In art, the artist learns that value contrast is critical in a picture. Without contrast, the picture will be weak—not having definable forms. Effective exaggeration also needs to have contrast between what is exaggerated and what is not. Exaggeration for no reason can also weaken an animation.

Contrast

Exaggeration should be thought of as punctuation. In animation, exaggeration is used to emphasize. Because of this, it should not be overused. If everything in an animation is exaggerated, nothing can be emphasized. It is kind of like going to a play where all of the actors shout at each other all the time. Shouting no longer has any emphasis. The same is true for exaggeration. If every aspect of an animated production is exaggerated, then exaggeration no longer can be used to emphasize. A whisper in a quiet room has more impact than a shout in a noisy room. It is the contrast that gives the sound emphasis.

Purpose

Animators need to remember that exaggeration needs a purpose for it to be worthwhile. Before you design your characters or develop any of the storyboards for an animation, you should decide what it is that you want to emphasize. Maybe you want the character to be cute by enlarging the eyes. Do all of the characters need to look cute with big eyes? Maybe it would emphasize how cute the main character was if she were the only one with the larger eyes. Style is also important. Too much exaggeration in realistic animations will look out of place.

Types of Exaggeration

Some of the ways that emotions can be exaggerated in a character are as follows:

- Exaggeration of a physical aspect of the character that relates to the emotions the character will be experiencing in the animation. For example, if the character will be sad, large eyes could help emphasize that emotion. If the character is going to be angry most of the time, then giving him heavy brows may help.
- Exaggeration of motion might help to convey an emotion. For example, a character that is excited might bounce around the scene while a character that is sad might mope around with slow lethargic movements.
- Exaggeration by distortion of a character to enlarge a particular part of the character's body during an emotion related action can help emphasize the emotion. For example, enlarging the character's head as he gets angry could give the viewer the feeling the character's head is about to explode. Enlarging the eyes and causing them to pop out of their sockets can emphasize surprise.

- Exaggeration in the composition of the scene can help direct attention. For example, using value contrast between the main character and the background will direct the audience's attention to the character.
- Exaggeration of the camera angle might help to better show an emotion. An extreme close-up of a clenched fist might show frustration. A long view of a character screaming can help to emphasize how loud the yell is.
- Exaggeration of the setting can help convey a mood for the entire scene. For example, a dark sinister looking background with a haunted house and trees without any leaves can heighten the feeling of suspense and fear. A bright sunny meadow with a multi-colored tent can help give the scene a feeling of happiness and excitement.
- Exaggeration of the music and sound effects in a scene can have a tremendous effect on the emotional feeling of a scene. For example, a loud marching rhythmic score can inspire, while a quiet melodious tune can calm.

These are just a few of the many ways that exaggeration can be used to emphasize emotions in animation. Let's take a closer look at each to see how they might be applied in an animated setting.

Physical Traits

Exaggeration of a physical attribute can have a significant impact on the audience's perception of the character. The exaggerations can be blatant like a heavy chest and thick arms on an adversary or they may be subtle like the slightly smaller hands on a heroine.

During the design phase of character development, the animator needs to take time to consider the character's personality so that the character can be designed to best express that personality. For example, look at the characters with exaggerated features shown in Figure 4.1.

Figure 4.1 Each of these characters has an exaggerated facial feature.

Exaggeration of the chin makes the first character look more masculine. Exaggeration of the eyes give the second character a more feminine look. Exaggeration of the nose makes the third character look older. Each of these traits is based on how we perceive the natural world. As people age their nose and ears continue to grow. We associate larger noses with older people. Men tend to have larger chins than women so exaggerating the chin moves the character toward a more masculine feeling. Larger eyes are associated with women and children. Women usually accent their eyes with make-up to make that feature more prominent.

NOTE

When I talk about exaggeration of physical traits, I mean those traits that are developed as part of the character's design and not those that are exaggerated as part of a specific animation. We will discuss distortion of the character as part of the movement in another section.

In the picture of the pirate shown in Figure 4.2, the character's muscles are exaggerated. The character has an enlarged chest and a reduced waist. All of these exaggerations have an effect on the character, making him seem powerful.

The example shown in Figure 4.3 is also a pirate character; however, instead of exaggerating the muscles of this pirate, the proportions are modified to give her a more athletic look. If you look, you can see that the character's legs are longer than those on a normal figure.

Figure 4.2 The exaggerations of the pirate make him look powerful.

Figure 4.3 This character's legs are longer than a normal figure.

Figure 4.4 Several elements are exaggerated on the girl to give her the look of a young child.

Sometimes many elements of a character are exaggerated. For example, in Figure 4.4 the character's head is much larger than the rest of her body. Her hair is also exaggerated and so is her ball cap. She has large eyes compared to the rest of her facial features. Her hands and feet are also larger. Together, these elements give her the appearance of being a young girl around the age of 7 or 8 years old.

Motion

Exaggeration in motion is a common aspect of animation. When an animator exaggerates a motion, he pushes it to its extreme to show a greater range of movement than what would be seen in real life. For example, in Figure 4.5, the character is swinging a large hammer. I have only included the beginning, back swing, and impact frames, but you can see that the motion is greatly exaggerated along with the size of the hammer.

The exaggeration of the motion makes the character look like he is really swinging the hammer with everything he has. This type of exaggeration is especially useful in emphasizing a particular action. The other actions of walking up to the hammer and picking it up would not be as exaggerated. It is the swing that is important so the emphasis is placed on that motion.

Figure 4.6 is another example of exaggerated motion. Here the girl is about to kick a soccer ball.

Notice the extreme angle of her kicking foot. The exaggeration of the windup before the kick makes the character appear as if this will be a very powerful kick.

The key to getting a good exaggeration of a motion is to pay attention to the action line in your characters. The action line is the imaginary line that runs through every character showing the main flow of action. In the case of Figure 4.6, the action line flows from her head down through her body and along the lifted foot, as shown in Figure 4.7.

The action line helps to keep the exaggerated motion unified. The best way to exaggerate a motion is to exaggerate the action line by making it more extreme.

Figure 4.5 Exaggerated motion gives the animation more impact.

Figure 4.6 The girl appears to be ready to really kick that ball.

Figure 4.7 Every character has an action line.

Distortion

Distortion is the changing of a part of a character during an action to emphasize that action. Distortion helps to deliver greater punch to an animation right when it is needed most.

The purpose of distortion is to draw attention to a specific aspect of the animation; therefore, the distortion should be designed and timed to a specific event. For example, in a punch animation, the animator enlarges the punching character's fist to emphasize the punch. It starts at normal size, then gets bigger as it heads for the point of impact. After impact, the fist is scaled back to normal size. The increase and decrease in size should be a smooth ramp up and down from the point of impact.

Figure 4.8 shows the character ready to punch.

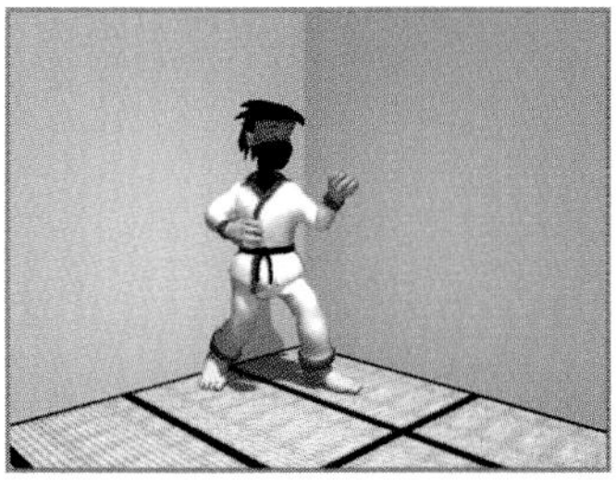

Figure 4.8 The hand starts out at normal size.

At the point of impact, shown in Figure 4.9, the hand is at its largest size.

Figure 4.9 The hand is largest at the point of impact.

After impact, the hand returns to normal size, as shown in Figure 4.10.

Figure 4.10 The hand returns to normal size after the punch.

You can use this technique in a number of ways to emphasize an emotional reaction. Enlarging the eyes and opening the mouth during a surprise is a very common technique. Enlarging a throbbing thumb after the character hits it with a hammer is another often-used technique to show pain. Stretching an arm when a character is reaching out for help is also used frequently.

The distortion does not always have to be blatant. Subtle variations in size can work well in animation where extreme changes will look out of place. Less noticeable yet effective ways to distort an animated character might be slightly enlarging the lifted eyebrow of a character that is showing interest. Another idea might be to slightly enlarge a hand offered in friendship. If done right, these subtle changes will go mostly unnoticed by the casual viewer, yet the slight change in scale will help to draw attention where you want the audience to be looking.

Composition

Exaggeration in composition can be a little more complex than other aspects of animation, but it does present a great opportunity for the animator to direct attention without being too heavy handed. Composition in animation is the arrangement of the scene. It is usually worked out first in the storyboards and then followed through in the layout and key frame stages of building animation. Understanding how to arrange your scenes for maximum impact on the audience is a great tool for creating effective animation. By exaggerating key aspects of a composition at opportune times, you will be able to better control the movement of the story and the overall experience.

The same principles that make a good composition for a painting also work for animation. This includes things like balance, contrast, character placement, focal points, and color.

✎ Balance composition is the concept that one side of a scene should not visually appear heavier than another side. Figure 4.11 illustrates an extreme example of a picture that is out of balance.

Figure 4.11 This picture is off balance.

Balance can be achieved by carefully centering elements in a scene so both sides are symmetrical or by offsetting visually heavier elements with lighter ones, as shown in Figure 4.12.

✎ Contrast is making something stand out by having it differ from its surroundings. The greater the difference from its surroundings, the more likely it will stand out and call attention to itself. For example, in Figure 4.13, the knight contrasts with the gray background. Contrast can also be achieved in color and movement in a scene.

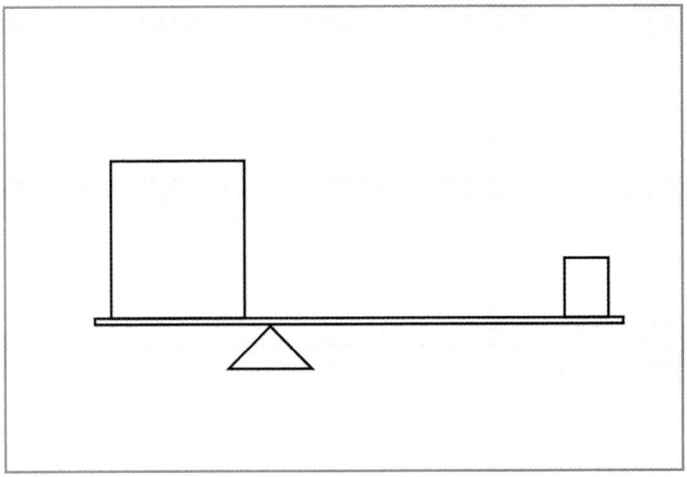

Figure 4.12 Distance and placement of objects from the center affects the appearance of balance.

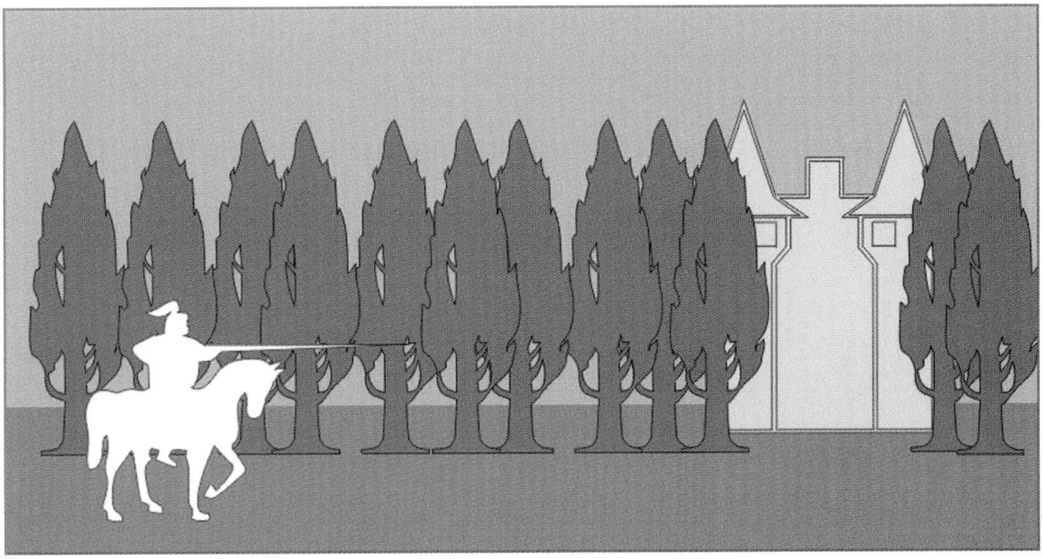

Figure 4.13 The white of the knight contrasts with the grays of the background.

If you want to emphasize a character or element in a scene, you can exaggerate the contrast. In 2D animation this may mean having the greatest value contrast in your main character. In 3D animation this may mean that you need to adjust the lighting to have greater contrast focused on the main character by having a brighter light on it than the other characters.

Contrast isn't just about light and dark value. It can be about many different aspects of a scene, like contrast in color, complexity, and motion. For example, look at Figure 4.14. Although the values in this picture are very similar, the yellow stands out from the other colors because there is a color contrast. The yellow only appears in one spot in the picture. The rest of the picture uses the other two primary colors of red and blue and their combinations.

Contrast can be exaggerated to bring more attention to an aspect of the animation. If you want a part of your animation to be more prominent than the rest of the scene, try giving it greater contrast.

Figure 4.14 You can use color contrast to emphasize a part of a scene.

✎ Character placement directs attention because there is a natural tendency to look at a character in a scene first before you look at the background elements. A common mistake beginning animators make is centering the main character on-screen and not considering any compositional work with the camera. While centering the main action on the screen is acceptable in most situations, if this is all that is done, many opportunities to do something really masterful with the camera are lost.

A character that is placed in the center of the screen will direct the audience's attention to the center of the screen. One that is placed to the side will direct attention to the side. You can direct attention to different parts of a scene just by the placement of your characters in the scene.

Exaggeration in character placement is achieved mostly by the motion of the character pulling the audience to look at the area. It is like your friend waving to you from a crowd. The movement of the hand calls your attention to where your friend is standing. Character placement combined with action is a powerful way to direct attention.

✎ A focal point is the area in a scene that attracts the audience's main attention. It is almost impossible to focus on an entire scene all at once. Usually we have to focus on one thing at a time. A big part of camera direction is using things like movement contrast and character placement to direct the audience's attention to the most important aspect of the story.

The natural focal point of any scene is the center of the scene, shown here in Figure 4.15.

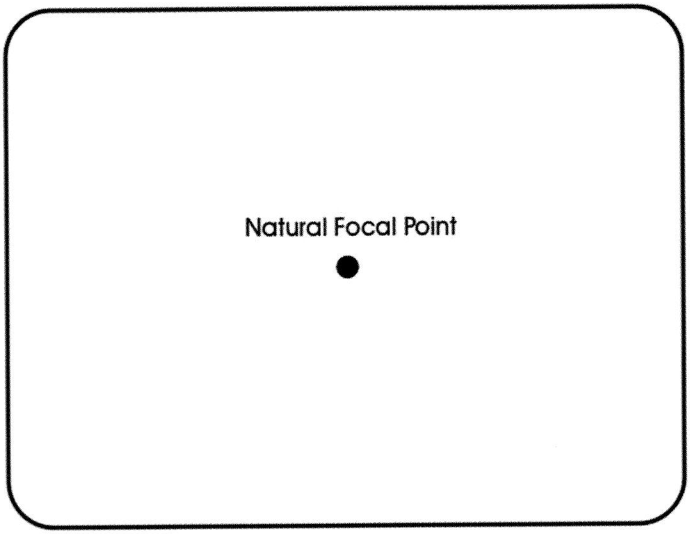

Figure 4.15 We tend to look to the natural focal point in the middle of a scene.

Most of your camera direction will be to keep the main action of the scene centered near the middle of the scene; however, always keeping the focal point in the center lacks variety and imagination. A better method is to direct the attention through the center by starting an action to the side and having it pass through the center by either moving elements in the scene or moving the camera.

✎ Color is an important aspect of composition. You can use color to direct attention as shown earlier under contrast. It can also be used to create a mood or help trigger emotional feelings. For example, blue is generally considered a cool color and is often associated with things like ice, the sky, and water. An overall blue color scheme is a good choice for a scene where you want the audience to feel a sense of detachment or aloofness. On the other hand, red and yellow are generally considered warm colors and are associated with fire, heat, and comfort. If you are designing a friendly setting for your animation, you might want to consider using reds and yellows as your dominant colors.

Much of exaggeration in color comes from contrasting one color from another. This can be done as shown in Figure 4.14 earlier by contrasting colors that are opposite each other in a color wheel, but it can also be done by contrasting intensity, thermal qualities, and purity. Contrasting pastel colors with a bright color uses intensity to show exaggeration. Contrasting cool colors with a warm color uses the colors' thermal qualities to exaggerate. Contrasting grayed colors with pure colors uses color purity to show exaggeration.

While composition may be less direct than other methods of exaggeration, it is one of the most effective ways to direct attention in a scene.

Camera Angle

Related to distortion, in that it focuses attention to a specific aspect of the animation, is the positioning of the camera. Camera angle refers to the audience's view of the scene. Because the animator has complete control of the view, he can use it to focus the audience's attention by creating camera angles that focus attention, like the newspaper in Figure 4.16.

There are many opportunities for you to shift the camera to emphasize an aspect of the animation. For example, let's say that a character is impatient. Instead of centering the camera on the character's head, you could try a quick cut to show the feet tapping the floor. The cut to the feet then back to the head emphasizes the emotion. Another example might be for you to show a character talking to another character. Instead of showing the talking character for the full conversation, you could show the listening character react to what the talking character is saying, thus heightening the emotional impact of the scene.

Figure 4.16 The camera angle helps to emphasize the newspaper.

Camera direction in animation is a complex and specialized skill. Entire volumes could be written on the subject. Rather than going into every aspect of how to direct a camera, I will give you a few pointers and then move on to how you might use the camera to emphasize an emotional reaction. But even in the concepts that govern good scene design, there are opportunities to use exaggeration to help direct attention. I will try to cover these as we go through each one.

Camera movement is an effective way to gain and keep attention. Movement attracts attention. Rather than holding the camera in one position during dialogue or other sequences, the camera could be in the process of a slow movement. This is a technique that is often used in live action when a person is giving a speech. The camera will start to back away from the speaker and then slowly zoom in.

Cutting to a different view is also a good technique to keep attention. Each time the camera cuts to a different view, the viewers have to process the new view. While processing usually only takes a split second in most cases, it does cause the audience to have to engage with what is going on in the animation.

The following are some concepts to help you with camera movements:

- For camera movement to be effective, it has to be smooth. In other words, the best camera movement is the movement that feels like it fits with the production and is enjoyed by the audience because it enhances the show. If the movement is not obvious to the audience, you have probably done a good job making the movement seem natural.
- Bad camera movement calls attention to itself. Usually, bad camera movement is accompanied by the audience not being able to follow the characters or a lack of ability to focus on any aspect of the scene. The camera moving too fast, abruptly changing direction, and showing the wrong part of the scene causes this discomfort and confusion. The best way to avoid bad camera movement is to keep the camera focused on the story. Plan out each scene in the storyboards and make sure that the focus of each scene is progressing the story.
- When the camera is moving, new aspects of the scene are introduced to the viewer. It takes time for the viewer to register and recognize every new element that is introduced to a scene. If the camera moves too fast across a scene, it can cause confusion. Motion blur helps because it limits the visual information, but even it may not be enough. Therefore, the camera should move at a comfortable speed unless there is a reason for an abrupt movement, like a character falling off a ledge or a quarterback throwing a pass. But even in these circumstances it may be better to show the beginning of the fast movement and then cut to the end so the audience has a better chance to keep up with the action.
- Abrupt changes in camera direction can disorient the viewer, particularly if the changes are in rapid succession. This is sometimes referred to as jerky camera movement. It is very noticeable to the audience and, in some cases, has been known to cause motion sickness. A good way to take the jerky camera out of your animation is to vary the speed of the camera movement. Start into a movement slowly and then pick up speed. Slow the movement as it comes to an end so the camera doesn't just stop. This is known as ease-in and ease-out in the industry.
- Sometimes the camera is not focused on the right action at the right time. Say, for example, the animation calls for a conversation between two of the main characters in a scene. It is common to have the camera focused on the character speaking, but what if the real story is told in what the character is speaking about, like a car crash or other dramatic event? If the camera is showing the speaking character and not the event, the story will be damaged. So, make sure your camera is focused correctly, and it shows all the essential elements of a scene for successful story telling.
- Line of action can also cause problems. For example, if you have a character walking from left to right across a scene and then in the next scene the character is facing left, you will likely confuse the audience. Line of action problems are more likely in 3D animation than they are in 2D animation because the animator may not consider it when placing multiple cameras in a scene. The Line of Action sidebar tells a story from the early days of television, and it may help illustrate the problem.

Line of Action

Many years ago, when television was first starting out, camera direction was experimental at best. A group of television pioneers decided that it might be a good idea to film the Kentucky Derby and broadcast it over the airways. They packed up all of their gear and went down to the racetrack.

Once they were there, they were faced with a problem. Where should they place the cameras to get a good shot of the entire race? You see the track was too big for just one camera to shoot so they needed to place cameras around the track so they could cover the whole race.

They placed a camera on one of the curves of the track to capture the horses coming down the straightaway and entering the turn. Next, they wanted to get the horses coming out of the turn and dashing toward the finish line so they placed a camera on the inside of the curve, as shown in Figure 4.17.

Can you see the problem with the camera placement?

Imagine watching your favorite horse as it enters the curve. On the TV screen, it is moving from left to right, then the camera switches from camera one to camera two and now the horses are moving from right to left. Where did your favorite horse go? You had her spotted in the scene before. Now everything is reversed.

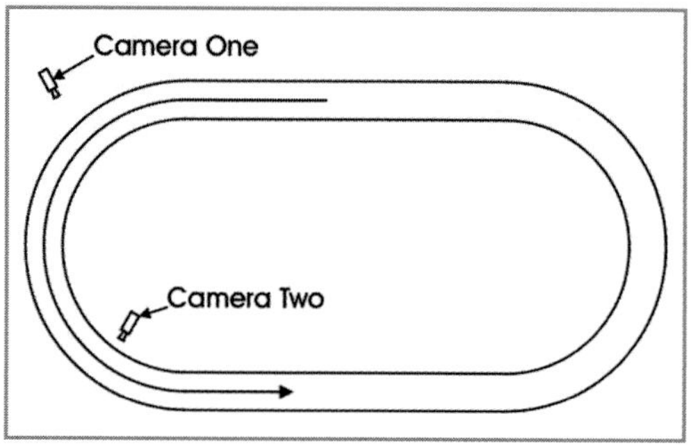

Figure 4.17 The cameras were placed on the inside and outside of the track.

Exaggeration in camera movement usually involves unusual angles. Normally we see the world from eye level. It is natural for us to look at an animation scene from the same level. However, when the eye level changes, it causes the audience to have to pay attention because they have to work a little harder to understand what the scene is really about. For example, a bird's eye view, like the one shown in Figure 4.18, where you are looking down on your characters, takes a little while for the audience to understand. While the view might be harder to understand, it adds variety to the production. It is also a great way to show relative distances.

Another technique for camera angles is to do a focused close-up view, as shown in Figure 4.19. Here the character is holding a scrap of paper in her fist. The camera focuses on the scrap of paper setting up the next scene where the writing on the paper will be revealed.

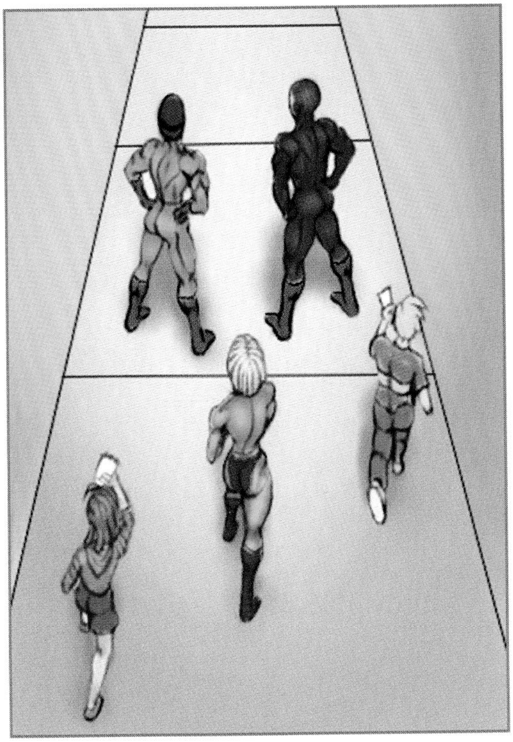

Figure 4.18 A bird's eye view is great for showing relative distances between characters.

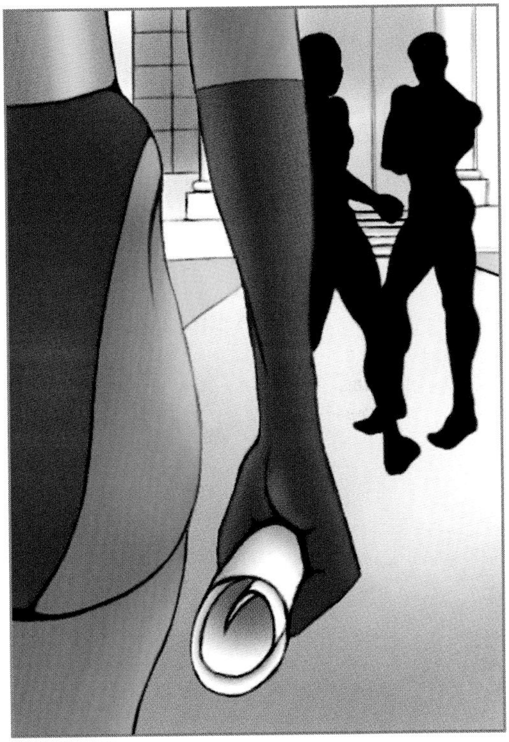

Figure 4.19 The camera focuses on the paper in the heroine's hand.

In the figure, the paper is held tightly in the character's fist showing that the character is angry about what is written on the paper. You could have shown the character reading the paper with an angry expression, but the same message is conveyed in this scene, plus the connection of the characters in the background who will soon hear all about this paper. Emotion doesn't always have to be shown by a facial expression.

Setting

Settings can also play a role in emphasizing an emotion by conveying a mood or ambiance to those watching an animation. The setting acts as the stage upon which you develop your story. The animated characters are the focal point of the animation, but the setting is the world in which your characters live so at least part of the audience's attention will be devoted to it. It would be a waste of visual real estate not to use the setting in expressing emotional messages to the audience.

In Chapter 7, we will cover building settings with emotion in detail. For now let's just look at a couple simple examples of settings and how they can affect the emotional ambiance of an animation.

Figure 4.20 is a simple animated character. Let's look at how even simple changes to a setting can affect how the animation might feel to the audience.

In the first example shown in Figure 4.21, the character is placed in a bright sunny setting. Notice how the setting changes the feeling of the scene. The bright vibrant colors give the scene a happy ambiance.

Just by moving the character into a dark setting, as shown in Figure 4.22, the entire mood of the scene is changed. It now has a more

Figure 4.21 A bright setting has a happy ambiance.

Figure 4.20 We will use this simple character to illustrate how a setting can affect the emotional mood of a scene.

Figure 4.22 Darker colors change the happy mood to a more mysterious feeling.

somber, maybe even sinister, feeling even though the character hasn't changed.

The setting is a great place to exaggerate the mood and feeling of an animation. If the script calls for a specific feeling at any time during a production, the first area you should consider is how you can express the feeling in the setting.

Audio

Sound is an important aspect of any animation and should be considered with any discussion of exaggeration in animation. While the animator may think of himself as a visual artist, he must also be a bit of an audio engineer and musician as well. Not that the animator needs to know how to write music or mix tracks, but he needs to understand the basic principles of audio to include it in his animation.

Music and sound effects are so much a natural part of productions that the audience may not even realize what they are listening to. In normal life, we seldom have a musical score to follow us around in our daily tasks. In TV, movies, and video games, music usually accompanies the characters as they go about their directed tasks. Music is part of the production because it has a significant impact on the audience, even if the audience doesn't realize it. In most cases, when a mood change is about to happen, the music changes. Watch a movie some time and listen to the soundtrack. You will notice that just before something bad is about to happen, the music will probably change. The movie *Jaws* is a great example and is often used to illustrate this point.

If you want to exaggerate the feelings and emotion in any setting, think about how the music score can help you emphasize the emotion.

Sound effects can also be exaggerated by turning up the volume in key instances, like the crash when a pot falls or the screech of tires on the pavement.

Multiple Exaggerations

With most animated productions, multiple exaggerations are combined to create the emotional feel of a scene. By combining an exaggerated setting with an extreme camera angle and a specific distorted movement, the exaggerated emotion becomes even more pronounced. If you then add music and sound effects to accompany the emotion, you begin to really emphasize the emotion.

Don't rely on one or two exaggeration methods in your animation; instead, think of the different methods of exaggerating emotion as a set of tools that give you power as the animator to direct the emotional quality of your animation.

In this chapter, we have only touched on a few of the many ways that emotion can be exaggerated and emphasized in animation. The opportunities for emphasizing emotion are almost endless. As you work on the emotional behavior of your characters and the overall emotional expression of your animation, look for opportunities to express emotion through exaggeration, but remember to not overdo it. Contrast your exaggerated animation with normal animation. Use exaggeration as a way to direct attention and emphasize emotion not as just a cool way to make your animation different. The smart use of exaggeration in animation is the hallmark of the great animator.

CHAPTER 5

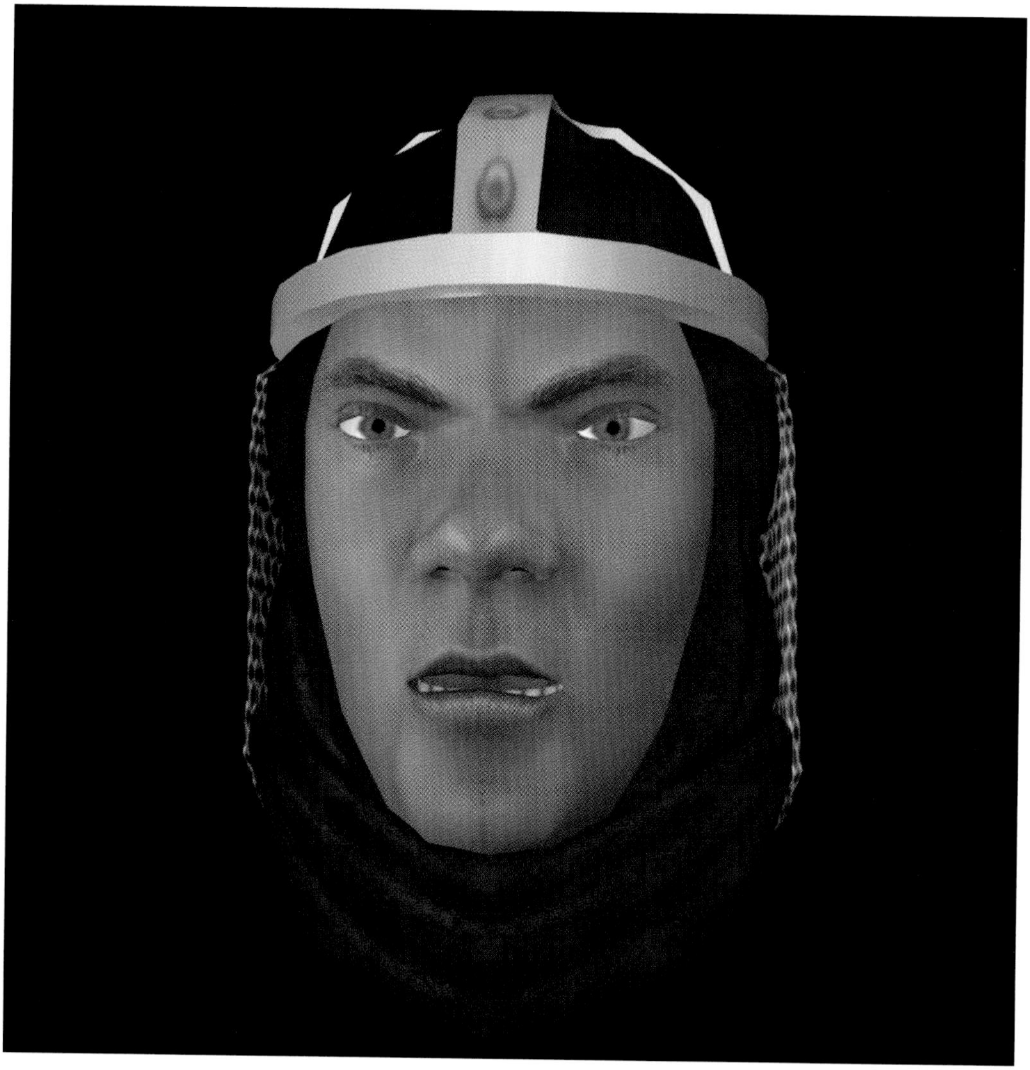

Facial Expressions

Of all the parts of the body, the head is probably the most emotionally expressive. It is hard to imagine a powerful emotion without the head as part of it. Our faces are very expressive. When we want to know how a person feels or how they react or think, we generally look at their face. You have to understand how to create great facial expressions to convincingly show emotion.

Expressions in Real Life

Our face is a window into our feelings and one of the best ways to observe how people are feeling is to watch closely the expressions they make as they go about their daily routine. If you are observant, you will notice that unconsciously most people show how they are feeling. You can tell whether they are sad or happy. You can see frustration or fatigue. You will be able to see confusion and confidence. All it takes is a little practice and you will be able to understand most expressions. Some will be obvious, like the anger shown in Figure 5.1. Others may be a little less obvious but still as powerful, like the anger shown in Figure 5.2.

Both of these examples show anger, but they do it in very different ways. One is so intense that it is almost comical, while the other is more economical in its expression, giving an almost chilling feeling to the emotion.

Now let's look at another picture shown in Figure 5.3. Notice that the girl is looking to the side like the man in Figure 5.2, and there are a few other similarities, yet her expression is very different from his.

The girl's emotion is obviously different from the man in Figure 5.2, yet her expression in the way she is holding her head and face is closer to the man in Figure 5.2 than the man in Figure 5.1. Showing emotion in facial expressions can be tricky. While there may be a few general rules, even a small change in the eyebrows or the mouth can completely alter the emotion.

Close study in life is essential to mastering facial expressions. You need to watch facial expressions to see the many changes that can happen. Great animators are great observers. They look for and derive inspiration from everyone around them.

Figure 5.1 This person is obviously angry. © istockphoto.com/ Oktay Ortakcioglu

Figure 5.2 This person is angry as well but the expression is different. © istockphoto.com/ Spauln

Figure 5.3 The girl's expression is similar to the man's in Figure 5.2, yet the feeling is very different. © istockphoto.com/ Miodrag Gajic

Understanding the Human Head

To really understand facial expressions, the artist must first understand the structure of the human head. It isn't enough to know that a raised eyebrow can show emotion, you need to understand how the eyebrow is raised. Understanding the mechanical aspect of facial changes will increase your expressive ability because the animation will look correct and believable.

The human head is unique compared to all of the other body parts. It is unique in what it contains, and it is unique in its structure. The head encompasses all of our sensory perception. Sight, smell, taste, touch, and hearing are all located in our heads. With our head, we can feel the wind on our face; we can taste a great meal; we can see a great work of art; we can hear a great symphony; and we can smell the fragrance of a beautiful flower. In addition to housing all of these important sensory perceptions, the head also houses our brain that interprets every perception. Because the brain and the rest of the organs of the head are so important, they need to be held in a structure that will protect and guard them from harm.

Bones of the Head

The human skull is different from other bones in our body. The skull is designed not only to support the important organs of the head; it is also designed to protect them. The skull is a hollow bone with much of it near the surface where it can protect what is within it. The skull is comprised of 22 bones that can be split into two main groups: the 8 bones of the cranium and the 14 facial bones. Figures 5.4 and 5.5 show some of the more prominent bones of the head.

It isn't important that you know every bone of the head by name, although it doesn't hurt, but it is important that you understand how the structure of the head affects the nature of a person's appearance. The bones of the skull are the framework upon which you will build your character and the anchor for all facial movements that indicate emotions. Most of these bones with the exception of the jaw bone don't actually noticeably move.

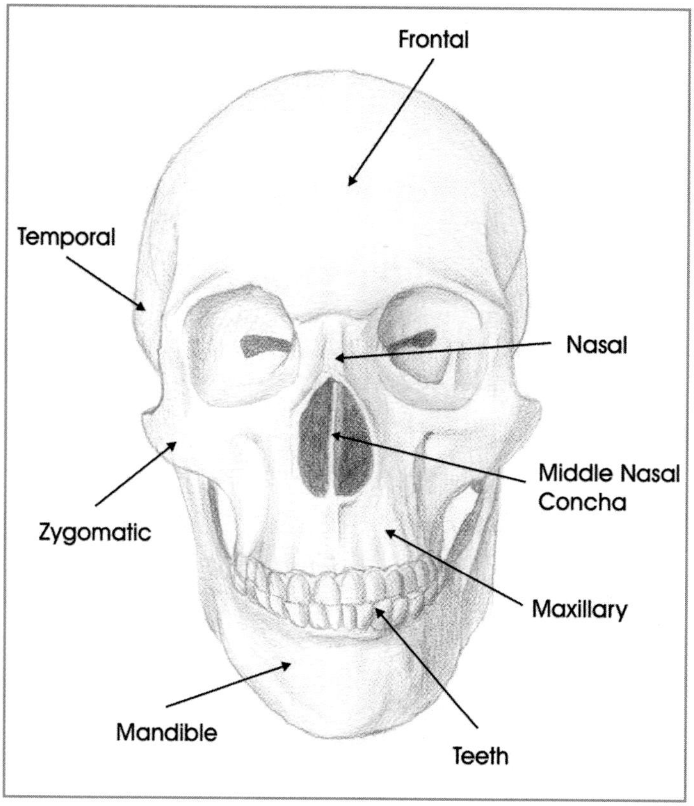

Figure 5.4 A front view of the human skull.

Some important aspects of the human skull you should be aware of are as follows:

- The most important bone of the cranium for facial expressions is the frontal bone because it determines the shape of the forehead and brow. The frontal bone curves back at the top of the head and flares out at the brow to protect the eyes. The flare above the eyes determines how heavy the brow is.
- The nasal bone forms the base of the nose but only extends partway down the nose. Cartilage forms the structure for the rest of the nose. The cartilage is more flexible than bone, enabling some movement of the nose. This bone also helps to determine the character's nose size.

- The zygomatic bone is also known as the cheek bone. It runs along the side of the face just below and to the side of the eyes. This bone has a lot to do with how a person looks. In some people, these bones are very pronounced and in others, they are not. They serve to protect the eyes and as an anchor for muscles of the face. Many western cultures consider high cheek bones beautiful.
- The mandible, also known as the jaw bone, is the only real moveable bone of the face. It is hinged to the skull near the ears. The mandible forms a person's jaw line. Heavy or large jaw bones are usually associated with masculinity in characters.

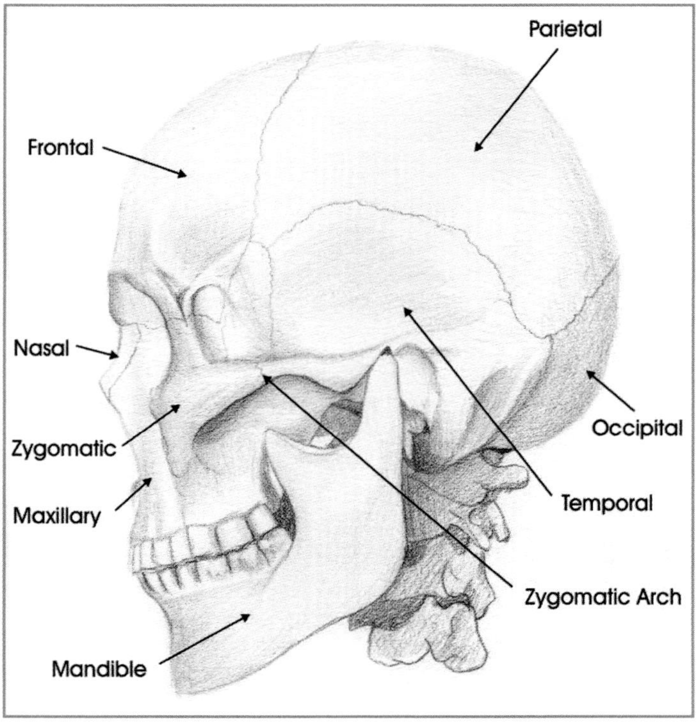

Figure 5.5 A side view of the human skull.

Muscles of the Head

The skull provides the structure of the head, but the muscles provide the movement. Both aspects are needed for facial expressions. Understanding how each muscle is attached to the skull and what its movement is will help you to better understand how to create believable facial expressions. Figure 5.6 is an overlay of the muscles of the head over the skull.

Most of the muscles of the head are located in and around the face. Some important aspects of the muscles of the head are as follows:

- The frontalis muscles run all along the brow. They are attached vertically so that the brow can be raised or lowered. They are very flexible allowing for independent movement of both brows.
- The orbicularis oculi muscles surround the eyes. They form both the upper and lower eyelids. The tissue of these muscles radiates outward concentrically from the eye.
- The orbicularis oris muscle groups surround the mouth, similar to the way the orbicularis oculi surround the eye. They control the movement of the upper and lower lips.

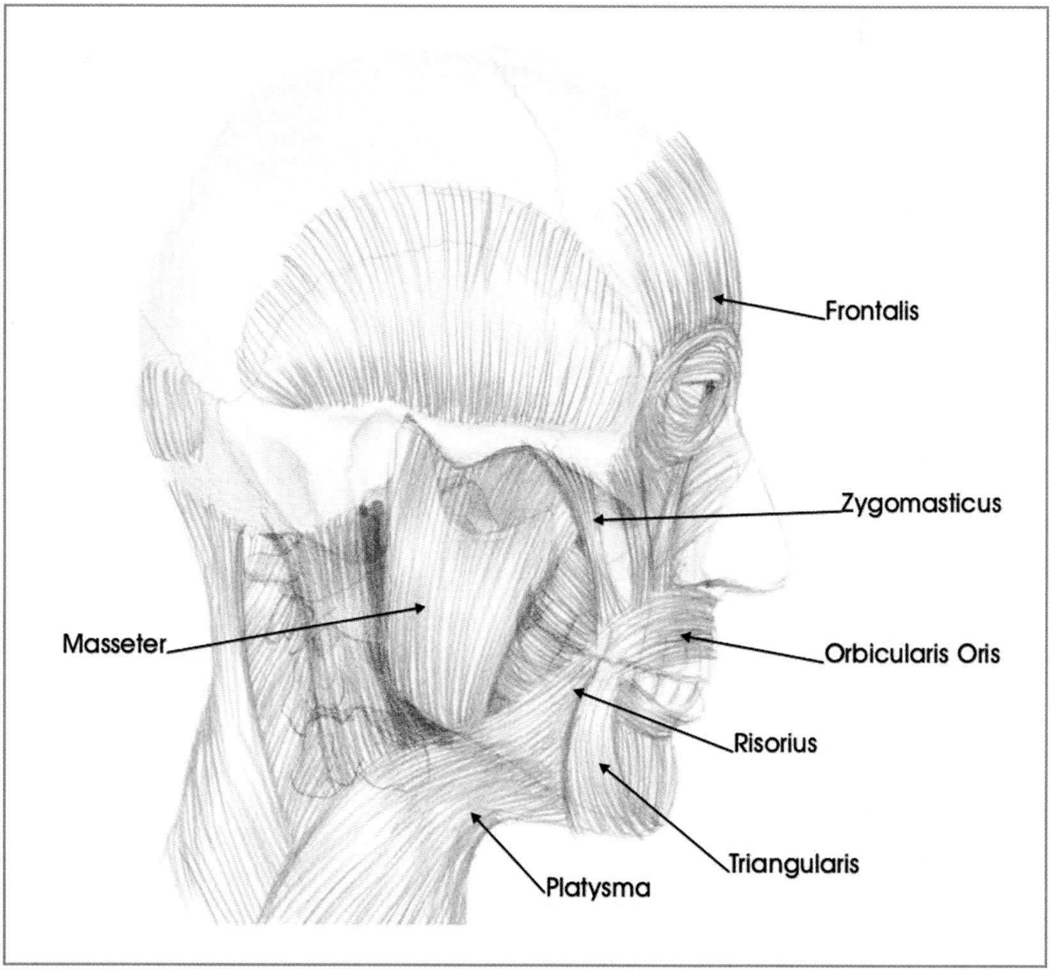

Figure 5.6 The muscles of the head control facial movement.

- The masseter muscles are powerful muscles that are used for biting. They are connected to the jaw and the zygomatic bones and are located toward the back of the cheeks. These muscles are evident when a person clenches his jaw.
- The platysma muscles are used to open the jaw and are located in the upper neck area.
- The zygomasticus muscles run from the zygomatic bones to the upper jaw. These muscles are what helps us to smile, along with the buccinator. The buccinator pulls the sides of the mouth back and the zygomasticus pulls the sides upward.
- Frowns are a result of the pulling back of the risorius muscles and the pulling down of the Triangularis muscles.

Now that you understand the muscles and bone structure of the head, let's look at a few emotions and what happens to create the corresponding facial expression.

Fear

In general, fear stretches the face vertically. The eyebrows shoot up and the jaw drops, as shown in Figure 5.7.

As you can see in the figure, the eyes and mouth are open wide. Fear, at least in the initial reaction phase, is very similar to surprise, but there are a few important differences. In a surprise reaction, the frontalis muscles of the forehead move upward all across the brow. In fright, the raised brow is more toward the nose and less toward the sides of the head. The mouth tends to be a little more open in surprise than in fear.

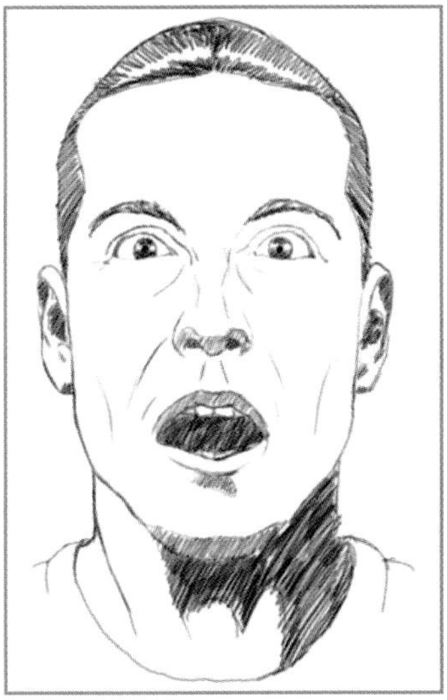

Figure 5.7 Fear affects the face vertically.

Anger

Anger is a tense emotion. Where fear tends to open the face vertically, anger tends to pull the face together, as shown in Figure 5.8.

The greatest tension is in the brow, which is often lowered and bunched together above the nose. The upper lip is also raised and the mouth narrowed, giving the face a pinched feeling. The eyes are less open than in most other expressions because the angry person is usually very intent on the source of the emotion. The eyelids are more pinched toward the center of the face. The nostrils flare.

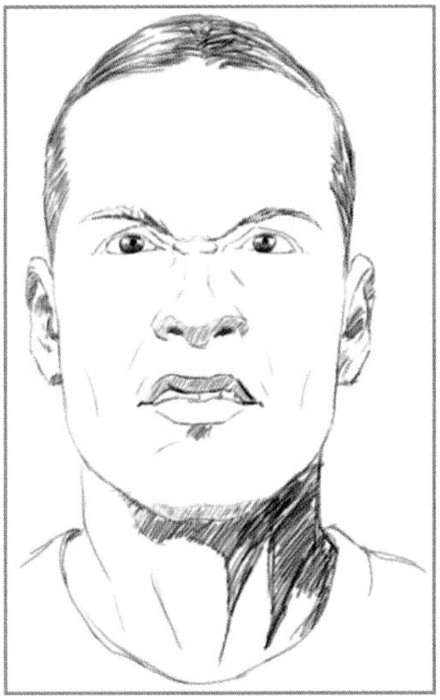

Figure 5.8 Anger causes the muscles of the face to push toward the center.

Worry

Worry causes the face to contract slightly around the eyes, as shown in Figure 5.9.

In a worried expression, the eyebrows are bunched together like in anger, but instead of the brow pushing downward, it is raised upward opening the eyes more. The mouth is usually slightly ajar and may be twisted up or down on one of the sides giving the face an uneven look.

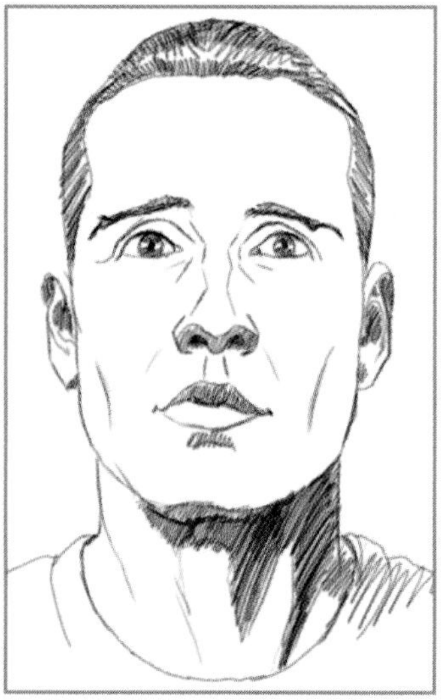

Figure 5.9 A worried expression is focused mostly around the eyes.

Animating the Head in 3D

Animating facial expressions in 3D is a complex process that requires more specialized knowledge than 2D animation. In 3D animation, there has to be care taken in how the model is built and how the model is rigged to the bones. If the model is built or rigged incorrectly, it will be difficult to animate so the emotions seem natural.

> **NOTE**
>
> 3D model construction and animation differs somewhat among 3D software programs. In the following example, I will be using Maya to show you how to animate facial expressions. If you are not familiar with how Maya works, see Appendix A. It is an introduction to Maya that may help you. It is an excerpt from my book that I co-authored with Mike Tidwell, *Autodesk Maya and Autodesk 3ds Max Side-by-Side*.

Building 3D Heads That Animate

In this next section, we will be dealing with the construction of the 3D head for facial animation. I will be using the head of the warrior character that I created for my book *Game Character Animation All in One*. A detailed step by step explanation of the head's construction can be found in that book. Additionally, if you want a copy of the Maya file, you can purchase it at www.turbosquid.com. There is a link on the CD that will take you to the file.

For a 3D head model to animate correctly, the polygons need to follow as closely as possible the flow of the muscles. That way when the vertices are influenced by the bones or other influencers, they will deform like the face in real life. For example, the orbicularis oculi muscles that surround the eye form concentric rings of muscle fiber. The polygons that surround and form the area around the eye should also form concentric rings, as shown in Figure 5.10.

The polygons of the forehead should follow the form of the frontalis muscles, as shown in Figure 5.11.

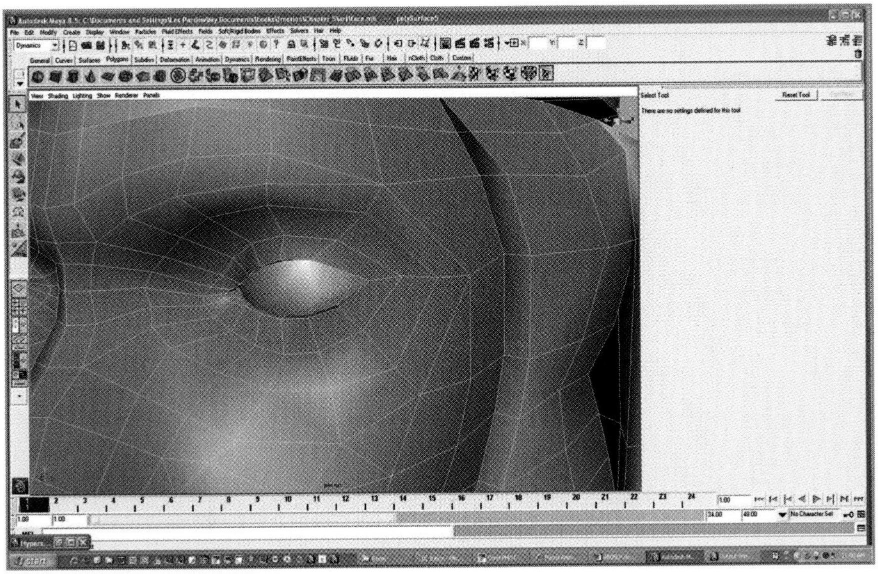

Figure 5.10
The polygons around the eye should follow the form of the muscles.

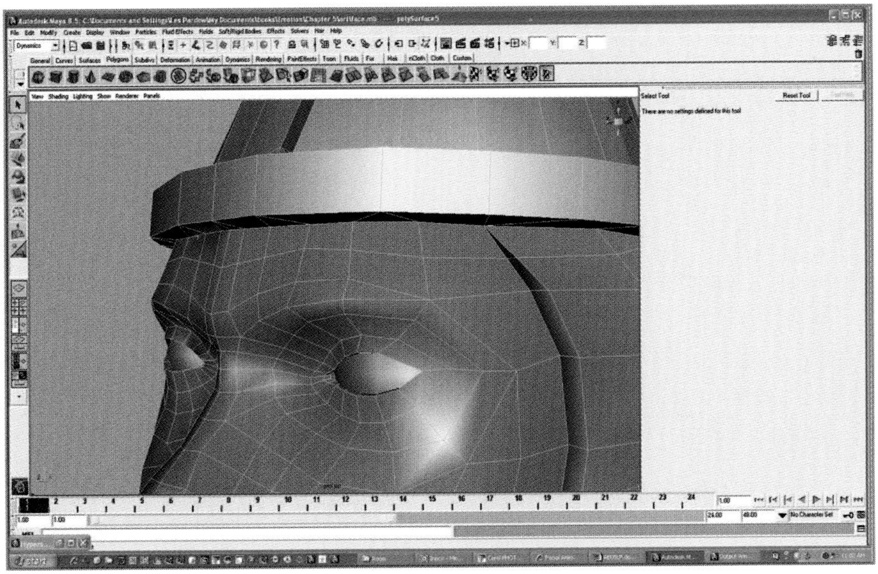

Figure 5.11
Have the polygons of the forehead follow the frontalis muscles.

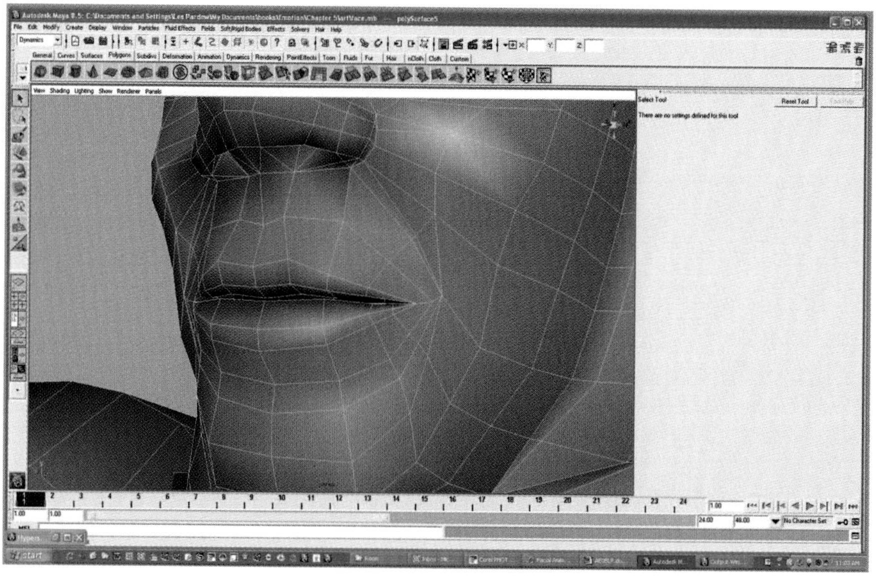

Figure 5.12 The polygons around the mouth should follow the obicularis oris muscles.

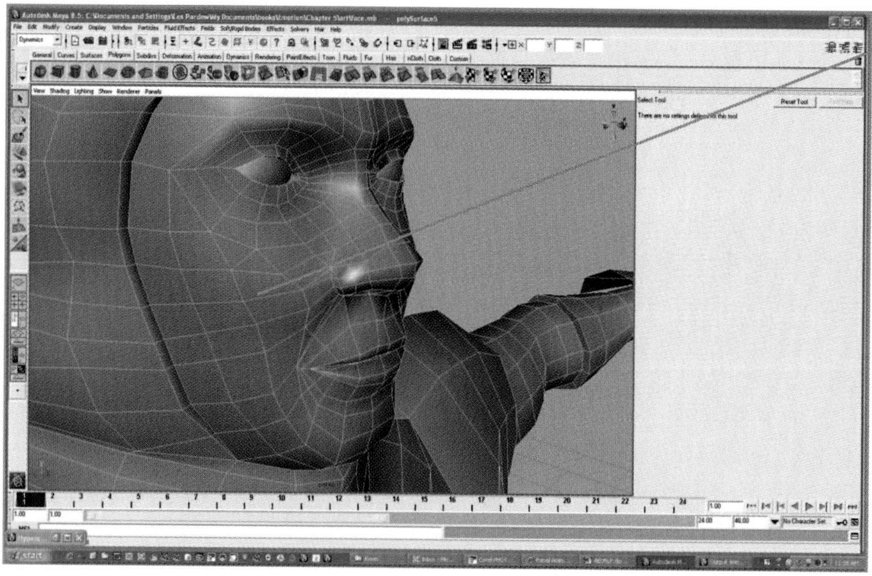

Figure 5.13 The cheeks should follow the masseter and zygomasiticus muscles.

The polygons around the mouth should follow the obicularis oris muscles and form concentric rings similar to those around the eyes, as shown in Figure 5.12.

The polygons of the cheeks should follow the masseter and the zygomasticus muscles so the cheeks can deform properly, as shown in Figure 5.13.

Organizing the polygons of the face to follow the muscle movement of the face will give the face a more natural appearance when it is animated, because the polygons can mimic the natural contours of the head.

Adding Influence

Once you have a head modeled, you will be ready to set it up for animation. 3D animation of facial expressions requires that the vertices of the head move to form different expressions. It is possible to move each vertex individually, but that becomes difficult the more vertices there are in your model. A better method is to create objects that can influence multiple vertices at the same time. These objects are called a rig and they act like the muscles and bones in our own skeleton. First, I will explain a little about rigging in general and then I will show how to build a rig for head animation.

Joints and Bones

The basic rig for a character model is made up of joints and bones similar to the ones we have in our own bodies. Figure 5.14 shows a completed skeleton for character animation. The round balls are joints and the cones are bones that connect the joints. Each joint influences assigned vertices in the model so when the joint is rotated or moved those vertices move with it.

If you look closely, you can see that the rig has many bones and joints that are similar to the ones in our own body. The main difference between our skeleton and the one in the figure is that rigs for animation are for controlling movement only and are not needed for protection of vital organs, thus there is no need for a ribcage or skull.

The joints in the character rig are the pivot points for the body. For example, by rotating the elbow joint, you can move the lower part of the arm and hand, as shown in Figure 5.15.

The 3D model is attached to the rig so that when the joints of the rig rotate, the model rotates with it. For the animation to look right, each joint has to influence specific assigned vertices. Figure 5.16 shows a rig in action inside a 3D model.

Some vertices are influenced by only one joint, while other vertices might be influenced by several joints. The amount of influence assigned to each joint for a vertex is called weighting. Almost all joints in our bodies are influenced by multiple muscles that are attached to different bones. Assigning more than one influencing joint to vertices simulates the complex movement of our bodies. For example, the movement of the shoulder is influenced by the shoulder joint but also by the spine and collarbone. Figure 5.17 shows the weighting of the pelvis joint for our 3D model. The whiter the area, the more influence the pelvis joint has on the vertices. The darker the area, the less influence the pelvis has on the vertices in that area.

A gradated influence of joints on vertices is called smooth binding and results in a more accurate representation of natural movement.

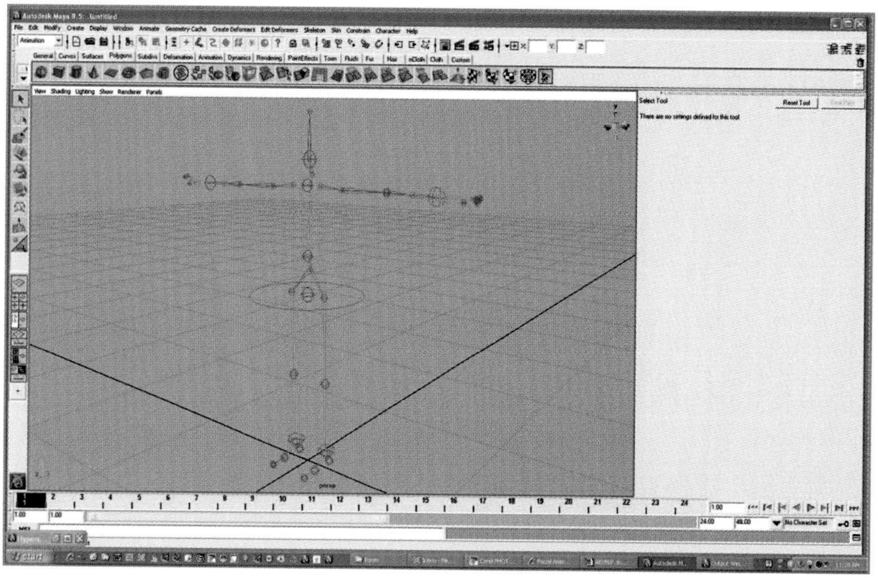

Figure 5.14 3D animators build skeletons that control the movement of the model.

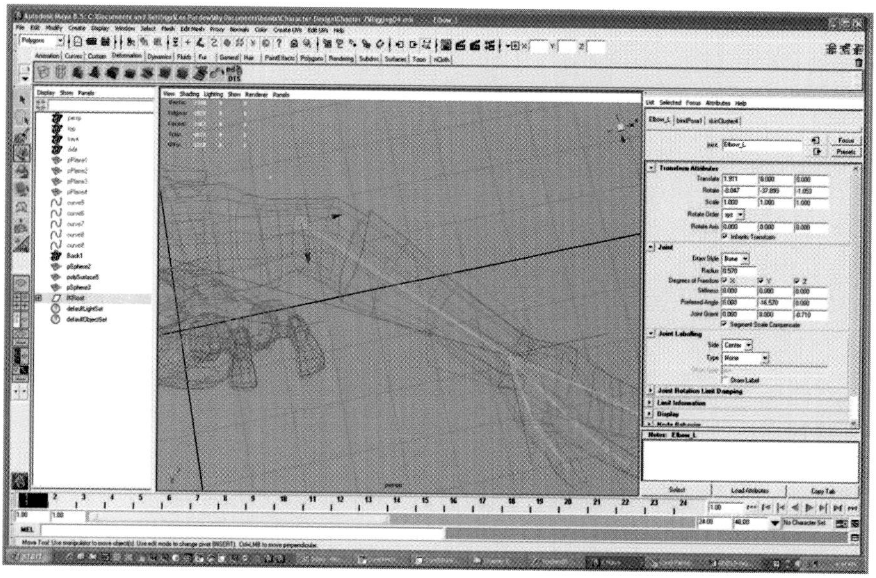

Figure 5.15 The joints rotate similar to the joints in our own body.

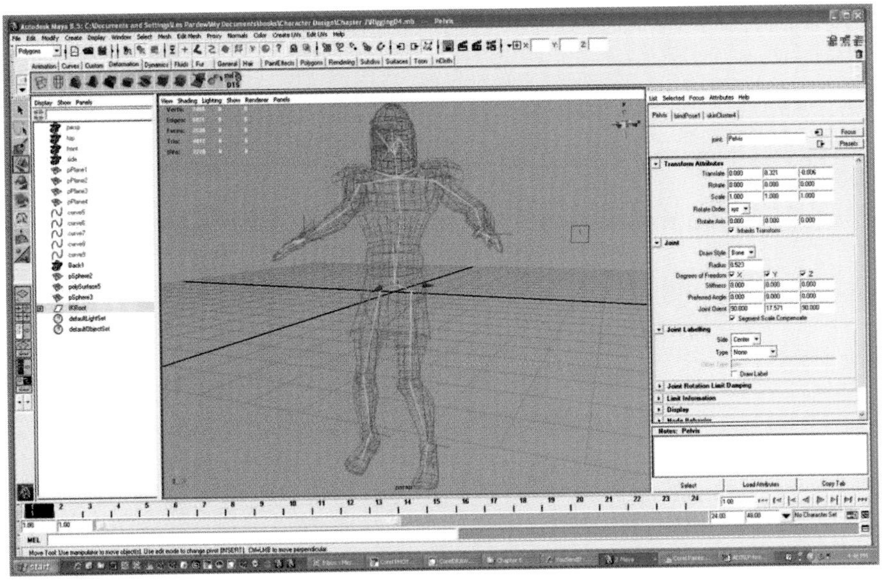

Figure 5.16
Each joint influences assigned vertices in the 3D model.

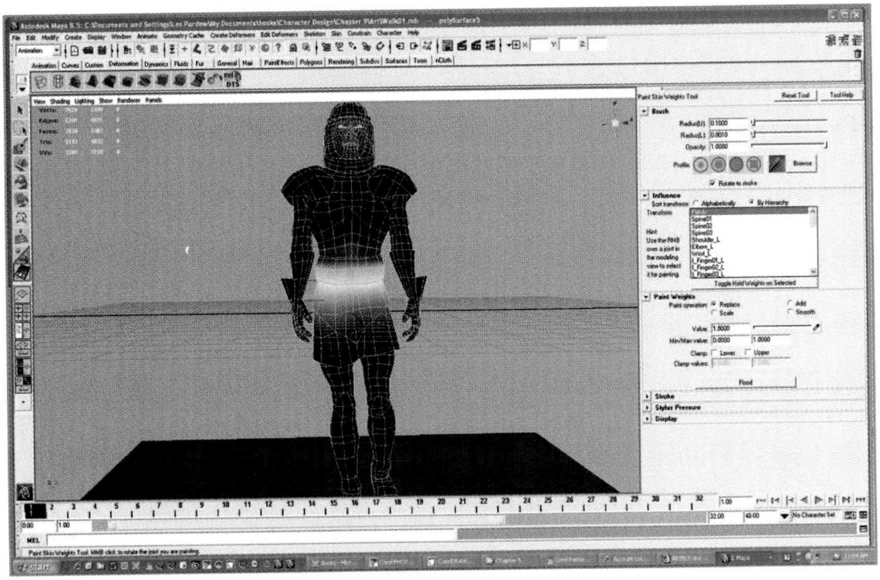

Figure 5.17
Greater influence is shown in white.

Facial Rigging

Joints work great for most parts of a character, but when it comes to the face, you need to create a fairly complex rigging system of bones. Additional influencers are needed to simulate the movement of the features for facial expressions. In this next section, you will learn one method of preparing a model for facial animations. Other methods of handling facial expressions include morph targets and blends.

STEP-BY-STEP

1

The first step in rigging a model for facial animation is to create the joints that will be the foundation of the movement of the face. The base joint for the head is the top of the spine or neck joint. If you are animating an entire character, it will be connected to the rest of the spine. In this example, we will just be binding the head. Make sure you are looking at the model in the side view. Place the neck joint using the Joint tool found in the Skeleton directory at the base of the neck, as shown in Figure 5.18. The neck joint moves the entire head.

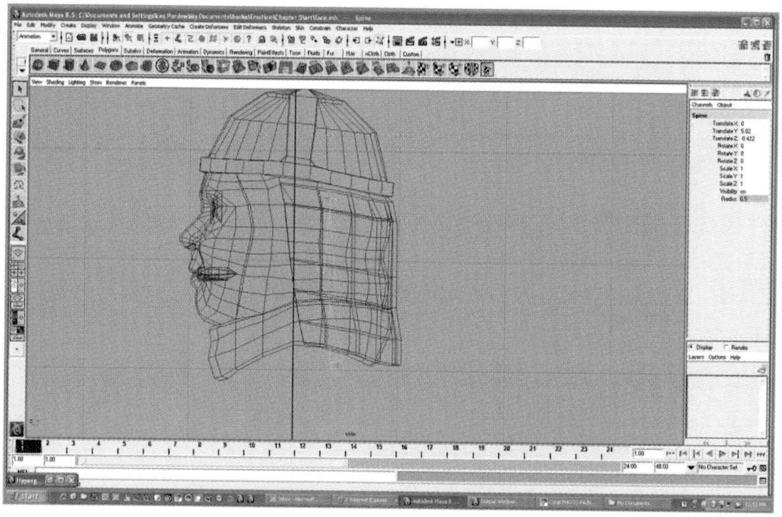

Figure 5.18 The base joint for the head is placed at the base of the neck.

2

The other two joints shown in Figure 5.19 are the head joint and the skull joint. The head joint is placed at the top of the neck and the skull joint is placed toward the back of the head just above the eyes. The head joint is the master joint for the head rigging and all other joints will extend from it. The skull joint will control all nonmoving parts of the head like the top and back of the skull.

3

Now you need to create a joint that will control the movement of the jaw. Place this joint near the base of the ear as shown in Figure 5.19, and then another joint near the chin.

4

Create a chain of joints for the tongue, as shown in Figure 5.20. These joints should be attached to the jaw joint. You can place a joint as the child of another joint by first selecting the child joint then Shift + clicking the parent joint and pressing the "p" key on the keyboard.

5

You will need some joints for the sides of the mouth. Figure 5.21 shows how these joints should be placed. One should be placed toward the back of the cheek and the other one right at the edge of the mouth. Make them the child of the jaw joint by selecting the joint at the back of the cheek, then Shift + clicking the jaw joint, and then pressing "p" on the keyboard.

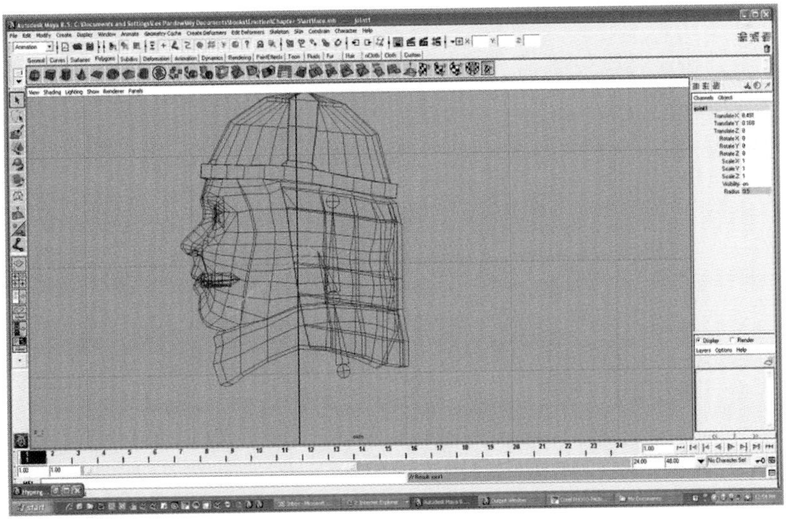

Figure 5.19
The jaw joint will control movement of the jaw.

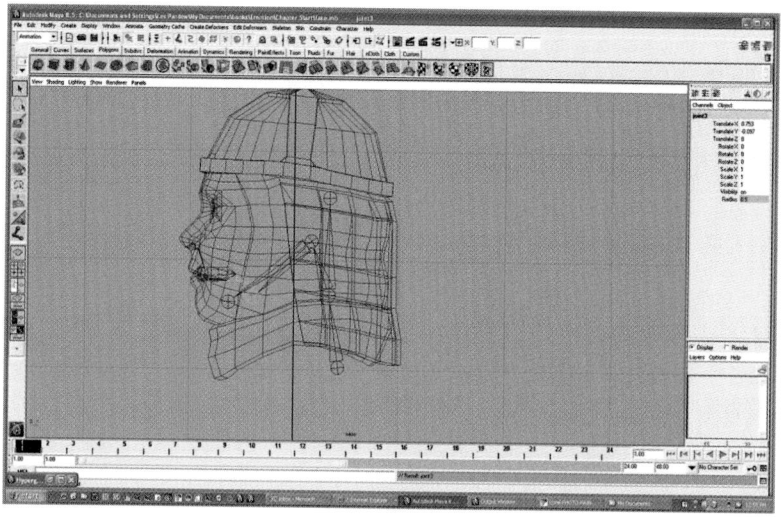

Figure 5.20
Create joints for the tongue.

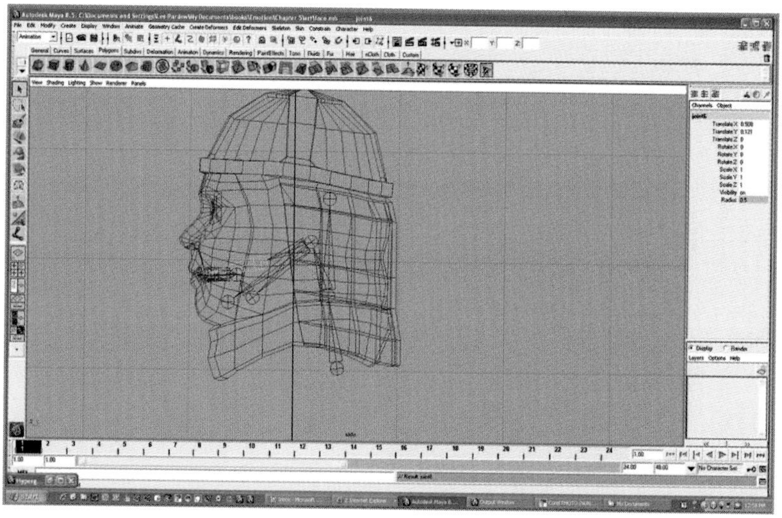

Figure 5.21
Place new joints for the sides of the mouth.

6

The eyeball joint needs to be placed in the center of the eyeball, as shown in Figure 5.22, and parented to the skull joint. Another joint needs to be placed in the upper cheek area as shown.

7

Now place two joints to control the eyebrow, as shown in Figure 5.23.

8

Place a joint at the end of the nose to influence that area.

9

The eye needs more control than just a single joint because there are three moving parts to the eye: the eyeball, the upper eyelid, and the lower eyelid. Duplicate the eyeball joint twice, labeling the first upper lid and the second lower lid.

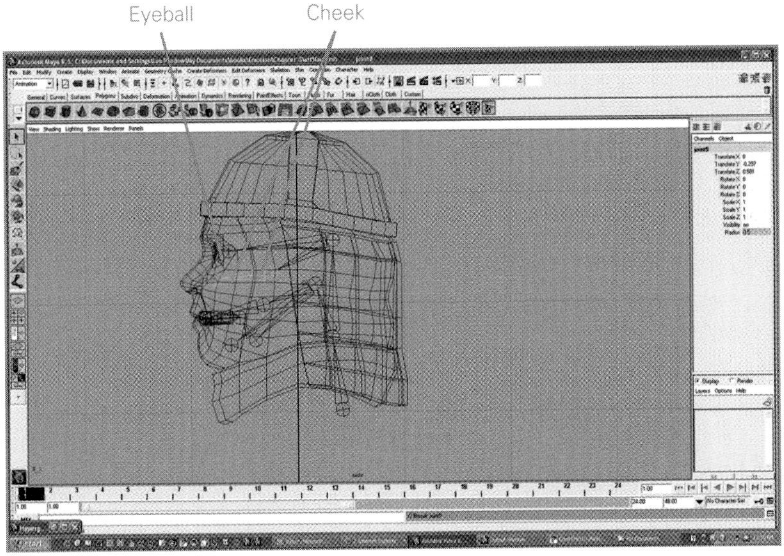

Figure 5.22 Place joints that control the eyeball and the cheek.

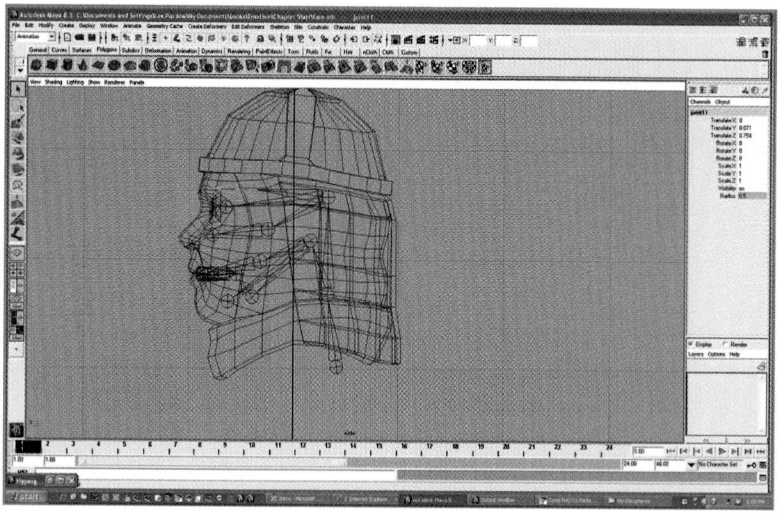

Figure 5.23 Add two joints for the eyebrow.

NOTE

Maya automatically names joints with a number, but they are a lot easier to keep track of if you name them yourself. I use the Outliner to name the joints because I can see each one and how they connect to the other joints. Figure 5.24 shows all of the joints so far and how I named them.

Later, when you are applying influences to the vertices of the model, you will find it a lot easier if you take the time now and name each joint.

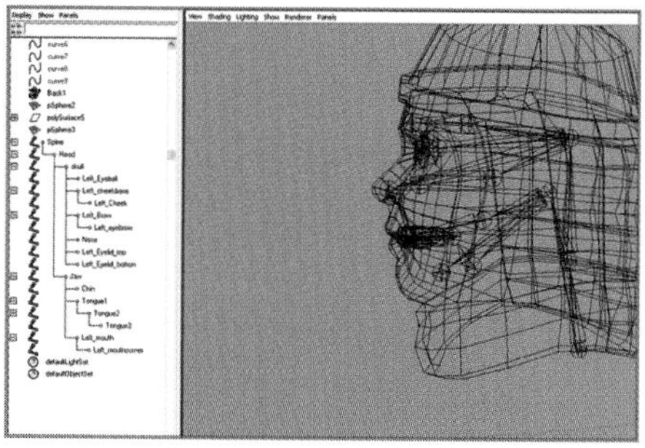

Figure 5.24 Naming the joints makes it easier to locate them later.

10

Now you need to change the views of the head to the front view and move the joints for the eyeball to the center of the eye. Figure 5.25 shows where the joints are placed.

11

Next, move the joints for the cheek to the left, as shown in Figure 5.26.

12

The mouth joints also need to be moved to the left, as shown in Figure 5.27.

13

The last joints that you need to move to the left side of the face are the eyebrow joints. Move them to the center of the eyebrow, as shown in Figure 5.28.

14

You will need joints for the right side of the mouth and the right eye to complete the joints for the face. Instead of duplicating and moving those joints, use Maya's Mirror Joint function found in the Skeleton directory. It is found in the Skeleton menu. Bring up the dialog box and change the settings to mirror across the YZ planes, as shown in Figure 5.29. You will be mirroring behavior so make sure that Behavior is checked. If you labeled the left side joints with the word "left," you can automatically rename the mirrored joint with the word "right" by using the Replacement Names for Duplicate Joints function. Select the Left_mouth joint and click Apply to mirror the joint.

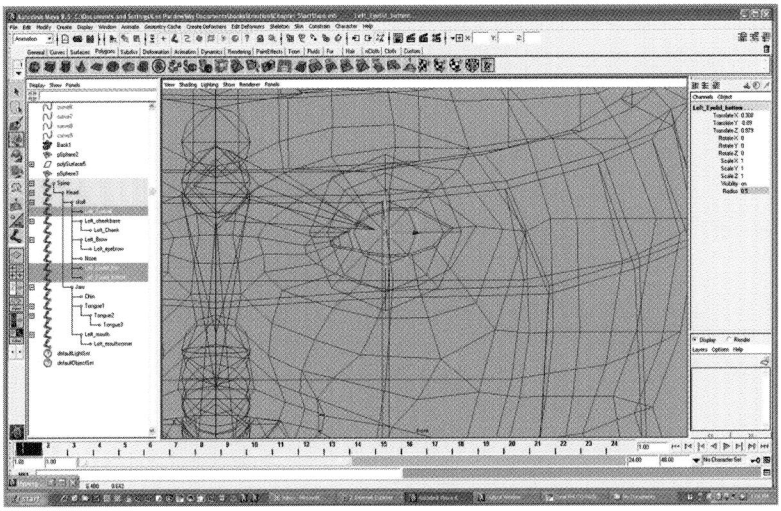

Figure 5.25
Move the eyeball joints to the left eye.

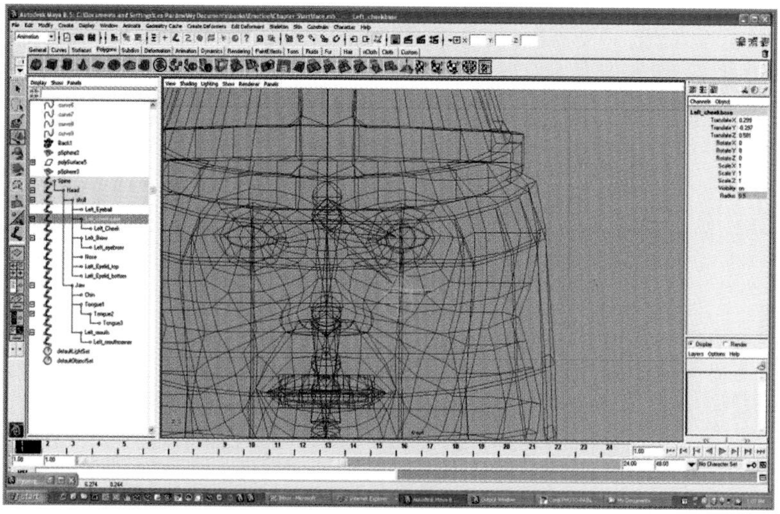

Figure 5.26 Move the cheek joints to the left.

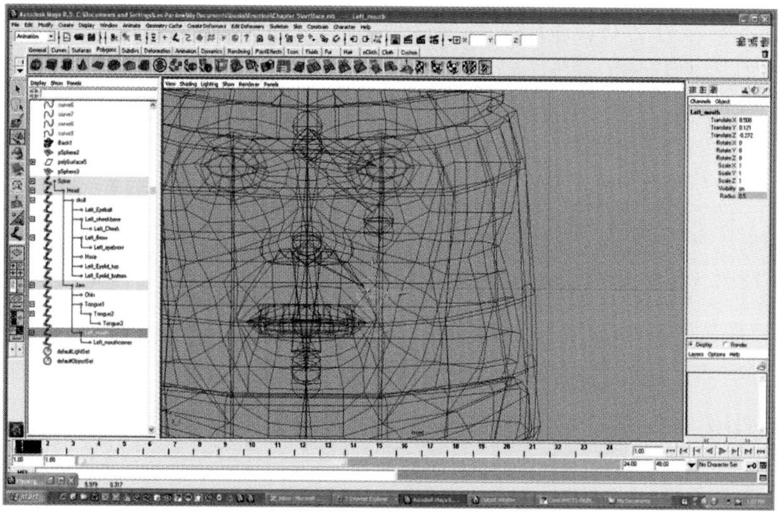

Figure 5.27 Move the mouth joints to the left corner of the mouth.

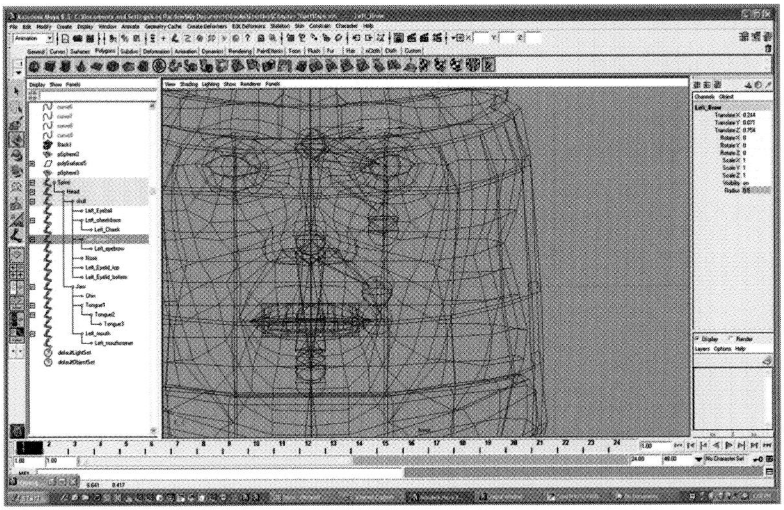

Figure 5.28
The eyebrow joints should also be moved to the left side of the face.

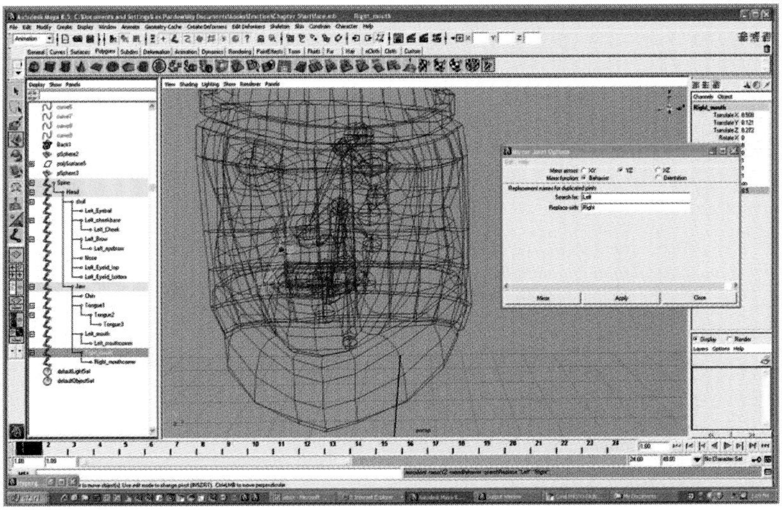

Figure 5.29
Mirror the left mouth joints to the right.

15

Repeat the process of mirroring joints for each of the three eye joints, the cheek joints, and the eyebrow joints, as shown in Figure 5.30.

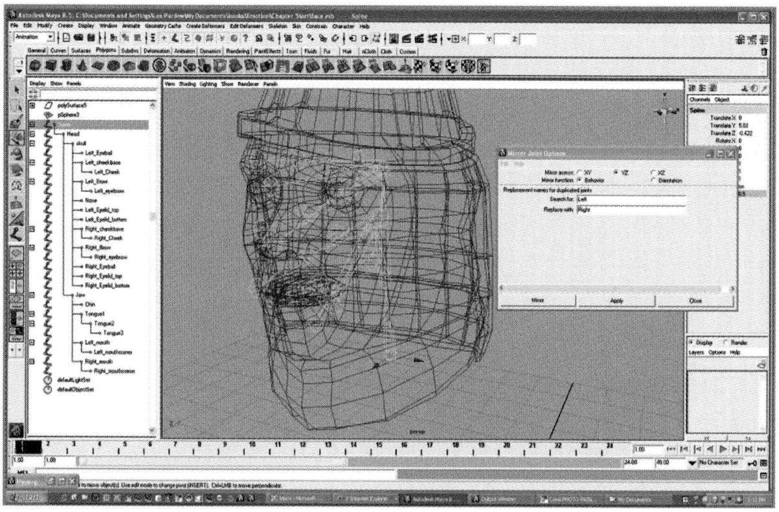

Figure 5.30 Mirror the eye joints to the right side of the face.

Now you have the basic bone structure for the head. This structure will be the foundation for building facial expressions in the 3D model. However, the structure is not complete. You still need a way to control the mouth. So far, all you have are the joints that control the edges. Many facial expressions require fine control of both the upper lip and the lower lip.

Rigging the Mouth

The mouth is unique in that it has two flexible lips that are capable of a huge variety of expressions. Next to the eyes, the mouth is probably the most viewed feature of the face. The mouth, however, is far more flexible and moveable than any other facial feature. Because of the extreme changes the mouth can achieve, special care should be given to rigging it.

Before you start, you should reduce the size of the joints so they don't clutter up the small area of the mouth. You can reduce the joint size by going to Display > Animation > Joint Size. A dialog box will appear. Change the size to .10, as shown in Figure 5.31.

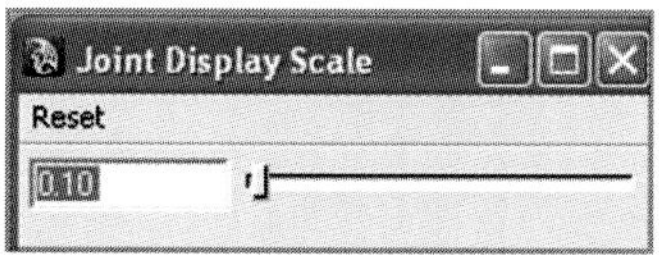

Figure 5.31 Change the joint size.

Now you are ready to start building the rig for the mouth.

STEP-BY-STEP

1

The first step to rigging the mouth is to place two new joints along the upper lip and make them the child of the left mouth joint, as shown in Figure 5.32. Notice that the joint in the middle of the lip sticks out from the mouth a little. This is to allow for stretching of the mouth.

2

Mirror the joints across the XZ plane starting with the Left_mouthcorner joint and move the joints down into place for the lower lip, as shown in Figure 5.33.

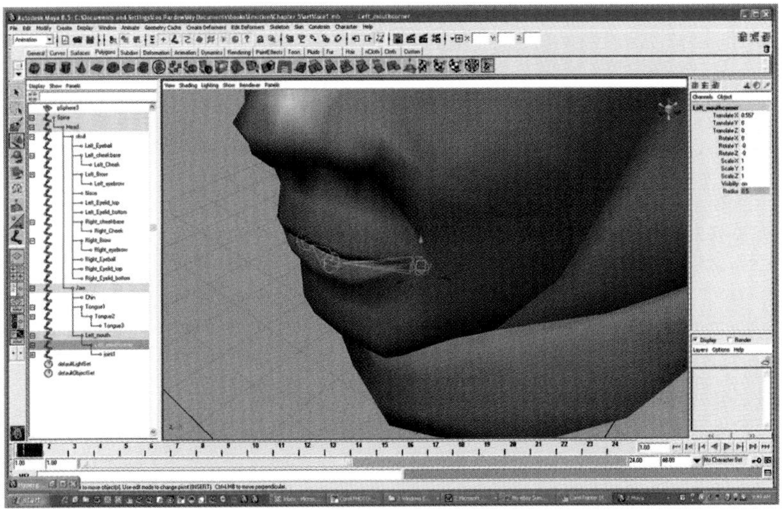

Figure 5.32
Start rigging the mouth by placing two joints along the upper lip.

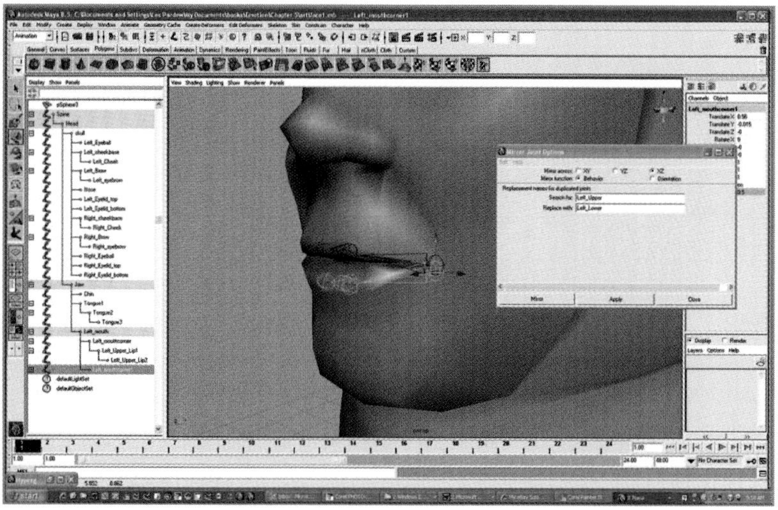

Figure 5.33 Mirror the joints for the lower lip.

3

We will be using an inverse kinematics handle or IK handle for short, to help animate the mouth. Inverse kinematics is a way to easily move chains of joints without having to rotate each individual joint. Before you can add an IK handle to the new upper lip joint chain, you need to set a preferred angle by first selecting the base of the joint chain at the Left_Mouth joint and then selecting the Set Preferred Angle feature from the Skeleton menu, as shown in Figure 5.34.

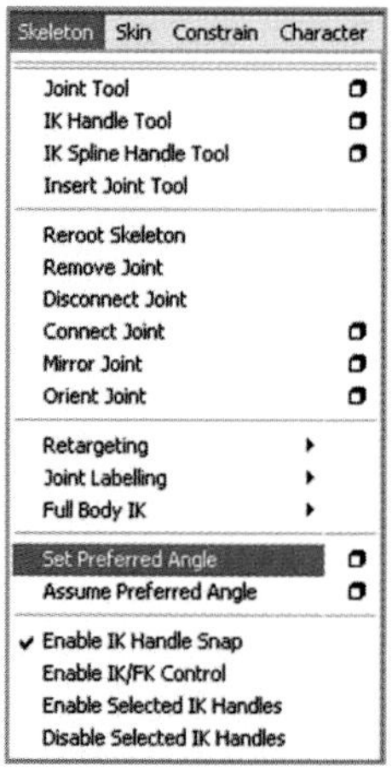

Figure 5.34 Set a preferred angle for the joint chain.

4

Now you can apply the IK handle by selecting it from the Skeleton menu and clicking first the Left_mouthcorner joint and then clicking the joint at the end of the chain near the upper center of the mouth, as shown in Figure 5.35. The handle will appear as three lines perpendicular to each other, originating at the center of the third joint.

5

Create an IK handle for the lower lip in the same way as you did for the upper lip, starting with Left_mouthcorner1 and ending with the joint in the center of the lower lip.

6

You can now create the joints for the right side of the mouth in the same way you did the left, but it is a lot easier to just take the left side and mirror it over to the right. If you decide to mirror the joints, you will need to delete the right mouth joints first or you will have two sets of joints on the right side. Figure 5.36 shows the mirrored joints.

7

The IK handles are not mirrored with the joints so you will have to create them for the right side of the mouth. Apply the IK handles to the right side so the mouth rig looks like Figure 5.37.

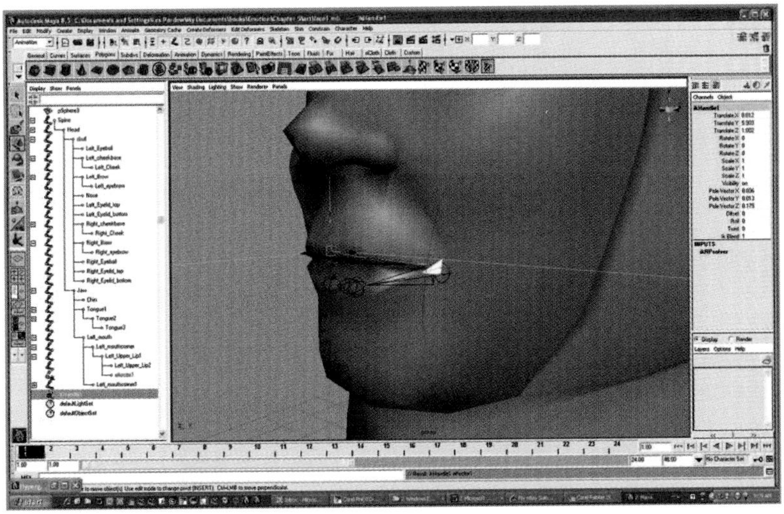

Figure 5.35
Add an IK handle to the upper lip.

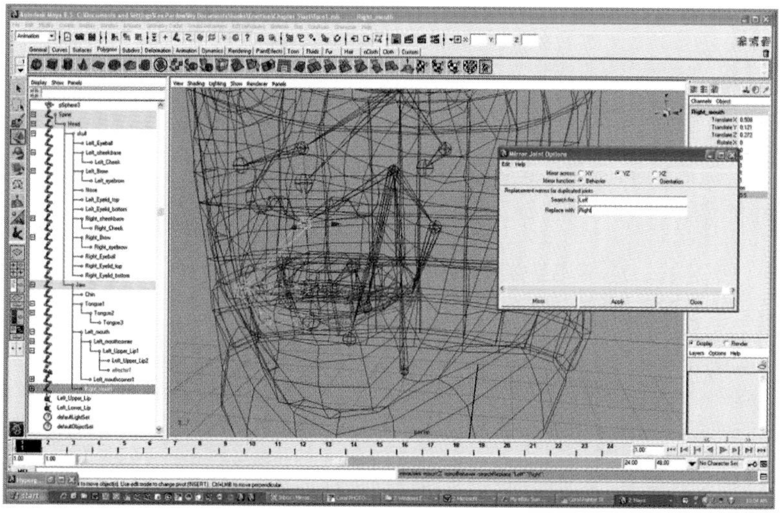

Figure 5.36
The left mouth rig can be mirrored to the right.

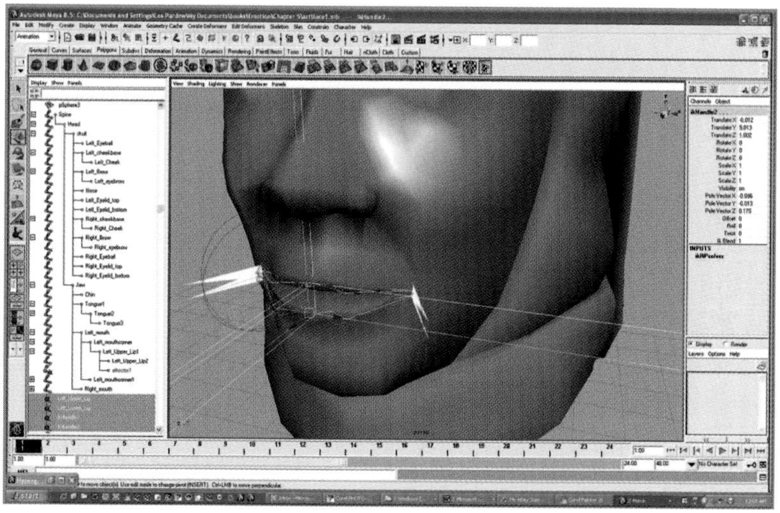

Figure 5.37
Create IK handles for the right side of the mouth rig.

8

Go to the Hypergraph found in the Windows directory. Notice that the IK handles are off to the side of the rig hierarchy. You need to parent the IK handles to joints in the hierarchy so they will work correctly. Select the IK handles for the upper lip and parent them to the skull, as shown in Figure 5.38.

9

Parent the IK handles for the lower lip to the jaw joint, as shown in Figure 5.39.

10

Rotate the jaw joint downward to open the mouth joints. If you created the hierarchy correctly, the upper lip joints should remain in place while the lower lip joints follow the movement of the jaw joints, as shown in Figure 5.40. We haven't attached the vertices of the model to the joints so only the joints will move and not the mesh.

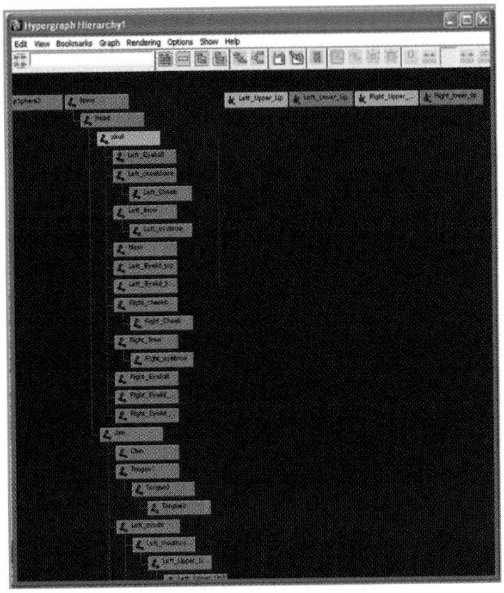

Figure 5.38 The IK handles for the upper lip are children of the skull joint.

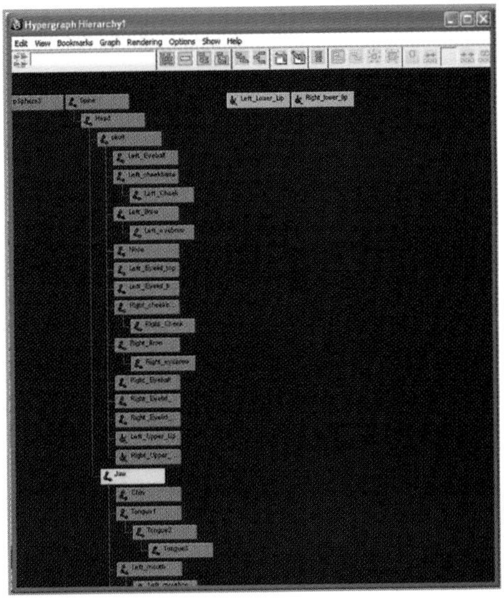

Figure 5.39 The lower lip IK handles need to be part of the jaw hierarchy.

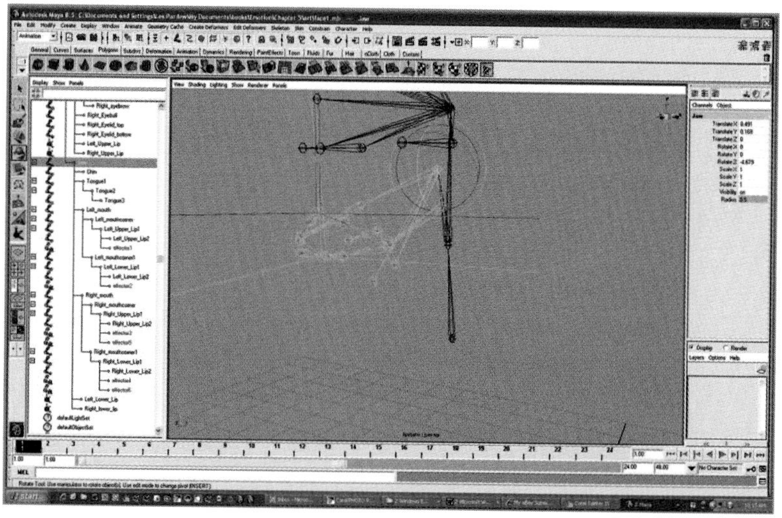

Figure 5.40 The mouth should open when you rotate the jaw.

The head rig is now finished and ready to attach to the model. This is a relatively simple facial rig; however, it should work for most facial expressions. If your model needs more control, you can add more joints to places like the eyebrows, cheeks, and mouth.

Binding the Head

The next step in getting the head ready for animation is to bind the geometry of the head to the bone structure you have just created. The process in Maya is called skinning. There are two ways to bind models to joints in Maya: one is called smooth binding and the other is called rigid binding. In smooth binding, vertices can share joint influences between several joints. In hard binding, only one joint can influence each vertex. Hard binding is basically for real-time applications where processing power limits the number of calculations for animation or for rigid robotic movements. Smooth binding is for more organic animations, like facial animations. We will be using smooth binding in our examples in this book.

STEP-BY-STEP

1

In the main menu go to Skin > Binding > Smooth Binding and bring up the dialog box shown in Figure 5.41. Set the Bind to Joint Hierarchy > Bind method to Closest in Hierarchy, which tells Maya to bind the model following the bone structure, and Maximum Influences to 4, which tells Maya to apply four influencing joints to the vertices of the model. Maintain Max Influences should be checked. Set the Dropoff rate to 4 and check Colorize Skeleton, as shown in the figure. To bind the head, first select the geometry of the head and then Shift + click the neck joint and click Apply.

2

The teeth are bound separately from the face because they are separate models. Because the upper teeth only need the influence of one joint, the Skull joint, you will need to change the Bind to Option to Selected Joints. Select the upper teeth and bind them to the skull joint, as shown in Figure 5.42.

3

Bind the lower teeth to the jaw joint. Binding the teeth separately makes it easier to work with the joint influences on the lips and tongue later.

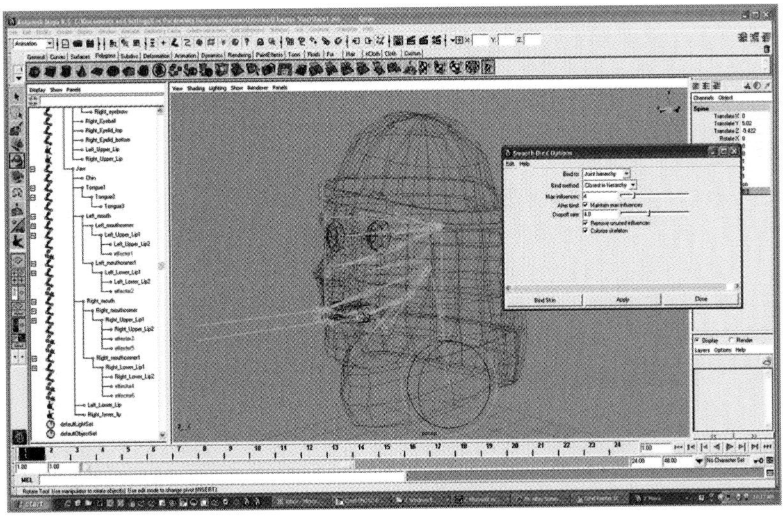

Figure 5.41
Bind the head geometry to the facial rig.

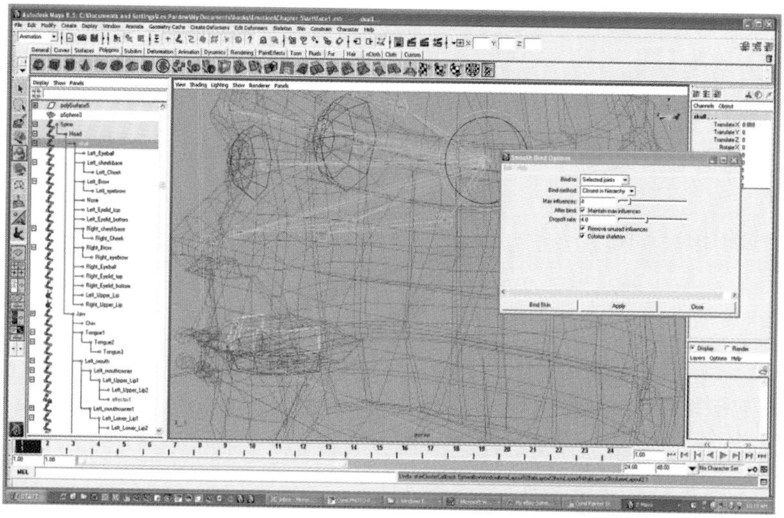

Figure 5.42 The upper teeth are bound to the skull joint.

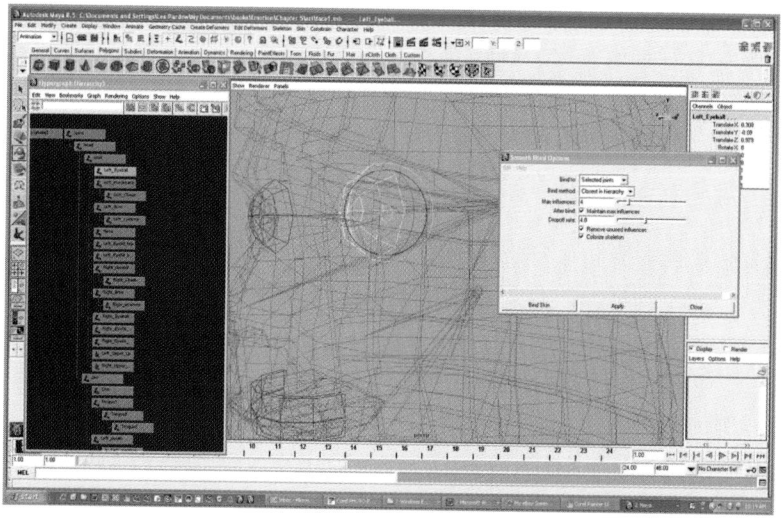

Figure 5.43 The Hypergraph utility is used to select the eyeball joint.

4

The eyeballs also need to be bound separately from the rest of the face. Now you can select the eyeball geometry and eyeball joint for binding. I use the Hypergraph utility found in the Windows menu for selecting the eyeball joint, as shown in Figure 5.43, because it is easier than trying to select the eyeball joint in the Workspace where three separate joints occupy the same place.

5

Repeat the binding process for the right eye, binding the right eye geometry to the right eyeball joint.

The model is now bound to the skeleton, but the binding is general for each joint and needs to be more specific to work correctly for facial animation. While Maya does the best it can with anticipating how you want the weighting of each vertex, it is impossible to use a general tool to get specific results.

For example, if you rotate the jaw joint, you will notice that there are problems with the weighting of the lips, as shown in Figure 5.44. They don't react to the movement of the jaw correctly because the weighting is wrong in that area.

You will need to adjust the influences or weighting of vertices in the model so they will work properly. This is called adjusting skin weights. There are two main ways to adjust smooth skin weights in Maya. One is to use the Paint Skin Weights tool and the other is to use the Component Editor. I will show you how to use both.

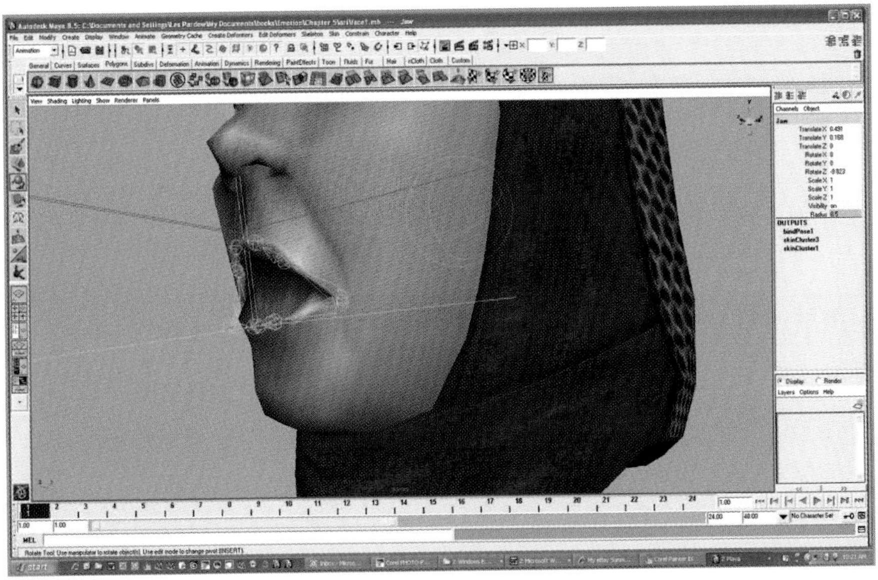

Figure 5.44
The general weighting of the mouth is wrong.

Component Editor

You can also use the Component Editor to adjust skin weighting to specific numbers. The Component Editor is found under General Editors in the Window menu. It is shown in Figure 5.45.

The Component Editor works similarly to a spreadsheet. It has several tabs along the top. Choose the Smooth Skins tab to edit smooth skin weights. Change the selection mode to Vertex on the model and select all of the vertices of the model, as shown in Figure 5.45.

All vertices will be listed along the left-hand column with each joint listed along the top row. The weighting of each vertex is shown in the rows and columns that correspond to the vertex and joint. The weighting is a number between 0 and 1, with 1 being full weighting and 0 being no weighting. By changing the numbers in these rows and columns, you adjust the weighting for each joint and vertex.

Now it is time to put this editor to work. Start with the character's helmet.

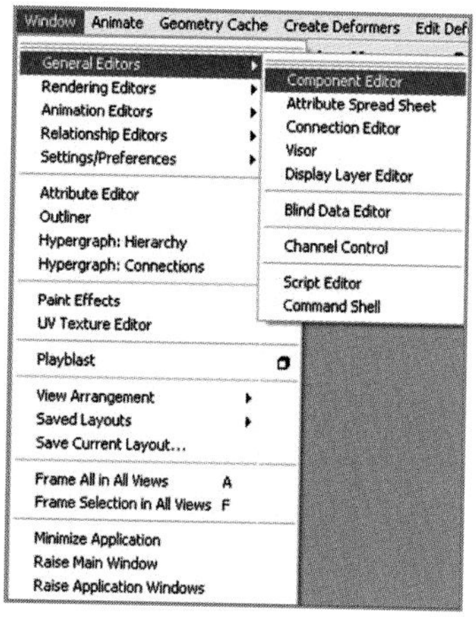

Figure 5.45 The Component Editor can be used to change specific weighting on each vertex.

STEP-BY-STEP

1

Change the display to Component Selection mode and select all of the vertices of the helmet.

2

Find the skull joint along the top of the editor and click on it.

3

You will notice that the column directly below skull turns black, indicating that all vertices in that column are selected. Find the slider along the bottom of the editor and slide it all the way to the right. This will change all the numbers in the column to 1, as shown in Figure 5.46. Changing the number to 1 forces all the vertices of the selected area to only have one influencer: the skull joint.

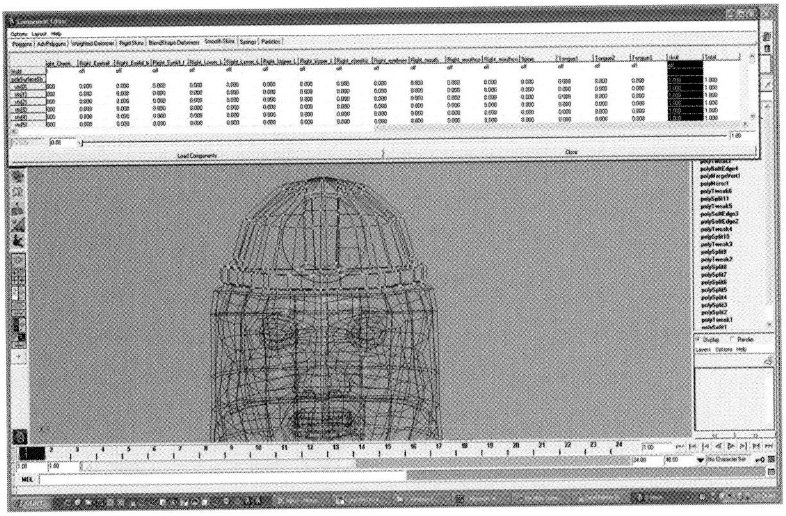

Figure 5.46
Change the weighting of all vertices of the helmet to 1.

In addition to being used to force weighting to a joint, the Component Editor can also be used to remove a joint's influence from the model. There are several joints in the rig that are used for pivots or whose weighting needs to be so finely adjusted that it is easier starting with no weighting than it is to use the default weighting supplied by Maya. For these joints, the Component Editor is ideal. Next is an example of how to remove the influences of a joint from the model.

STEP-BY-STEP

1

Select all of the vertices of the model by dragging a bounding box over it.

2

Find the Left_eyelid_top joint and select the top vertex in that column.

3

Scroll down to the bottom of the column and Shift + click the last vertex in the column. This should select all of the vertices in that column.

4

Now type in the number that you want all of the vertices to have for this joint. In this case, the number will be 0 because you want to remove the Left_eyelid_top joint's influences from the model. A 0 indicates that this joint has no influence on any of the selected vertices.

5

Press Enter on the keyboard and all the numbers in that column will change to 0, as shown in Figure 5.47.

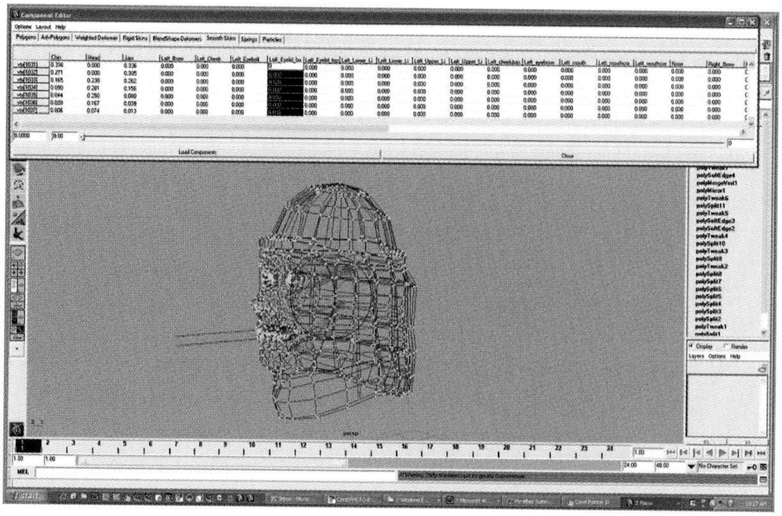

Figure 5.47 Remove the influences of the Left_eyelid_top joint from the model.

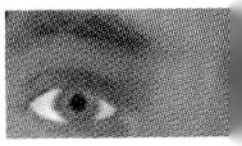

There are several other joints that need to have their influences removed from the model. The following list contains these joints:

- Left_cheekbase
- Right_cheekbase
- Left_Brow
- Right_Brow
- Left_Eyeball
- Left_Eyelid_top
- Left_Eyelid_Bottom
- Right_Eyeball
- Right_Eyelid_top
- Right_Eyelid_Bottom
- Tongue1
- Tongue2
- Tongue3
- Left_mouth
- Right_mouth

Go through the process of eliminating the influences of these joints from the model. Using the Component Editor is a good way to adjust skin weights, but it isn't very intuitive. Another way to refine the weighting on a model is to paint it on the model using Maya's Paint Skin Weights feature.

Paint Skin Weights

The Paint Skin Weights feature in Maya makes it possible for you to use Maya's 3D paint feature to apply skin weights to models using the Artisan brush tools. This feature gives you a visual view of how the weights are applied to the model, making it easier to see and adjust them.

First, bring up the Paint Skin Weights tool found in the Edit Smooth Skin submenu of the Skin menu. The tool is pictured in use in Figure 5.48.

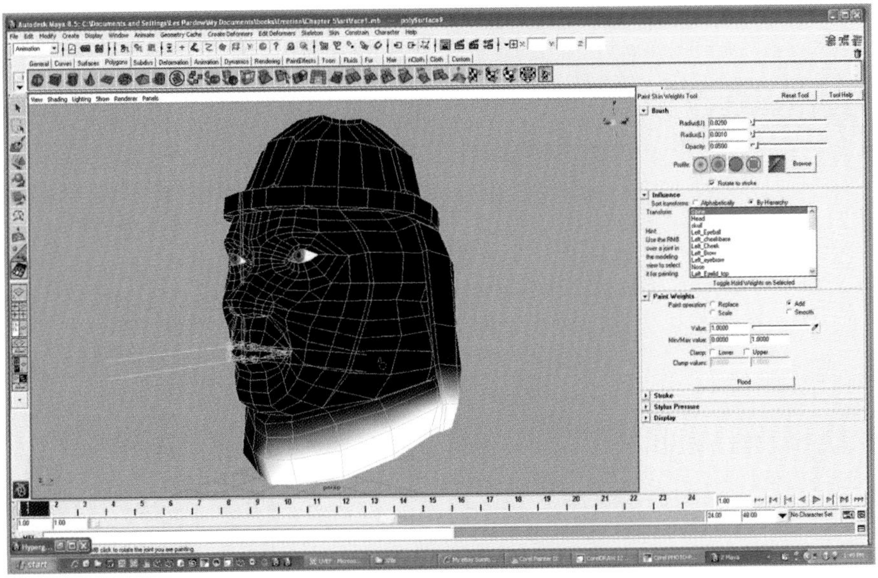

Figure 5.48
The Paint Skin Weights tool has many features.

The Paint Skin Weights tool allows you to adjust the weighting of each vertex as if you were painting them on the surface. Darker areas represent less weighting and lighter areas represent more weighting. In Figure 5.48, the Spine joint is selected. The white areas around the base of the model are the vertices that are assigned to the Spine joint.

There are three main options that you need to concern yourself with when painting skin weights: Brush, Influence, and Paint Weights. These options appear on the right side of the screen. The Brush options let you control the size and type of brush you paint with. The Influence options let you choose what joint you are working with. The Paint Weights options let you choose how your painting affects the model.

To give the painting skin weights a try, select the spine joint and paint the area indicated in the figure above. Use the Paint Skin Weights tool to replace other influences in this area with those of spine joint.

You can also use the Paint Skin Weights tool to see how each joint influences the model by clicking the joints in the Influences Options area. Try running through a few of the joints to see their influences. You should notice that several of the joints that you zeroed out with the Component Editor show no white areas.

Painting skin weights is an interactive process where you must adjust weighting between several joints to get each one to look right. For this reason, I can't really show the process as a step by step procedure. Instead, what I will do is take each of the joints that have weighting and show you how they should look when you are done painting the weights.

- Start with the spine joint shown earlier in Figure 5.48. The spine joint should only influence the area around the base of the neck. This is so when the head joint is animated, the area around the base remains in place, making it appear to be connected to the character's shoulders.

  As you paint the weighting, you will notice that the spine joint's influences extend above the area shown in the figure. In order to remove the weighting in these areas, you will have to paint those areas with other joint influences. For now, paint these areas with the head joint.

  The weights only need to be painted on the left side because the model and rig are symmetrical and you can mirror the weights from the left side to the right side.

- The head joint is primarily there as a pivot point for the entire head. Most of the weighting of the head is influenced by joints that are children of the head joint. Only the small area shown in Figure 5.49 is influenced by the head joint directly.
- The majority of the model is influenced by the skull joint, as shown in Figure 5.50. Take a close look at the figure. You will notice that in some places the areas are completely white and in other areas they are gray. Try to match the weighting in the figure with that on your own model.
- The Left_Cheek joint influences the area just below the eye, as shown in Figure 5.51. Notice that there is really no area that is completely white and the weighting blends into the areas around the cheek.
- The Left_Eyebrow joint's weighting is similar to the cheek. It controls the area just above the eye, as shown in Figure 5.52. Because this model is wearing a helmet, the weighting only extends up the forehead to the edge of the helmet. In a model without a helmet, the weighting would extend up near the hairline.

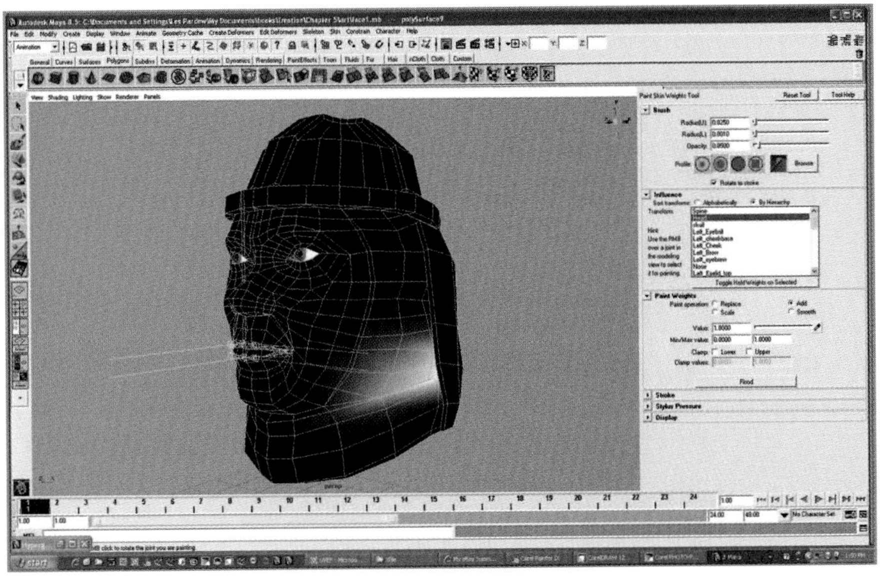

Figure 5.49
The area influenced by the head joint is relatively small.

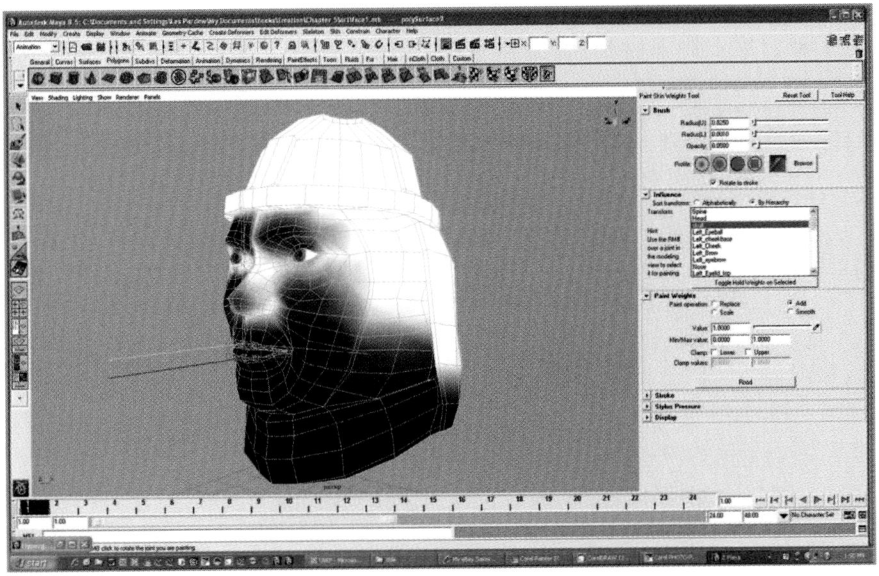

Figure 5.50
Much of the model is influenced by the skull joint.

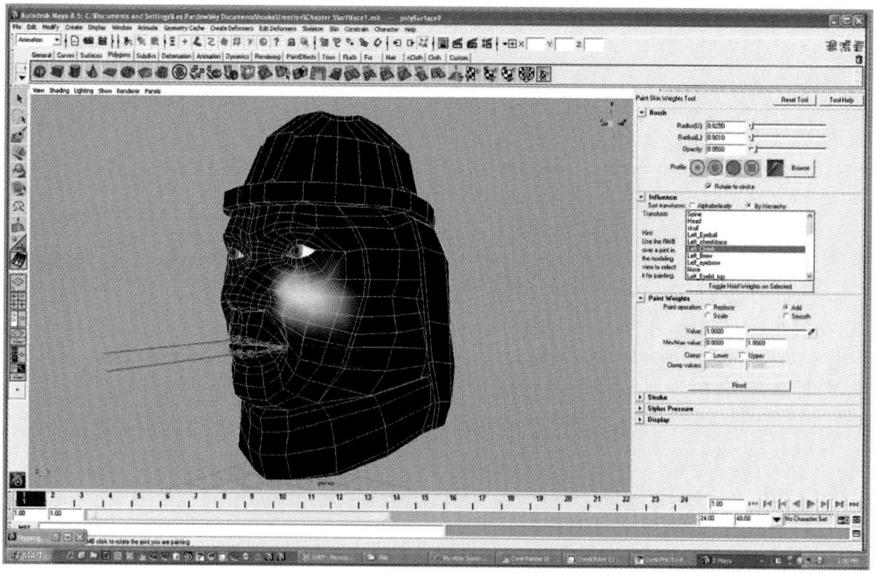

Figure 5.51 The weighting of the Left_Cheek joint is just below the eye.

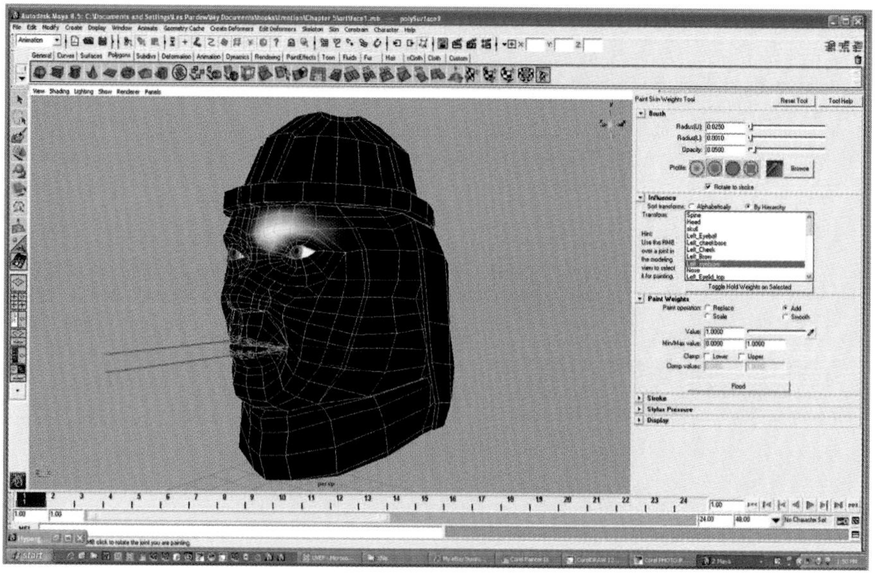

Figure 5.52 The Left_Eyebrow joint controls the area just above the eye.

- The nose joint just influences the tip of the nose, as shown in Figure 5.53. This joint is not necessary for all models, but it can give the animation a more natural look if you can make minor adjustments of the nose.
- Some of the most delicate weighting takes place around the eye. Figure 5.54 shows the weighting of the Left_Eyelid_top joint.
- The weighting of the Left_Eyelid_bottom is shown in Figure 5.55. This weighting is even more subtle than the upper lid. It is so slight that you have to really look to see it.
- You should check the weighting of the eyelids by rotating the joints to have the model close his eye, as shown in Figure 5.56. The top lid should move downward most of the way, but the bottom lid should also move up just a little.
- The weighting of the jaw joint is shown in Figure 5.57. Notice the blending that occurs between the jaw joint and the spine and head joints.
- The chin joint is placed in the model so the weighting of the jaw can extend all the way from the ear to the end of the chin. This joint doesn't actually animate, but it is there for binding purposes. Figure 5.58 shows the weighting of the chin joint.

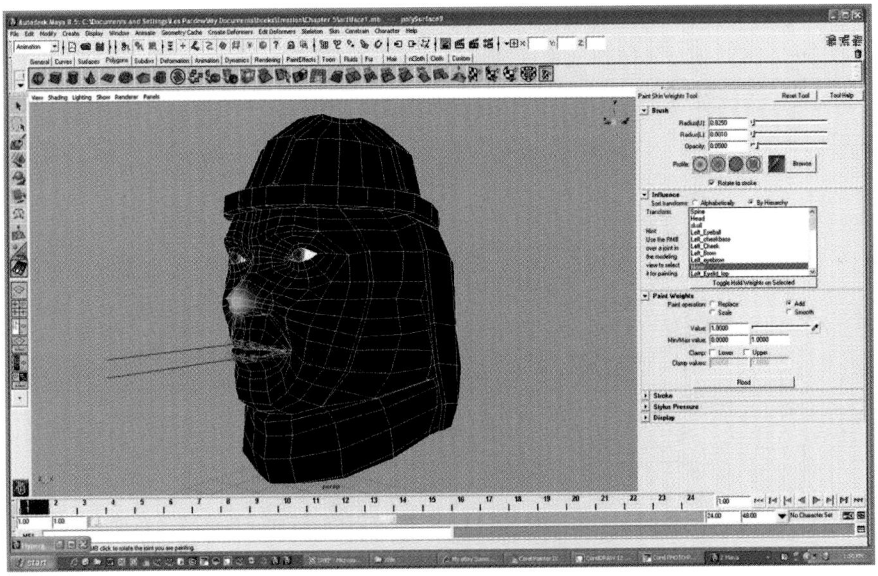

Figure 5.53
The nose joint has a small area of influence.

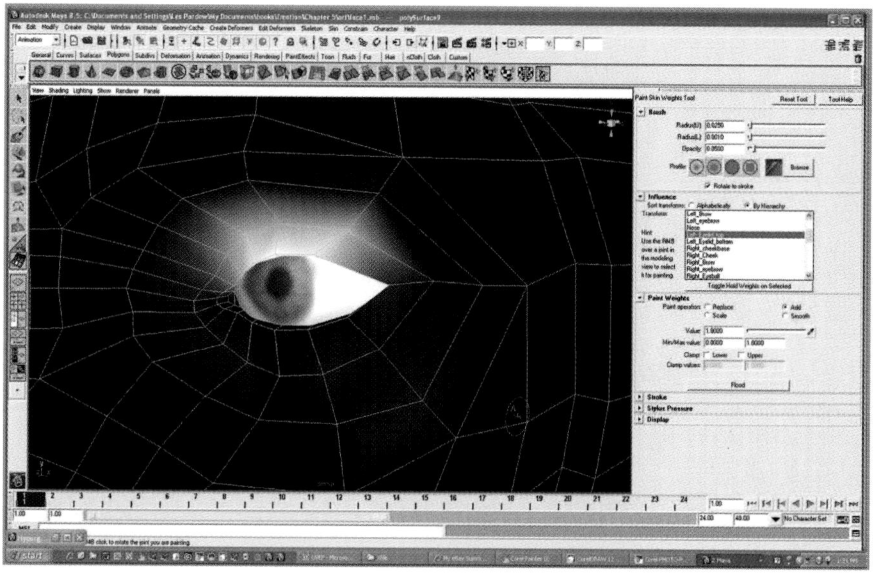

Figure 5.54
Weighting around the eye is delicate.

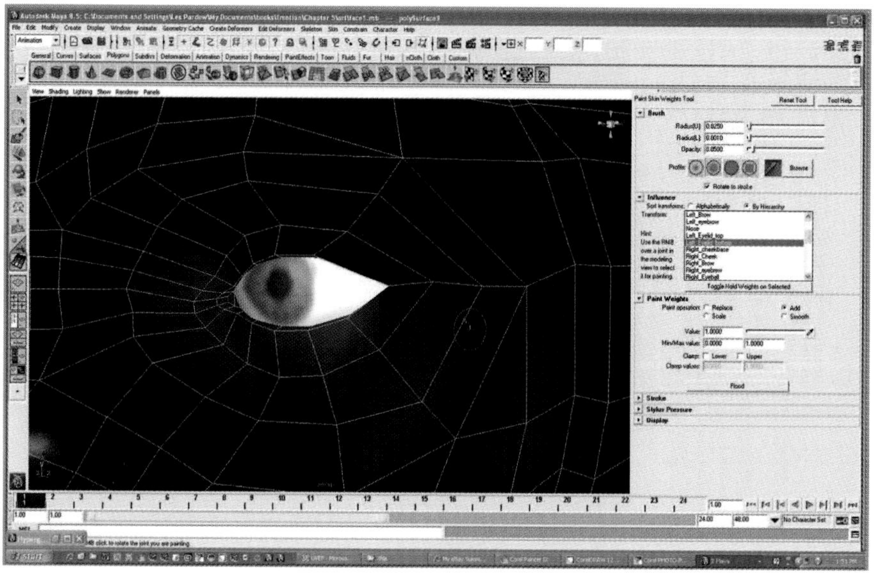

Figure 5.55
The lower eyelid has very subtle weighting.

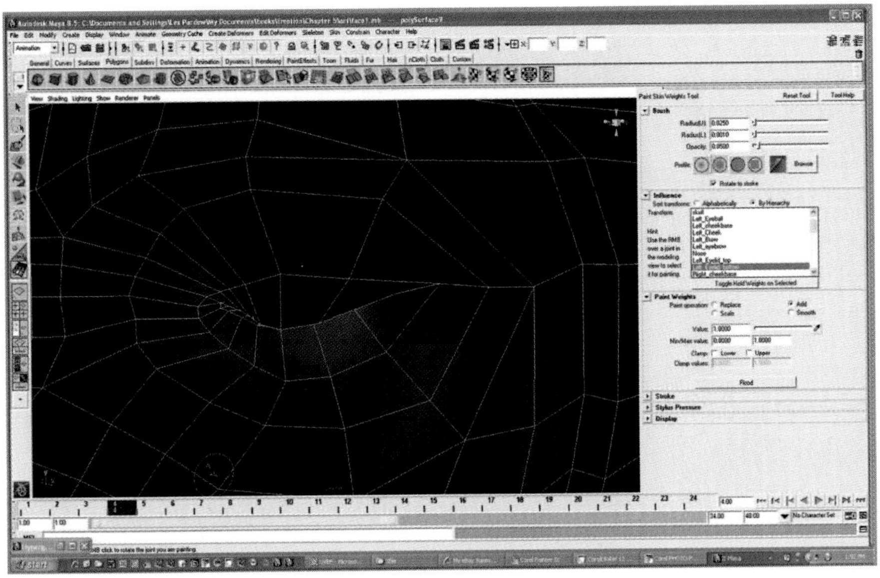

Figure 5.56
Check the weighting by animating the eyelids.

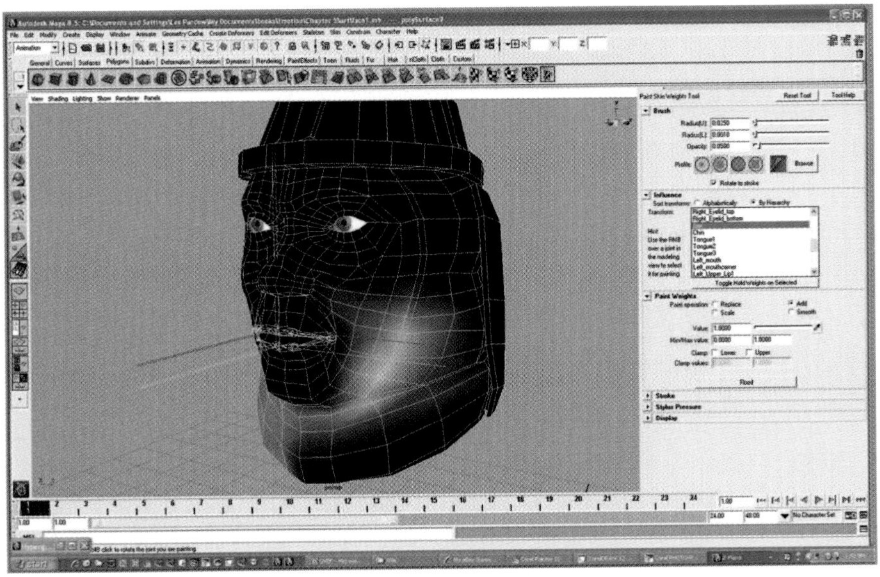

Figure 5.57
The jaw joint controls the character's jaw movement.

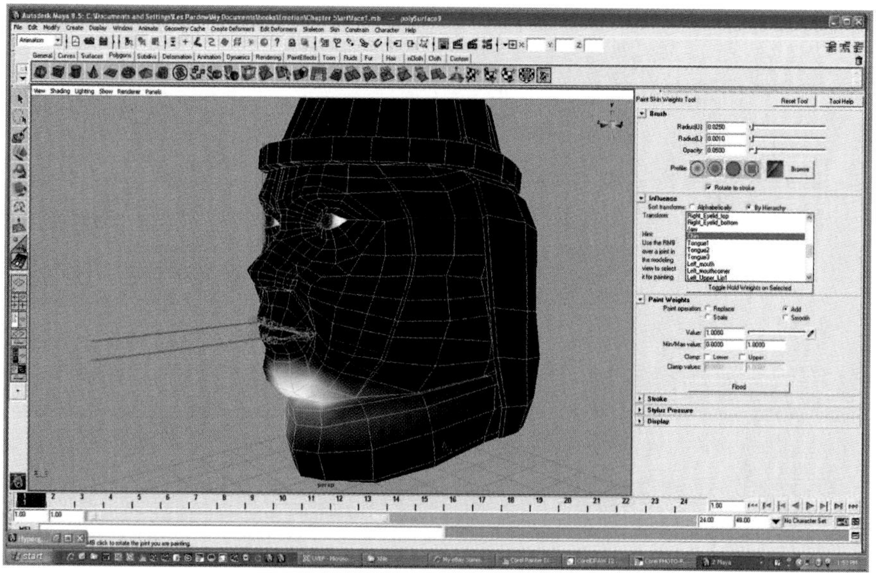

Figure 5.58
The weighting of the chin joint controls the movement of the chin.

- Most of the weighting of the mouth will be around the corners controlled by the Left_mouthcorner joint, as shown in Figure 5.59. Notice that the weighting of this joint extends out to the cheek and up to the nose as well.
- Only minimal weighting is applied for the Left_Upper_Lip1 joint, as shown in Figure 5.60, because the primary purpose of this joint is to supply the stretching of the mouth when the mouth opens.
- The Left_Upper_lip2 joint influences the area just below the nose, as shown in Figure 5.61.
- The Left_mouthcorner1 joint is similar to the Left_mouthcorner joint in its influence, which extends outward from the mouth, as shown in Figure 5.62.
- The lower lip is bound similar to the upper lip, with little influence given to the Left_Lower_Lip1 joint, as shown in Figure 5.63.
- Finally the Left_Lower_Lip2 joint influences the area of the middle of the lower lip above the chin, as shown in Figure 5.64.
- The rigging of the tongue is not easy to show in pictures because it is inside the head. All you really need to know is to bind the tip of the tongue to the Tongue3 joint and the base of the tongue to the Tongue2 joint. Tongue1 joint should have no weighting.

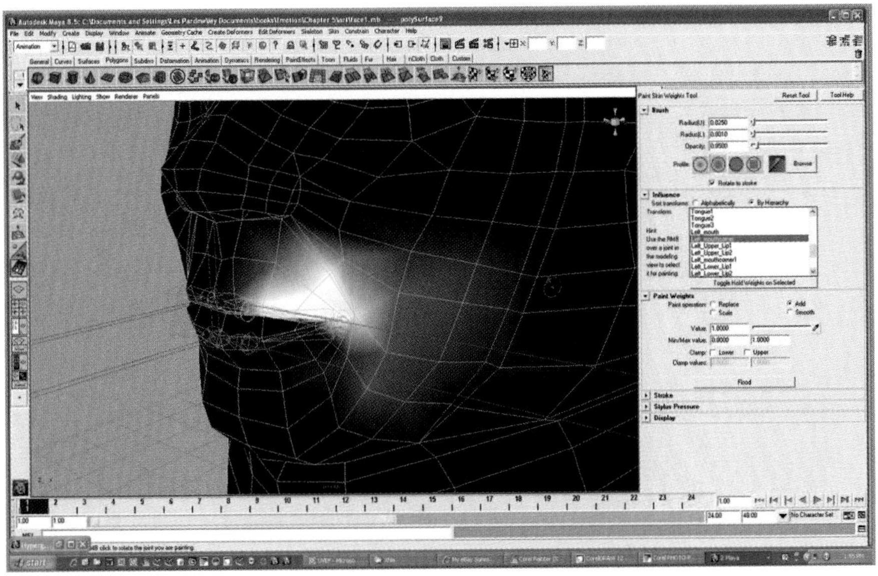

Figure 5.59
The weighting of the mouth extends outward toward the cheek.

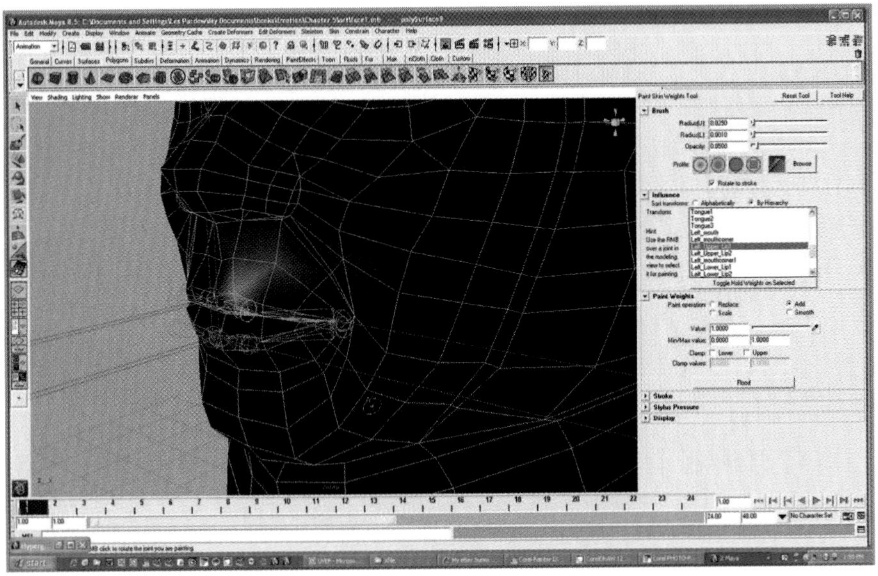

Figure 5.60
The Left_Upper_Lip1 joint only has a little weighting on the model.

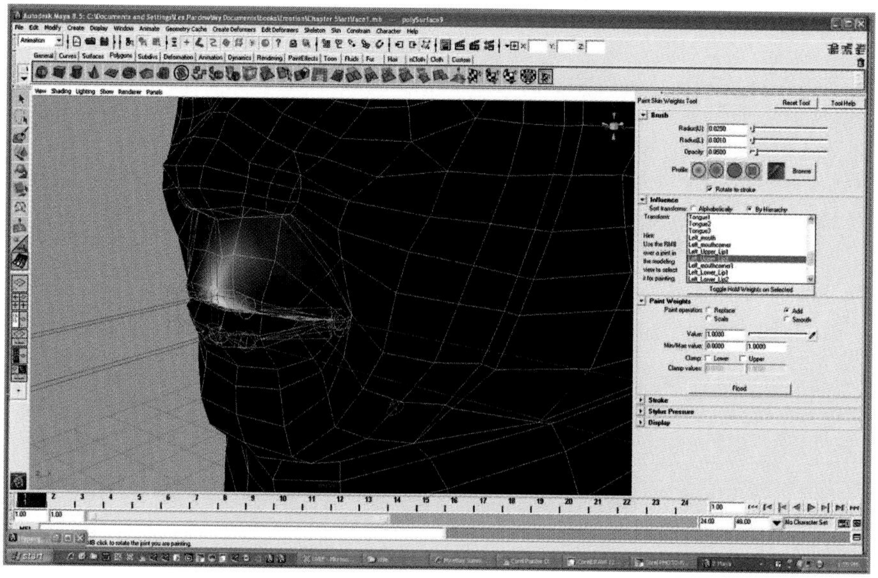

Figure 5.61 The weighting of the Left_Upper_lip2 joint extends up toward the nose.

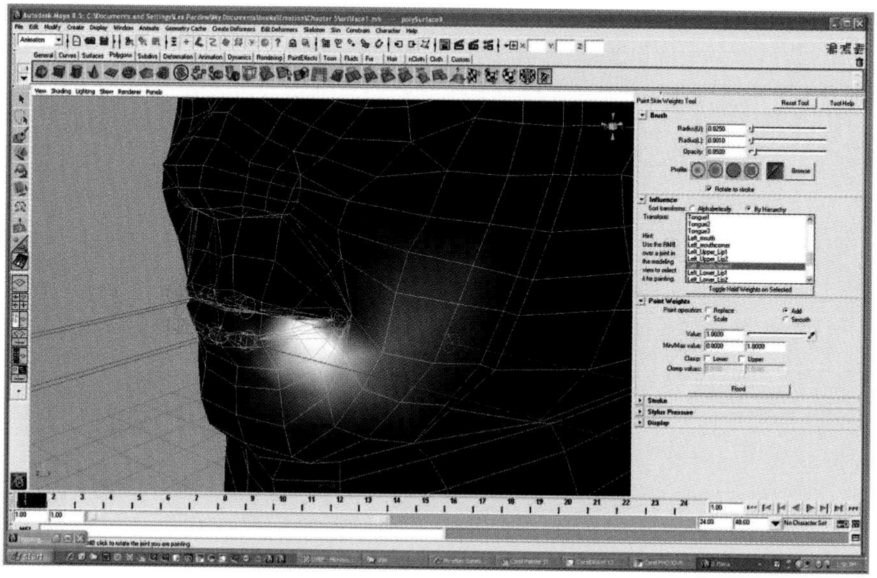

Figure 5.62 The Left_mouthcorner1 joint controls the lower and outer area of the mouth.

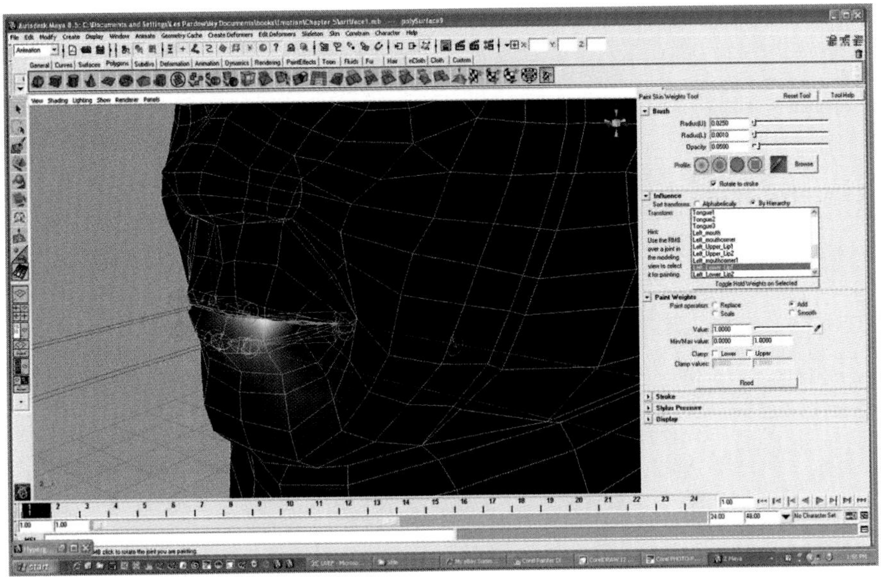

Figure 5.63
The Left_Lower_Lip1 joint receives little weighting.

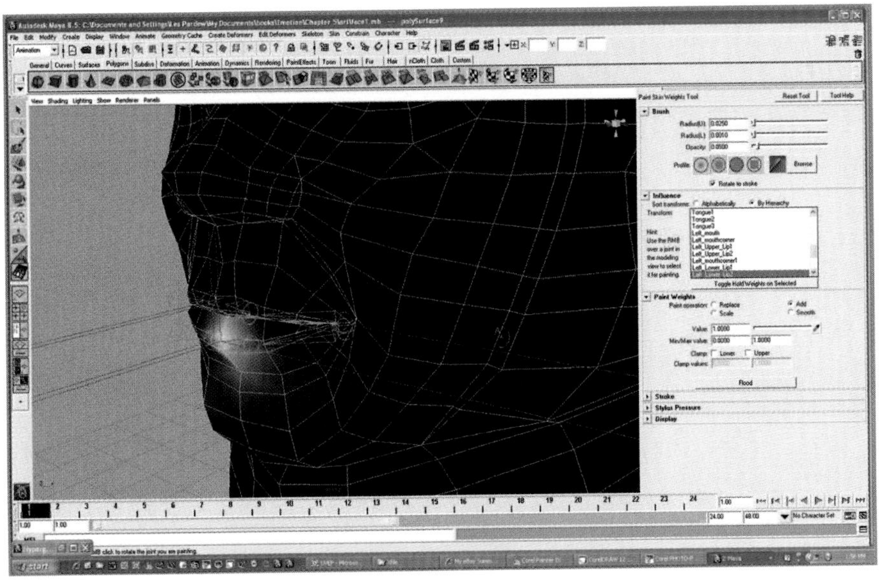

Figure 5.64
The center of the lower lip is controlled by the Left_Lower_Lip2 joint.

If you followed the weighting, your model should be almost ready for animating. You have two important steps that you need to finish before the model is ready, however. The first thing you need to do is mirror the skin weights from one side of your model to the other side. Use the Mirror Skin Weights tool found in the Edit Smooth Skin menu of the Skin menu shown here in Figure 5.65. Mirrored skin weights automatically overwrite the old skin weights so if you accidentally weighted some of the joints on the other side don't worry about it.

There remains one thing that you need to do before your model will be ready for animating facial expressions. Recall that you have two joints on the upper and lower lips that are basically influencing a single row of vertices down the center of the mouth. These vertices need to be evenly divided between the two joints or the mouth will be distorted while animating. To fix the problem, you will need to use the Component Editor again. Bring up the editor and select the three vertices of the upper lip, as shown in Figure 5.66.

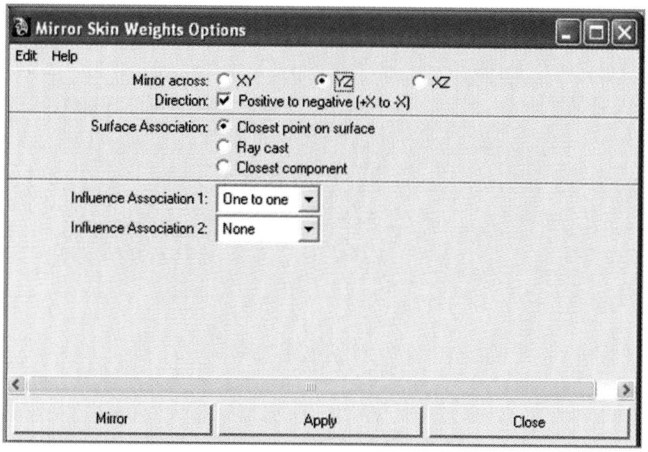

Figure 5.65 Use the Mirror Skin Weights tool to mirror the weights across the YZ plane.

Fixing the weighting requires two steps. First, you need to find the Left_Upper_Lip2 joint and change the weighting for the joint to 1. This will force all of the weighting to that joint. Next, you will need to find Right_Upper_Lip2 joint and change the weighting to .5. Now the weighting of the vertices should be exactly .5 for both joints.

You will also need to repeat the process for the lower lips, as shown in Figure 5.67.

The model is now weighted and ready for animation. Try moving a few of the joints and see how the face reacts. Now that it is ready, you need to run it through a few animations to test it. Very seldom does your initial binding work completely. Testing each joint will tell you if the skinning needs to be adjusted. Test the joint by rotating it and watching closely the movement of the face. Figures 5.68 through 5.71 are a few of the facial expressions that I came up with.

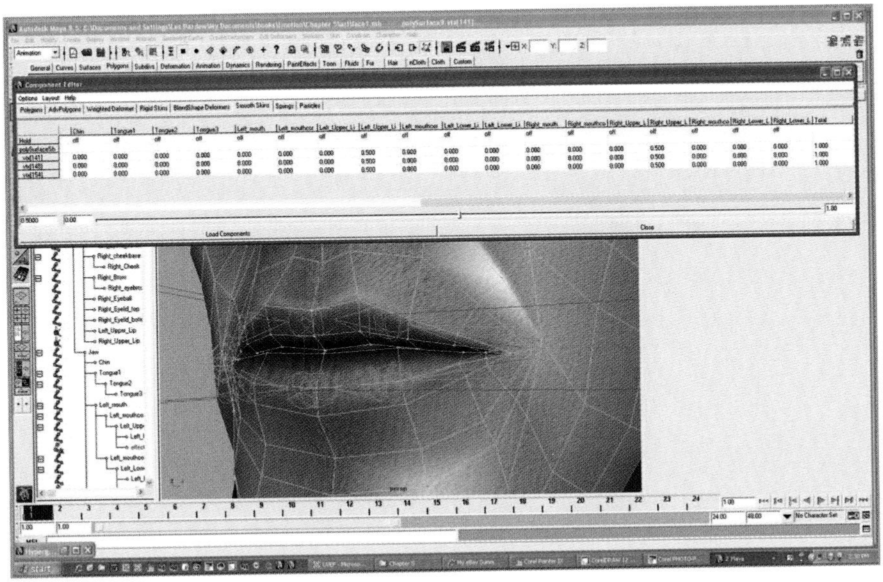

Figure 5.66
The center vertices of the upper lip should be evenly divided between the joints.

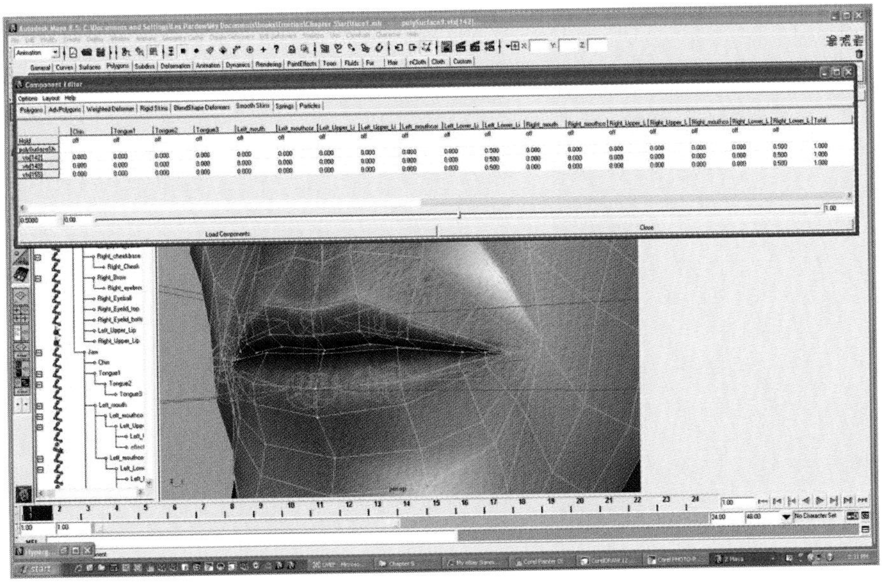

Figure 5.67
Divide the weighting between the joints for the lower lip.

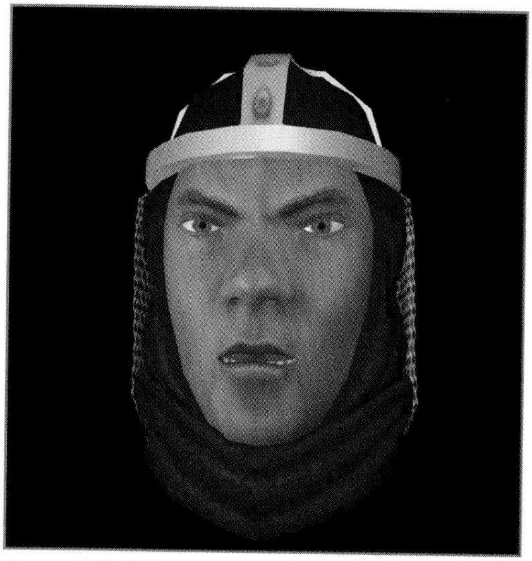

Figure 5.68 This character is angry.

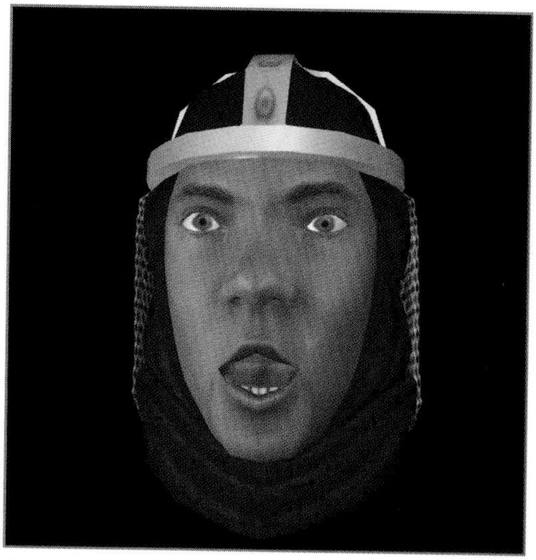

Figure 5.69 Here the model is yelling.

Figure 5.70 The model is smiling.

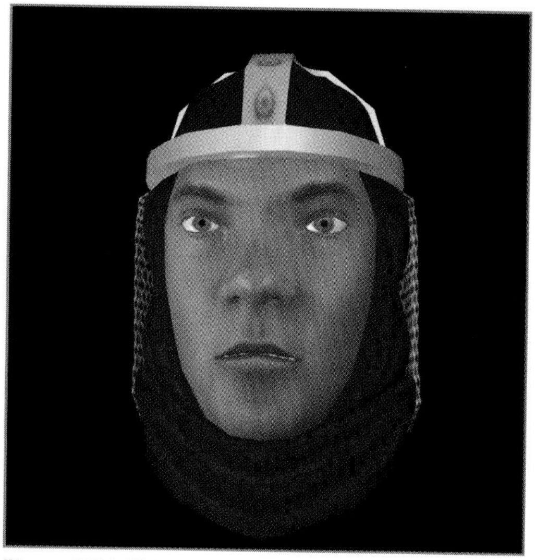

Figure 5.71 This model is sad.

I know that the process for rigging a 3D model for animation is long and tedious, but if you do it right, your model will be able to have facial expressions forever. The beauty of a 3D model is that even though they take some time to develop, once they are finished, they can animate forever. It may take longer to create a 3D model than draw an animation, but in the long run, if the character will be used repeatedly, you will never have to build the model again.

I know this chapter was a bit longer than the other chapters. That is because we had a lot to cover here. I hope that you understand how to animate facial expressions a little better at this point. With this as the base, you should be ready to explore some of your own territory in emotional expression. Try developing some facial expressions of your own.

CHAPTER 6

Emotion and Timing

In animation, like in life, timing is everything. Timing is what makes a joke funny. Timing is what causes something to be scary or calming. Timing in animation is the control of placement, events, movements, and story in a scene and throughout the show. The animator has to be aware of every aspect of a scene and coordinate them so that everything happens when and how it is supposed to happen.

In this chapter, we will be dealing with timing as it relates to developing emotion in an animated production.

Types of Timing

There are basically three types of timing that you need to be familiar with to create emotion in your animation. Each type deals with a specific aspect of animation, starting small and getting more universal. I will explain them in order so that you can understand why each is important to your animation.

- Internal timing
- External timing
- Story timing

Internal Timing

Internal timing is the timing of an individual character's movements. We already touched on internal timing in Chapter 3 for emotional reactions. This type of timing has to do with having a character's movements' look and feel correct for the desired emotional effect. In other words, the character appears to move in a natural believable manner for the specific animated movement.

To better understand how internal timing works, you need to understand spacing. Spacing is the distance an animation travels between frames. For example, a fast-moving object will have more movement between frames as compared to a slow-moving object, as shown in Figure 6.1.

Timing and spacing go hand in hand. They are both important aspects of the same principle of achieving natural-seeming believable motion. Even exaggerated cartoon motion can seem appropriate if the timing is correct.

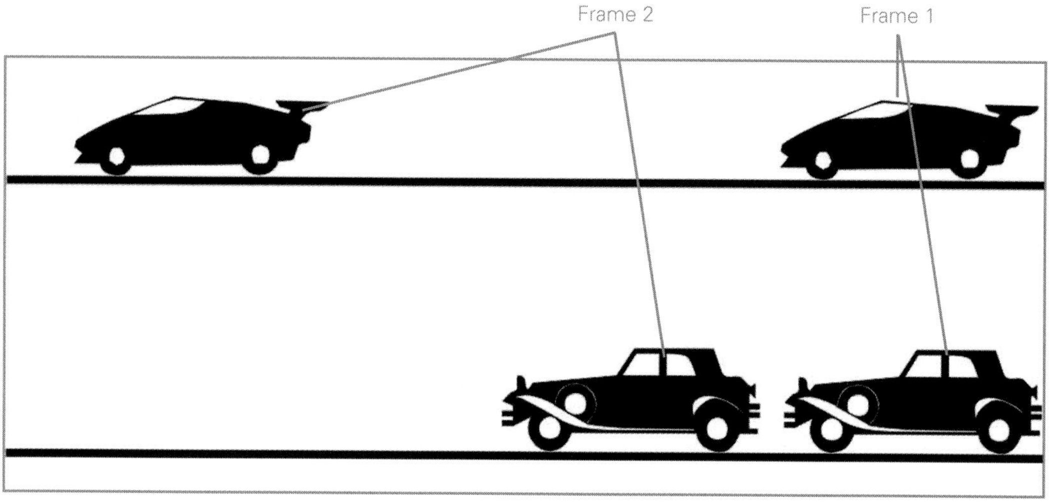

Figure 6.1 There is greater distance between frames in a faster moving object.

Have you ever watched a movie where the audio was not synced with the video? If you have, you will understand how incorrect timing can be very uncomfortable. The characters' mouths are moving, but they are either a step ahead or behind the audio. The same thing can happen with internal timing. A character can move, but it doesn't feel right because the movement is not timed and spaced according to natural movement.

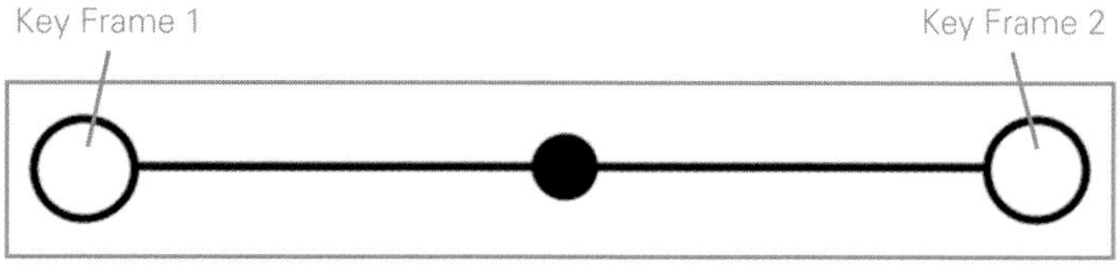

Figure 6.2 The two key frames have the ball on opposite sides of the scene.

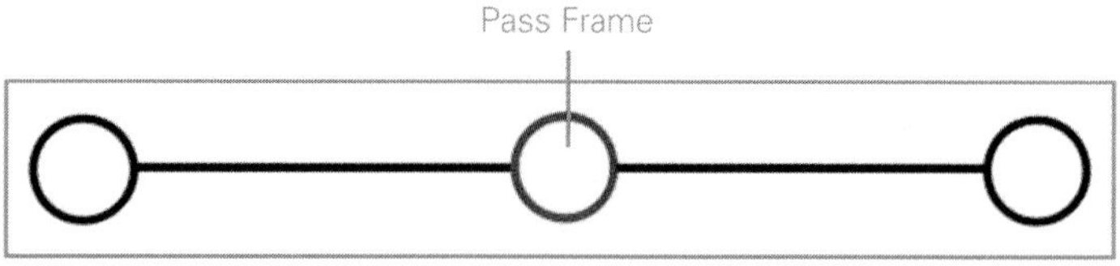

Figure 6.3 The pass frame falls in the middle if broken down directly.

Understanding Timing and Spacing

To understand how timing and spacing work together, let's look at a simple example. Figure 6.2 shows two key frames of a ball on a string.

If you were to break down the movement between the two key drawings directly, the breakdown or pass frame would fall somewhere near the center of the screen, as shown in Figure 6.3 in red. Pass frames are the frames that fall between key frames in an animation sequence. The pass frame defines the line of motion from one key frame to another and is usually located at the apex of an arc.

Notice how the animation changes dramatically if the breakdown places the ball on a swinging arc from the right to the left, as shown in red in Figure 6.4.

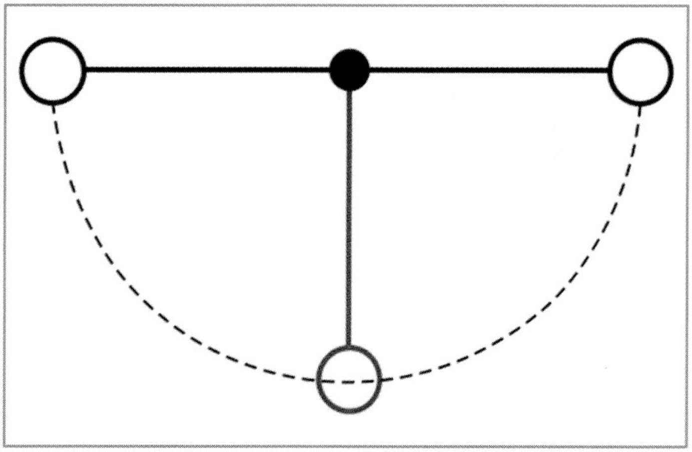
Figure 6.4 The ball traveling on an arc is more interesting.

NOTE

As you can see from the example, the placement of the pass frame is very important to the motion. This is where the animator is better than a computer for breaking down motion. When a computer creates in-between frames, the computer creates a direct path from one frame to the next. The animator, on the other hand, knows that an arc will look better and creates a better movement. When creating 3D motion and using an animation program to calculate the in-betweens, the animator is better off creating extra key frames to indicate the arcs that the animation should follow.

To take this one step further, let's break down the frames of the swinging ball. If we divide the distance between each frame evenly, the animation will look like that shown in Figure 6.5.

The timing shown in Figure 6.5 is even and smooth, but it is very mechanical like the movement of the second hand on a clock. It has an even smooth swing. This type of spacing is okay if you are animating a robot, but it is not very good for most other types of animation.

Now look at Figure 6.6, where there is an ease in and ease out added to the animation. Ease in and ease out are animation terms that mean the motion starts and ends slow but is faster in the middle of the motion.

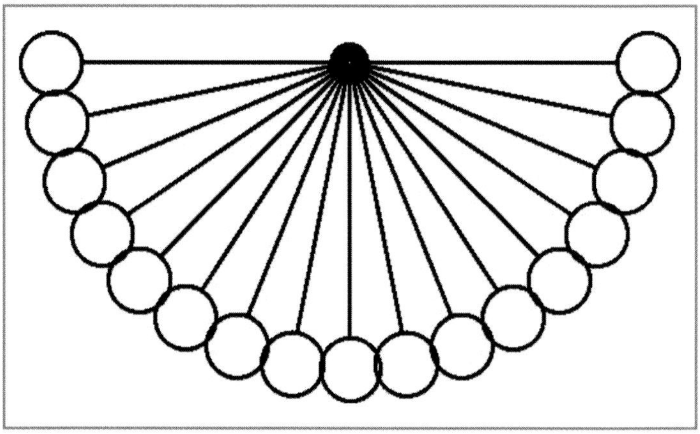

Figure 6.5 Even spacing creates mechanical movement.

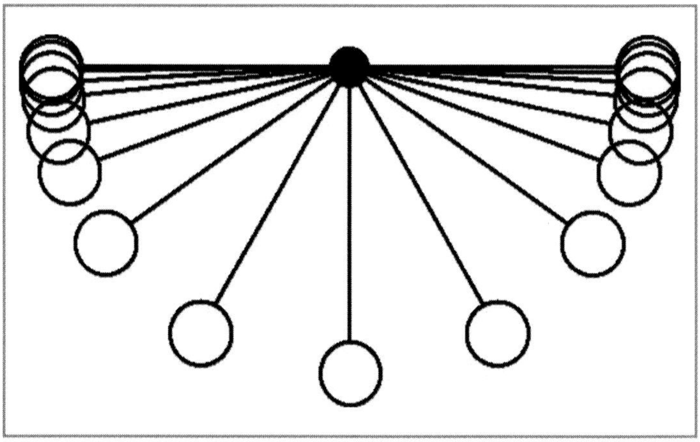

Figure 6.6 The movement is better for a more natural-looking swing.

The two animations are very different, yet the two key frames and the pass frame remain the same. The second animation achieves a more natural feel because it is simulating the way gravity acts on an object. In nature, a falling object accelerates as if falls. The momentum of the object then pushes the object past the lowest point and upward in a pendulum motion because the ball is attached to a string. As the ball continues upward, it slows because gravity is pulling against the upward motion.

Even though the observer may not know the physical laws that govern the motion of the ball and string, because it follows natural laws of motion, it will feel right to the observer.

Figures 6.5 and 6.6 are smooth animations because there are no sharp changes in the distance between frames. In Figure 6.5, the distance remains constant. In Figure 6.6, the distance ramps up and down in a consistent manner. If you plotted the motion of the two animations, it would look like the chart in Figure 6.7, with time as the vertical axis and distance as the horizontal axis.

The first animation of the ball is represented in blue and the second in red on the graph. I know this seems a little like a math class, but this is a very important concept in animation. You don't have to mathematically plot your motions as an animator, but you do have to understand the underlying principles that deal with motion and momentum. Timing is not just the division of a scene into separate movements. It is also the acceleration and deceleration of those movements. In nature, very seldom is a motion in constant speed. Objects and actions are almost always either in the process of speeding up or slowing down. That is one of the reasons that animators should think of motion as a curve or arc, as shown in the graph.

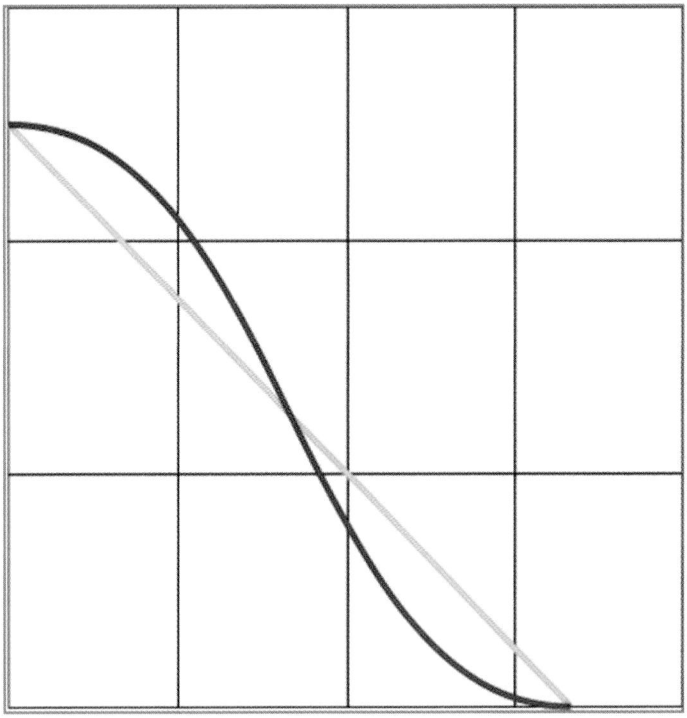

Figure 6.7 The movement of the two animations can be compared in a graph.

Even a walk cycle will have variations in speed from one part of a step to another. The body slows as it catches its balance between steps and speeds up as it descends from the pass position to the step position. While the entire movement might look okay to have the character move at an even, steady rate, it will look more natural if there is just a little variance in the spacing.

Learning the Laws

If you are going to be an animator, one of the most important things you will learn is to understand the laws that govern momentum and movement in the natural world. Understanding these laws will give you a greater ability to create convincing animated movements in your own characters.

Momentum is defined as a measure of the motion of a body, combining mass and velocity. Okay, that sounds a little scientific, and science doesn't always have much emotion. Bear with me a little here. If it weren't important that you understand this, I wouldn't have put it in the book. What does it mean to the animator? It means that a bigger heavier object or character takes more effort to move than a smaller lighter object. A firefly can zip around a scene with very little effort, whereas an elephant requires large powerful muscles to move around or to stop moving.

When you are animating a character that is large and heavy, it will not look natural if the character appears to move with little or no effort. It is like the young slim female game character that can with no apparent effort hold a 300 pound automatic cannon in one arm. It just looks odd. In fact, one of the best ways that you make a large heavy character look large and heavy is to have the character require effort to move around. If you want something to look heavy, make your characters have to work to lift it.

To be a good animator, you have to understand a little about physics. I know, I know, science is boring, but believe me, any time you spend learning about the physics of motion will be well worth it as you animate. Understanding the physics of motion is indispensable to developing believable timing and spacing in your characters.

Time for a Short Physics Lesson

Let's look at Sir Isaac Newton's first law of motion.

Newton's First Law of Motion

I. Every object in a state of uniform motion tends to remain in that state of motion unless an external force is applied to it.

This law applies to all objects. It means that if an object is moving, it will continue to move, and if an object is not moving, it will continue not moving. Sounds pretty simple, doesn't it? External force is required to change the state of movement of any object. Let's look at an example.

Picture a baseball game. The pitcher applies force to the baseball to pitch it toward the batter. If the ball is hit by the batter, a new force (the bat) causes the ball to change directions. Without the new force of the bat, the ball would continue to travel in the direction the pitcher threw it until it hit the catcher's mitt where a new force stops the ball. If the bat hits the ball, it sails up into the air but its direction changes because gravity is pulling it back to earth. Without gravity, it would continue to sail forever. The outfielder stops the motion of the ball by catching it in his glove. If the outfielder misses, the ball bounces and falls to a stop because of gravity and friction. So in this one simple example we see several outside forces acting on the ball.

So what does this mean to the animator? Well, if you have a character who is about to move from one place to another, you need to show that the character is using effort to move. You can increase the naturalness of the animation by not having everything on the character move all at once. For example, as the character starts to move, you could show a slight delay in the character's head and arms. This is called secondary motion, and it is present in almost every character movement.

Newton also had a second law of motion that is a little more complex than the first law. It is shown in the following sidebar.

Newton's Second Law of Motion

II. The rate of change of momentum of a body is proportional to the resultant force acting on the body and is in the same direction.

Basically, what Newton is saying is that change in momentum of an object over time is directly proportional to the amount of force applied to the object. He goes on to state that any change of direction in momentum is determined by the angle of the new force exerted on the object. The baseball scenario showed this earlier when the ball changed direction based on the bat hitting the ball. The new direction was determined by the angle of the swing of the bat versus the angle of the pitch of the ball. The new direction is a combination of the two previous directions of the objects.

This is important because for things to look correct to the viewer, changes in direction of moving objects have to be a direct reaction to the angle of the new force applied to them. This is true not only in how a baseball might change direction when hit by a bat but also in the subtle changes of direction in a character's walk or the movement of a character's hair when in frustration she flips it out of her eyes. If you understand the law and know what to look for, you will see it in many aspects of life.

Now for Newton's third law of motion.

Newton's Third Law of Motion

III. For every action there is an equal and opposite reaction.

This law is important to the animator because it explains what happens when a character runs into a tree or any other collision. For the resulting collision to look realistic, the force of the impact has to have a reaction. What happens in this instance is that the character hits the tree. The tree absorbs the impact moving slightly and transfers some of it back to the character causing him to bounce off the tree. The total force of the impact is equal to the total force of the reaction to the impact.

Okay, so how do you as an animator use these laws to create better animation? First of all, you have to understand that most people will expect your characters to move and react in accordance to these laws even if they don't understand the laws themselves. Second, by following or even exaggerating the reactions to these laws, you can enhance and emphasize the actions of your characters. Third, you can break these laws to get across a specific effect. For example, one character bounces off another character with no effect on the second character. Because the natural laws state that there should have been a reaction to the impact, the second character obviously must be significantly more massive than the first character—kind of like walking into Superman.

Timing for Personality

Timing can be used to add personality and interest to a character or object. In fact, it is probably the most powerful method of adding personality of anything you can do in animation. We often think of an emotional reaction as body language or a facial expression. In truth, these are important aspects of showing character emotion, but the key to really being able to get them to work is in the timing. The reaction has to happen at the right time and in the right way to carry the story.

The speed at which an action is performed can greatly affect how that action is perceived. For example, if a character raises a hand to fix a stray lock of hair very slowly, the audience may think he is preoccupied. If, on the other hand, the action is quick, the character may be thought of as impatient. If the character is walking fast, he is in a hurry. If he is walking slowly, he isn't in a hurry.

Timing is part of every action because every action takes time. Even subtle animations like the flick of a wrist or raising of an eyebrow take time. That's why it is important to understand how much time it takes to perform every action in animation. If you try to put too many actions in a given amount of time, the animation will seem rushed. If, on the other hand, you don't put enough in a given amount of time, the animation will seem slow or lethargic.

The timing of motion can be deliberate, erratic, graceful, uncertain, quick, slow, majestic, sneaky, cautious, and the list goes on and on. If you think about it, timing can take on almost any emotion or feeling and show it in animation. Even if the character doesn't have any arms or legs or even a face, the timing of how the character moves can reveal much about its personality.

External Timing

External timing is the control of events, characters, and objects in a scene. In other words, it dictates the staging of everything that goes on in a scene. External timing is used to have characters or objects in the right place at the right time.

Every aspect of an animation is timed. When a character walks across the scene, each foot step is timed so the character reaches the right place at the right time. Real problems can result if the timing gets off even a little from the plan. For example, if you have 80 frames to get a character from one side of the scene to the other to knock on a door, you need to divide the distance moved in those 80 frames. If your character takes 96 frames to move across the scene, the animation of the door opening will have to be delayed, as will every succeeding animation in the show. If several scenes are longer than expected, then the whole show runs longer.

Mistiming an animation can cause a domino effect that could increase costs and in some cases cause drastic problems for the production. In many cases, animation is for a set time, particularly anything that is shown on television. A TV show has a specific time slot, and the show has to fill that slot to the second. Every member of the animation team needs to understand the time limitations of the project including when the show will break for a commercial.

Dividing Scenes

The animation director often has to work from the general to the specific when figuring scene length. However, at the same time, he also has to work from the specific to the general to make sure the individual animations appear natural. In order to divide the total number of frames between the various scenes, the director has to understand the action that will need to take place in each scene.

The process starts with determining the total number of frames available for animation. For example, if the animation is for a half-hour TV show, there will be about 23 minutes of animation with 7 minutes of commercials. That amounts to 33,120 frames.

Next, the director divides the show into separate scenes based on the script. If there is any dialogue in the show, the animation director can roughly divide the frames into scenes based on the recorded dialogue. If the dialogue is not recorded, a rough estimate can be achieved by reading the script out loud and timing the reading; however, a recorded, edited sound track is needed for accurate timing breakdowns.

In addition to the dialogue in an animated show, there is also a certain amount of essential action that takes place without any dialogue. For example, a character might be walking down a country lane to go fishing with no dialogue. The director has to time out these actions and include them in their individual scenes. This requires that the animation director have a good feel for how long it takes something to happen.

Once all critical action and dialogue have been accounted for, the frames are added together and compared to the total number of frames needed in the show. Hopefully, it will be close but not over the frame count for the show. If there are too many frames, some of the dialogue or actions will have to be shortened. If the frame count is below that needed for the show, the animation director then has an opportunity to add some personality and interest in each scene.

So you can see that the animation director has to understand the general requirements for the entire show and use specifics to build the show to an exact number of frames. The result will be a set number of frames for each scene and also a set number of frames for each action.

Sometimes the animation director will loosely define the actions and give the lead animator some freedom within the total number of frames for that scene. The lead animator then breaks down the scene into individual actions and camera movements and defines the timing for the scene. Whether it is the animation director or lead animator, someone has to determine the frame counts for each action in each scene, all of which have to be synchronized in order for the animation to work. This may sound complicated, but it is a reality that every animator has to live with.

Figure Interaction

In a scene with multiple characters interacting with one another, you, the animator, have to orchestrate events so they happen exactly when they are supposed to. This requires that you keep track of all of the characters on-screen and time events for multiple characters. This is a big job and requires close attention to detail.

Animating a single character is hard enough, but when it comes to animating several characters in a scene, the complexity goes way up. The issue is mostly with the timing of actions and reactions. With a single character, timing is mostly internal and all about getting the movements to look correct. With multiple characters, in addition to having each movement look correct, the animator must also coordinate the movements of each character so critical actions occur at specific interaction points.

Interaction Points

Interaction points are points in time and space where the actions of two or more characters coincide with each other. An example of this is in a fight scene where one character punches another. Both characters have to be in position, and the punch has to be timed right so that the action of the punching character matches the reaction of the punched character, like in Figure 6.8.

It would look pretty odd for the character getting punched to react even a little before or after the punch was thrown. The timing has to be perfect for the punch to have the right effect. This means that the internal timing of both characters has to synchronize at the exact moment of the punch striking.

The moment the punch connects is a critical interaction point. When working with multiple figures on the screen, interaction points have to be identified well in advance of drawing the animation. When breaking down a scene, the lead animator has to define all interaction points before any key frames are drawn. This is a very important task and requires a good understanding of what constitutes an

Figure 6.8 The timing of the punch has to be perfect.

interaction point because some of them might not be as evident as others. For example, a punch is easy to find, but a character reacting to the antics of another character may not be so evident and may not be indicated in the script. You have to visualize the scene before it goes to layout to find both the obvious and not so obvious interaction points. A not so obvious interaction point might be a character laughing at a joke.

Once the interaction points are all identified, the animator can use them to plan out the rest of the scene by creating interaction key frames for each interaction point. The interaction key frames need to be placed within the frames available for the scene. In other words, the interaction points need to be assigned specific frames within the scene.

For example, look at Figure 6.9. In this scene, the female super hero is approaching the two male super heroes. The interaction point of this scene will be when the talking super heroes notice her approach and turn to look at her. The critical interaction will be between her and one of the male heroes. The non-critical actions are those of the supporting characters in the scene.

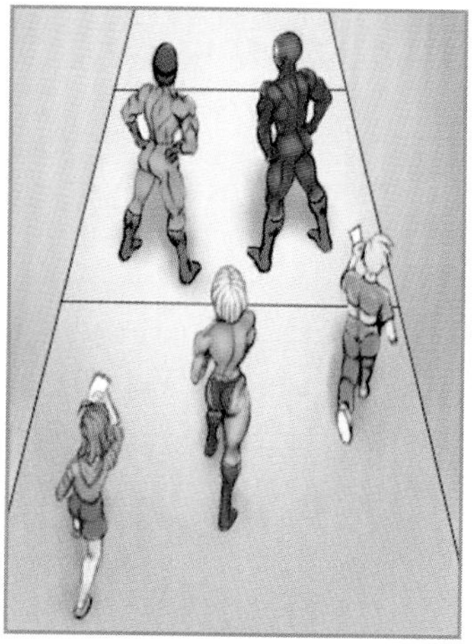

Figure 6.9 The critical interaction point is when one character notices the approach of the other.

Once the interaction point is defined, you can then time the lead into the interaction point and lead out of the interaction point. The supporting characters can also be timed so as not to interfere with the critical action.

Creating interaction point key frames doesn't just have to be about interaction with multiple characters. It is also useful in coordinating animated objects in a scene or coordinating characters with objects. For example, if a ball hits the character rather than a punch, the interaction point of the ball hitting the player is just as important as the punch was.

All of this may seem like the "nuts and bolts" of animation and not directly related to personality, but it is essential to pulling off a good show. It is true that a lot of the emotional impact of a scene is in the internal timing and spacing of a character. If the internal timing happens at the wrong time or in the wrong place, the intended effect is lost. A scene that is supposed to be dramatic will become comical.

Continual Interaction

There are some cases in animation where the interaction of the characters will not be at a specific point or there are too many interaction points to practically plot them in preproduction. The interaction might be continuous or near continuous. This type of character interaction requires a different approach from the interactive point key frame method.

A good example of this type of continuous interaction is when two characters are dancing with each other. When two characters dance with each other, they are more like a single character than they are two characters, and you need to treat them as if they were a single character and animate them together. This also happens with characters that are wrestling or fighting with each other. Other examples include characters riding other characters or objects like a horse or scooter, characters handling objects like a rope or sword, and characters who are affected by the same force, like falling together or walking into a stiff gusting wind. All of these examples require that the characters and objects react in at least a near continuous manner.

In dealing with these situations, it is a good idea to combine the characters or objects and animate them as if they were a single entity, like the couple in Figure 6.10.

Figure 6.10 These dancers are animated together.

It would be very difficult for two animators to coordinate the interaction of a dance scene. Often a single animator is responsible for a single character in a large animation production. This can cause problems if there is a scene where two or more characters are involved in continuous interaction with each other. The best way to handle animating this type of interaction is to have one animator develop the animation as if the two characters were a single character. By doing this, the interaction points become internal timing rather than external timing, and the external timing then deals with points when the dancing pair needs to react to other elements in the scene, like tripping over a stool or the end of the song.

Story Timing

Story timing is the overall timing of events as they relate to the progression of the story in an animated show. Every scene and action in an animated show should play a role in developing the story. In other words, the story is a sequence of events that together constitute a cohesive whole.

At the heart of every great animated show is a good story. Motion picture studios understand this and pay millions of dollars a year for screenplays and novel rights. Top screen writers are some of the best paid writers in the world, sometimes commanding huge sums for a single script. The rights for a popular novel can run into millions of dollars. Understanding how to create good stories is big business.

Why do producers pay so much for a story? Because they know that the foundation of any good movie, whether it is animated or not, is the story. Have you ever walked out of a movie disappointed because the story was lame? The effects might be spectacular. The characters might be intriguing. The soundtrack might be inspiring. But if the story is lame, the movie is lame.

As an animator, you have to learn how to interpret a story and carry the story to the audience. A good animator uses the script as an inspiration for unfolding the story to the audience. Animation isn't just a matter of having the characters go through the motions and say the lines in the script. The real job of the animator is to bring the story to life in the minds and hearts of the audience.

Think of some of your favorite stories. If you give it a little thought, I am sure you can remember the stories with a significant amount of detail. The reason you remember the stories so well is because they had an emotional impact on you. You identified with the stories in some way. Good storytelling touches the hearts and minds of the audience.

The script writer might write the story for the animated production, but it is the animator who tells that story. When you animate your characters, you tell a story. Will your story be good or bad? A lot depends on how you set up the sequence of events within the story or, in other words, the story timing.

Stories and Emotion

There are two ways that the human brain learns: repetition and emotional impact. Anyone who has tried to learn to play the piano or written out spelling words for school assignments knows a little about the power of repetition for retaining knowledge. Repetition is good, but it isn't as powerful as emotional impact. Emotion is by far the stronger source for imprinting an event or situation on a person's mind.

Think of the best meal you have ever had in your life. Can you remember what you ate? Of course you can remember because there was something about what you ate that impressed you. Now, think about what you had to eat three weeks ago on Thursday for lunch. Do you even remember what you ate? Eating is something you repeat every day, yet you don't often remember what you ate beyond a few minor details. However, a truly great meal is often remembered fondly and with some detail.

How many television (TV) shows and movies do you remember? The ones you remember well are the ones that were somehow important to you. They are remembered because of their emotional impact in your life.

I remember as a small child going to see a movie called "The Night of the Grizzly." The movie was about a family that lived in the woods and a vicious grizzly bear that was in the area. As a small child, the movie had a powerful impact on me. I was truly frightened of the grizzly bear. Even today I remember the more dramatic scenes in the movie that I saw only one time almost forty years ago. I have seen hundreds of movies since that time, most of which I remember very little.

Is it the same way with you? Are there specific movies that you remember very well even years later because they had an emotional impact on your life?

Now think about your animation. Do you want people to remember your work, or do you want it to gain a quick round of applause and then have the audience move on to the next show? You have to connect with your audience emotionally if you want them to appreciate and remember all your hard animation work.

Emotional connections happen when the animation causes the audience to react to it. The reaction can be to laugh, cry, shrink in fright, glow with warmth, or just about any other feeling. Think about possibilities. You as the animator hold the keys to unlock emotional feelings in your audience through your storytelling.

A good story weaves emotional reactions seamlessly into a production without being overtly obvious to the viewer. When you go through a potential script for an animated production, you need to search for the emotion that the writer is hoping to invoke in the audience.

Planning the Story

The first step to telling your story is in the storyboards you create in preproduction. There is a reason why they are called storyboards—they tell the story. The foundation of your story needs to be conveyed in the storyboards. Just by looking at the storyboards, the viewer should be able to understand the essence of the story.

As you set up your story in the storyboards, think about the timing of events and how they will play a role in the progression of the story. Think about the camera angles, the characters, the setting, and all the elements that are part of the story. How can you get them to work together to have the best chance to touch the emotions of your audience?

Once you understand the basic plot of the story and the sequence of events that develop that plot, you can then start to visualize how the story can unfold in your mind.

The emotional purpose of a story is to cause the audience to respond emotionally to whatever is happening on-screen. The emotional response might be powerful in a dramatic show or hilarious in a comedy. The important thing for you, the animator, to understand is to identify those times in the progression of the story that need heightened emotional impact. For some stories, it might be a tender moment. For other stories, it might be the punch line of a joke. Whatever it is, you need to be aware of these important points in time and plan the animation so that it delivers the emotional feeling to the audience.

In many ways story timing is similar to internal timing. Think about the emotional reactions you studied in Chapter 3. Remember the sequence of events? There was a lead in, a reaction, and a let down. Story timing is similar in that the delivering of emotional events usually comes in waves.

It is hard to sustain a single emotion throughout an entire show. The audience needs background and contrast to feel the intended emotion, just as a painter needs contrast to paint a picture. A picture without any contrast would not be much more than a single color. Using contrast between different emotions can help to strengthen each individual emotion.

Map out the key emotional moments in your animated production. Sometimes this is best done with the scriptwriter so that key moments can be better identified, and, in some cases, the script can be modified to better take advantage of these key moments.

Once identified, the key emotional points can then be plotted so that all animators understand how the drama will unfold. It is also a good way for you to see if there are any long drawn out lulls or rapid successions of emotions. These may need to be modified to better enhance the flow of the story.

Controlling these emotional waves is an important aspect of story timing. It is how you, as an animator, can become a good storyteller. The timing of each wave is important to the overall emotional feeling of the show.

Timing and Emotions

As you can see from the breakdown of timing in this chapter, there are three main areas that you need to understand to create a great animation with regard to timing. In dealing with the subject, we started with the small and worked toward the overall.

Internal timing deals with the movements of a character or object. It has to do with timing and spacing of movements performed by a character, and it is critical to showing emotion in a character. Internal timing is how a character acts or reacts on-screen. The important thing to remember about developing good internal timing is that the motion needs to be believable. Believability is based on natural laws that govern most movement. Personality is developed by understanding and using the natural laws in conjunction with the attributes of the character.

External timing deals with the movement and position of all characters and objects within any given scene. External timing is important to the timing of events and coordination of interaction between characters and their environments.

Good external timing has things happen where and when they should happen. It requires a precise understanding of the time available and how to work within those limits.

Story timing is timing that deals with the progression of the story and the overall emotional impact of the production. Story timing works with emotional waves that flow throughout the sequence of events within the story. By controlling the progression of the story, you become a better storyteller.

Although I approached the topic from small to large, in a production the three types of timing are reversed. You, the animator, first deal with story timing, then with external timing, and lastly with internal timing.

Hopefully you have a better understanding of timing and how it works to create emotion in your animation. Some of the information may seem a little technical, but learning it will help you to be more creative because you will then understand how to get the feelings and reactions you want from your characters and the audience.

CHAPTER 7

Emotions, Story, and Environments

So far most of our discussion has centered on emotion in characters, but there is a lot more to emotion in animation that just the character. In this chapter, we will look at how the environment can affect emotion. I use the word *environment* instead of *setting* because I am including things like lighting, camera angles, and audio. So environment means all aspects that make up the world in which your animated characters will perform.

To begin with, we will look at designing environments. Then we will go on to talk about the emotional aspects of environments. The last part of the chapter will deal with creating an environment.

Characters and Settings

Integrating characters with a background may sound simple, but in reality, there are lots of elements a good animator needs be aware of to make the characters look like they belong in the setting. These elements are as follows:

- Perspective
- Contrast
- Style
- Color
- Lighting

Perspective

One of the most glaring errors that an animator can make when creating an animated production is to draw characters out of perspective with the setting, as shown in Figure 7.1. Keeping your characters in perspective with your setting isn't necessarily hard, but it does take an understanding of linear perspective.

If you have taken a drawing course, you probably already know a little about linear perspective. With that training, you should understand how to draw any object or character using linear perspective. If you haven't had much experience with linear perspective, then I suggest you take some time and develop some skill in that area. Linear perspective is an essential tool for getting your characters to look like they belong in your settings. If you plot the two characters in Figure 7.1 using linear perspective, you can see that there is an extreme difference between them, as shown in Figure 7.2. The biggest difference is that the horizon lines for each character are different. The horizon line is the horizontal line that represents the horizon.

Figure 7.1 These characters look out of place with each other.

Figure 7.2 The character looks out of place in this setting.

As you can see from Figure 7.2, it is important to always have consistent perspective between the character and the background. It is a good idea to check the perspective of your characters with the scene every few frames to make sure it is still correct. One of the purposes of animation layouts is to establish the perspective of a scene.

Contrast

The character needs to contrast in some way with the background so that it is easily distinguishable to the viewer.

Years ago while working on an animated production for a company that sold military defense systems, I had the opportunity to animate a missile launcher. The engineers at the company were very specific about the launcher having camouflage paint. They wanted it to look like the launchers in the field. Unable to convince them that there was an inherent problem with camouflage, I animated the launcher as directed knowing that it wouldn't work. When the launcher was reviewed, they complained that they couldn't see the launcher. "Well if it wasn't painted to blend into the background, it might be easier to see." I responded. In the end we had to highlight the launcher so the audience could see it.

Motion is the most powerful contrast that you can use to distinguish characters from backgrounds. Our eyes are drawn to movement. By having your character always in motion, even if it is subtle, you will be contrasting your character with the background. But motion alone isn't the only way to contrast your character from the background. In addition to motion, the animator can also use value contrast and color contrast. A combination of value and color contrast will help keep your character easily distinguishable even when it isn't in motion. Figures 7.3 and 7.4 show value contrast and color contrast, respectively.

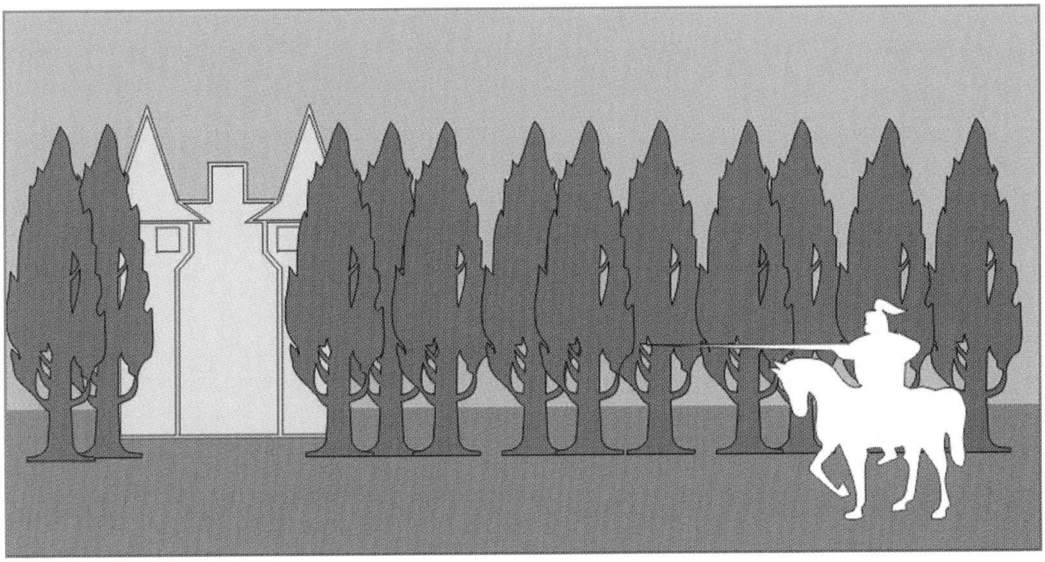

Figure 7.3 This example shows how value contrast emphasizes the knight.

Figure 7.4 This example shows how color contrast emphasizes the trophy.

Style

The style of the character should match the style of the setting. In other words, if the setting is painted in soft pastels, the character should not be all sharp angles and bright colors if you want your audience to believe that your charac[illegible] belongs in that background.

Most animated productions will have a style guide. The guide is meant to keep the style for all aspects of the show consistent. Often the background artists in animated productions are not the same artists who animate the characters. Because many artists work on animation together, they usually always have to follow a style guide to keep the overall style of the show consistent.

Style is something that is determined very early on in a production, during the preproduction phase. In fact, most of the creative part of animating is worked out in the preproduction phase. During the production phase, there are very strict guidelines for all animators to follow. Good examples of consistent style are the Pixar movies. All elements in these movies fit into the universe they create.

Lighting

The lighting of a character should match the lighting in a scene. For example, if the character is walking outside in a bright sunny scene and then enters a dark cave, the lighting on the character should change with the lighting of the scene. In 2D animation where the characters are drawn separately from the background, animators must carefully follow scene guides to keep the character colors consistent with the background colors. Often 3D animation has the characters and backgrounds sharing the same lighting when rendering. If, however, the character is rendered separately from the background, there will often be lighting problems on the characters and in the shadows.

In this section, we covered several ways that you can improve the integration of the character with the setting. These rules should be looked upon as guidelines and not hard and fast rules. In some cases, you may want to break some of the rules to achieve a specific effect. For example, you may want to have the drawing style of the character be different than the setting to make the character seem out of place in the world, or you may want to have the lighting of the character be brighter than the background to gain greater contrast. If done on purpose and for a reason, the results could be very effective. In Disney's *Pinocchio,* the soft water color backgrounds were contrasted with the cell drawn animation to good effect. However, in most situations, it is safer to stick with the guidelines above.

Dramatic Effect

For the purposes of this section, we will define dramatic effect as those elements that cause audience involvement in the animated show. While not all of these will relate directly to settings, they are all important considerations in developing emotion in animation. I am including them in this chapter to help set the stage for setting design. The goal of any animator is to somehow get the audience involved. To do this, the animator can use a number of dramatic tools. Some of these tools are as follows:

- Humor
- Suspense
- Sentiment
- Surprise
- Fear
- Anger
- Intrigue
- Interest

Humor

Humor is more often associated with animation than many other emotions because of the history of cartoon animation. Many of the early animated shows were designed as comical short productions as lead-ins for movies and later for television cartoons.

Animation is a great medium for conveying humor to an audience because of the tremendous opportunity for exaggeration. A character who hits his thumb with a hammer can have a huge throbbing thumb. A character that is angry can have steam coming out his ears. Environments can also be exaggerated with odd-looking buildings or zany plants and animals like in some of the Dr. Seuss movies.

Humor is achieved when an unexpected event happens that the audience identifies as being funny. This could be something that the character says or does at an unexpected time or something that happens at an unexpected moment.

Humor usually requires bright happy settings that put the audience in a light buoyant mood; however, that is not always the case. Sometimes a comical exchange in a somber or suspenseful setting can be very effective like the witty remarks Spiderman makes as he struggles with the bad guys.

Suspense

With the possible exception of anime, suspense is not as associated with animation as it is with other forms of cinema, but it is a valid part of an animator's arsenal. Suspense is a product of anticipation. In other words, the audience is anticipating something will happen and is anxiously waiting for it to happen.

Unlike humor the animator lets the audience know something is going to happen instead of having it just come at them unexpectedly. One of the best ways to do this is to set the stage by creating a suspenseful mood with the setting. A dark, dangerous looking setting can go a long way to prepare the audience for suspense. Suspense is the art of anticipation. It draws the audience into the scene because it causes them to hang on every word and guess at every turn.

Sentiment

Sentiment is the aspect of the animated show that the audience identifies with. Maybe it reminds them of something about themselves or their childhood. The idea of using sentiment is to have the audience recognize something in the production that they remember from their own life.

Some animators will use specific settings or situations that they know will give many in the audience a nostalgic tug. That is one of the reasons that Christmas shows are so popular. There are many pleasant memories associated with Christmas for most people. Other settings or situations that may bring back fond memories are country homes, camping trips, walks in the park, amusement parks, and tender moments with a loved one.

Sentiment can be a place or a situation, but most often it is an emotion. The reason emotion is so effective is because almost everyone has felt a range of emotions from sad to joyful or scared to angry. Not everyone, on the other hand, has been to a specific place or had a specific experience. However, there are times when the target audience is so well identified that the animator can use an event or situation effectively like referencing types of flowers to a group of florists or battles to a group of veterans.

Surprise

Surprise is like humor in that something happens unexpectedly, but instead of just being funny, it surprises the audience. Surprises in animated shows can be anything that causes the audience to think, "Hey I didn't expect that." You can surprise the audience with an unexpected character or an unexpected event. You can surprise them with a plot twist or even something as simple as a few words of dialogue. Many times the animator can surprise the audience with something in the setting like an unexpected item or location.

Surprise is a short-lived event and won't often keep the audience's attention for an entire show. It should be used to grab attention and pull the audience into an important event. In a way, it can be considered attention shock therapy. It is always good to sprinkle a few surprises throughout your show just to keep the audience awake like characters coming out at unexpected times.

Fear

Fear is a powerful emotion, and it can be very effective in keeping an audience's attention. Fear comes when the audience expects something bad to happen to a character. In order for it to work, the audience has to become attached to the character so they have a sense of worry for the character's well being. While suspense can encompass any and all anticipation, including the anticipation of a happy ending, fear is more for anticipating something bad to happen.

Settings play a large role in developing a situation where the characters and audience will experience fear. Dark spooky houses or environments set the stage for the emotion. It is hard to express fear in a bright pastel-colored landscape. It is much easier to develop a sense of fear in a dark menacing dungeon.

Fear is not as commonly used in animation as in other cinema because it is a little more difficult for the audience to identify with and have empathy for a drawn character than it is for a live human being. However, that doesn't mean that it is impossible. If a character has qualities that the audience can relate to, there can be a great deal of empathy for that character.

Anger

Like fear, anger is another powerful emotion. Anger in the sense that we are talking about here is not a character getting angry on-screen, but rather the audience getting angry at what they perceive as an injustice.

Anger is not directly related to setting, but setting plays a role because the perceived injustice has to happen somewhere. For example, the setting of a prison is a key part of developing anger about a person unjustly incarcerated.

Again for anger to work, the audience has to relate to the character and have empathy for them. Then if something unjust happens to the character, the audience may very well feel some strong feelings of righteous indignation. If you can get an audience to feel anger in an animated production, you have a great chance of keeping their attention.

Intrigue

Intrigue is the art of getting the audience to think about what is happening and to be interested in the outcome. If someone is intrigued, he sees something that causes him to want to investigate, thus keeping his attention on the show.

Some shows will show an opening scene that gives just enough information to get the audience to want to see the show because they are intrigued about the outcome. They want to know how things will turn out.

Intrigue can also be developed when the audience learns something new. Learning something new is always a good way to gain and hold attention particularly if it is part of the story development.

Interest

In some cases, the audience is just interested in the show. People's interests vary so it is difficult to be interesting to everyone. Sometimes an animated production will be targeted to a special interest group. For example, an animated short on rock climbing might be targeted specifically to a narrow group of rock climbers who use a specific type of equipment.

Location and setting can play a role in gaining interest. For example, a fantasy setting may excite the thousands of fantasy fans across the country. Another good way to gain interest is to create something interesting about your setting like ambient animation or unique lighting.

A good way to gain interest from the audience is to know your audience and what they are interested in. Targeting your animation to a specific audience often is more effective for having a successful animation than trying for general interests.

Dramatic Techniques

So now that you understand a little about dramatic effect, let's look at some of the dramatic techniques that an animator can use to grab and keep an audience's attention. They include the following:

- Timing
- Camera movement
- Expression
- Emotion
- Lighting
- Sound effects
- Dialogue
- Music

Timing

Timing is probably the most important technique an animator can use to engage the audience. Timing is an element in all dramatic effects. Whether it is humor or suspense, dramatic effects rely on timing to impact the audience.

The timing or pacing of the dramatic events in a show can have a large bearing on holding the audience's interest. When designing a show, the animation director should arrange dramatic events to continuously appear throughout the show. If there are no dramatic events for a period of time, the show can have dead spots where the audience's attention wanders.

Camera Movement

Camera movement is an effective way to gain and keep the audience's attention. Movement attracts attention. For example, rather than holding the camera in one position during dialogue or other sequences, the camera could be in the process of a slow movement. This is a technique that is often used in live action when a person is giving a speech. The camera will start to back away from the speaker and then slowly zoom in or start in close then slowly pull back.

Cutting to a different view is also a good technique to keep attention. Each time the camera cuts to a different view, the viewers have to process the new view. While processing usually only takes a split second in most cases, it does cause the audience to have to engage with what is going on in the animation.

Before you get carried away with camera movement and view changes, let me caution you. While these techniques are effective, they can also be distracting. If you use them too much, the audience will become numb to them. In some cases, overuse can also cause audience discomfort. It is better to plan your camera movement for a reason. Try to imagine interesting camera angles that enhance the experience while showing the best views of the scene.

As the animator, you have the advantage of being able to place the camera anywhere it is needed. Unlike live action that is limited by a physical camera, the animator uses an imaginary camera that views the setting from any angle that the animation director likes. Use this freedom wisely.

Expression

Expression is acting. In order to express an emotion or feeling, you have to bring the character to life with sound acting principles like those discussed earlier in the book in conjunction with expressing emotions.

For character animation to hold a person's attention, it needs to be expressive. It has to carry a message to the audience. Animated characters can express messages about themselves, their surroundings, their situations, their feelings, their hopes, and their personality, all through acting.

When a character expresses emotion on-screen, it makes the character more real. It adds depth to the character and gives him or her a personality that some members of the audience might be able to identify with. Everyone feels emotion to some extent, and if the emotion expressed is somehow familiar with the audience, there will be recognition of shared feelings that can result in empathy for the character.

Lighting

Lighting has a big impact on the dramatic mood of a scene, as discussed earlier in this chapter. Bright lighting can make a scene feel open and joyful. Dark lighting can make a scene feel intimidating and sinister.

When developing lighting for an animated show, think of the places where specific lighting can enhance the mood of the scene. It could be that you want to highlight something in the scene. Why not shine a spotlight on it? Maybe you want a character to be mysterious. Try putting him in the shadows. There are lots of ways to use lighting to help keep a scene interesting. Don't just settle for bland generic lighting.

Sound Effects

Sound effects can play a big role in helping things stay interesting by adding a greater feeling of reality. Take just a minute right now and listen to the background sounds around you. Try to isolate them. Depending on the time of day and location, there may be just a few sounds or there may be many. You might hear cars on the road. Maybe you can hear people talking. There might be the hum of your computer fan. These sounds can be called ambient sounds.

In addition to ambient sounds you can also have specific sounds that demand immediate attention. It might be the pounding of the character's heart when he is frightened. It might be a shout from a maiden in distress. It might even be the whine of an approaching dive-bomber. These are sound effects that tell the audience something is about to happen. They demand attention because they build anticipation in an approaching event.

If you use ambient sound in your scenes, you can emphasize specific sounds by having the ambient sound fade out just before a more important sound occurs.

Dialogue

A character's dialogue or speech can have a tremendous effect on a motion picture. For example, the Scottish accent for the character Shrek had a major impact on the character. Voice talent can bring character dialogue alive in ways that would be hard to achieve by the animation alone. When you develop your stories for animation, you should carefully plan how you want your characters to talk and let the voice talent know so they can create the character audio to match the drawn character.

Music

Early in the development of the film industry, directors learned about the powerful effect music had on the mood of the audience. If you listen carefully to any movie or TV show, you're going to usually hear music playing in the background. It has become so commonplace that we accept it without even realizing music is playing.

If you listen closely to one of your favorite movies, you will notice a number of different types of music depending on the scene and the situation in the show. The music changes depending on what emotion the director wants the audience to feel. It carries the mood of the show to the audience. Because music is so often going in the background, silence can also be used to effectively get the audience's attention.

As you select the background music for your show, take some time and think about what mood you want your audience in during any specific part of the show. Try to find music that enhances the feelings you want the audience to feel, like upbeat tempos for action scenes.

Drama in Your Production

We have covered a lot of ground with regard to drama in your animated productions. It is important that you consider these elements as you plan and develop your animation. Keep the above lists for dramatic effect and dramatic technique handy and review them while you are developing your show to help remind you of some of the many tools that you have available. Remember that the setting or environment includes a great deal more that just background art. The background is just one component in the total feeling of the environment.

Creating a 3D Set

Now that we have covered many of the elements that go together to create emotion in an environment, let's go to work and create a set for animation. This next section deals with the creation of a fantasy setting in 3D. We will create the set from concept to completion in a step-by-step procedure so you can follow along.

The first step in creating the set is to have a solid idea of what you are going to create. The best way to get a good visual image is to draw it on paper. Figure 7.5 shows a sketch of our set.

Figure 7.5 Draw a sketch before you start to build your 3D set.

We will be creating a set that includes the home of a gnome in the side of an embankment under a dead tree, as shown in the sketch. You can use this sketch to build your model. The sketch is located on the CD that came with this book in the resources directory. The directory also contains the textures that we will use to create the set.

We will be using Maya to create the background, so if you are ready to start, bring it up on your computer and let's get building.

STEP-BY-STEP

1

Begin by creating a polygon plane to use as a guide for building your model, as shown in Figure 7.6.

2

Create a Lambert material and load the sketch into it.

3

Apply the texture to the polygon plane and scale it to fit the picture, as shown in Figure 7.7.

4

Start by creating a cylinder for the tree, as shown in Figure 7.8. Make sure the cylinder has at least 32 divisions around the axis and eight along the height.

5

Scale the cylinder to fit the guide in the drawing.

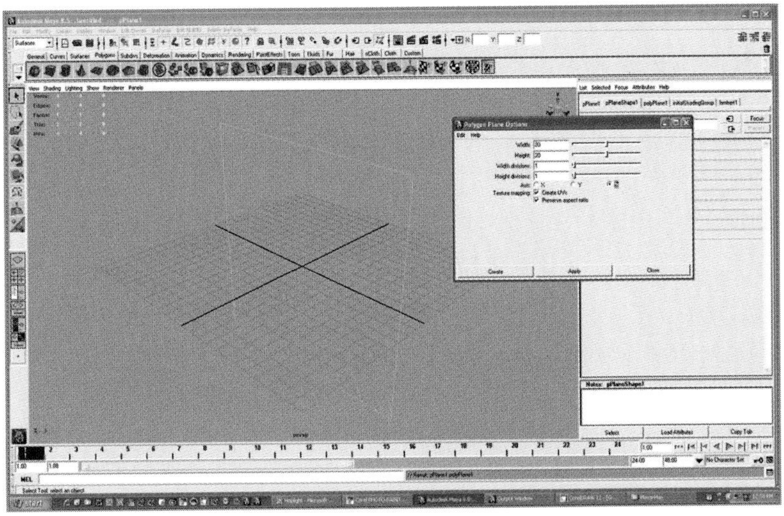

Figure 7.6
Create a single polygon plane.

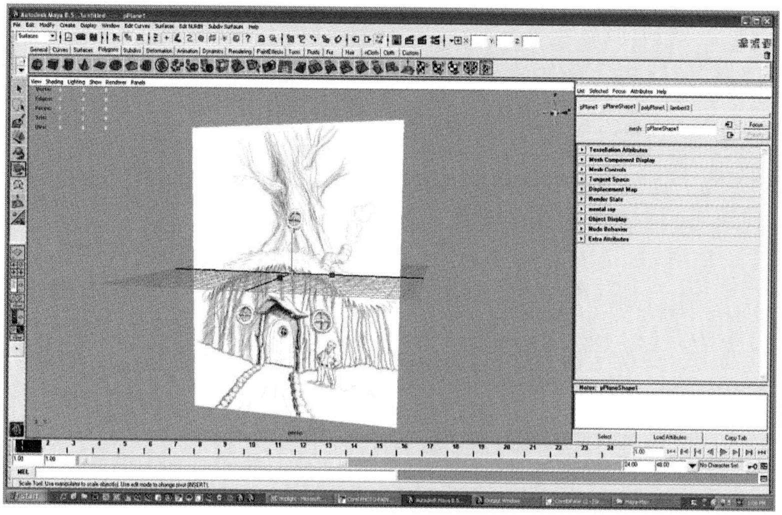

Figure 7.7 Load the picture so you can use it for a guide.

Figure 7.8 Create a cylinder for the tree trunk.

6

Select the faces at the bottom of the cylinder and extrude them down and around following the guide to form the top of the house, as shown in Figure 7.9.

7

Continue to extrude down the sides of the house and then delete the bottom faces so the model looks similar to Figure 7.10.

8

The house will be part of an embankment. Go around to the back of the house and delete the faces on the back side, as shown in Figure 7.11. This is where the house will join the embankment.

9

Extrude the edges outward from the house along the sides of the house where you deleted the back, as shown in Figure 7.12, to create the embankment.

10

Now we will create the ridge behind the house. Select the edges along the top of the embankment and the back of the house and extrude them up and back as shown in Figure 7.13. The ridge doesn't have to be steep.

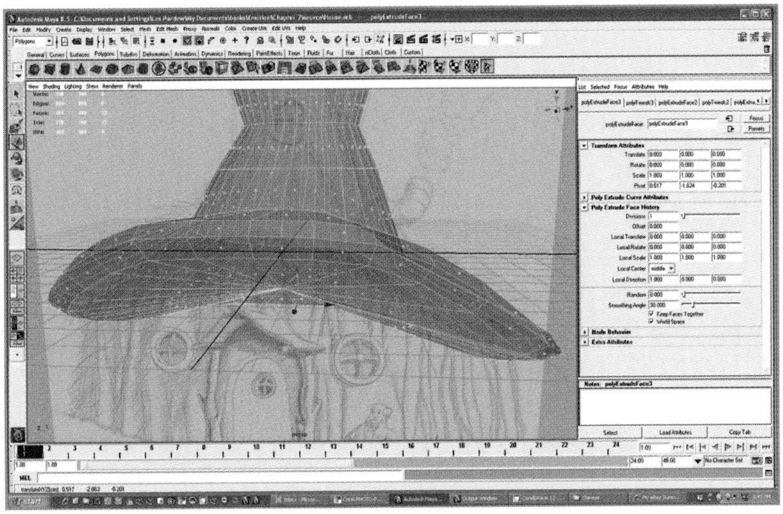

Figure 7.9
Create the roof of the house from the bottom of the tree.

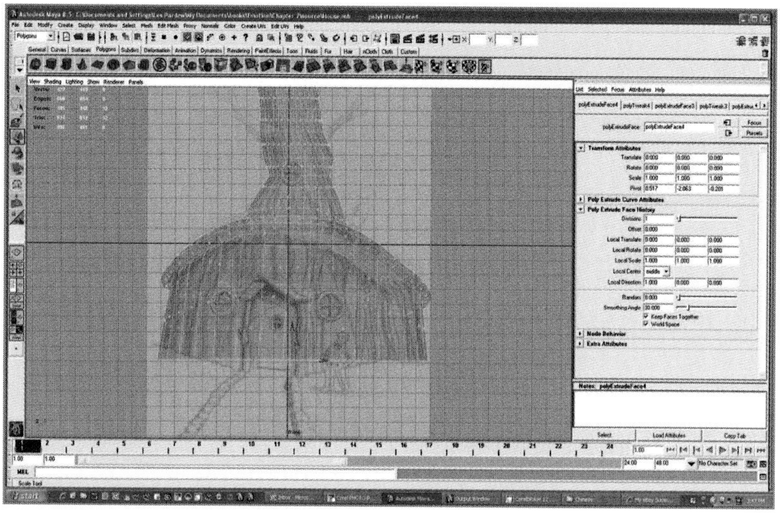

Figure 7.10 Create the sides of the house.

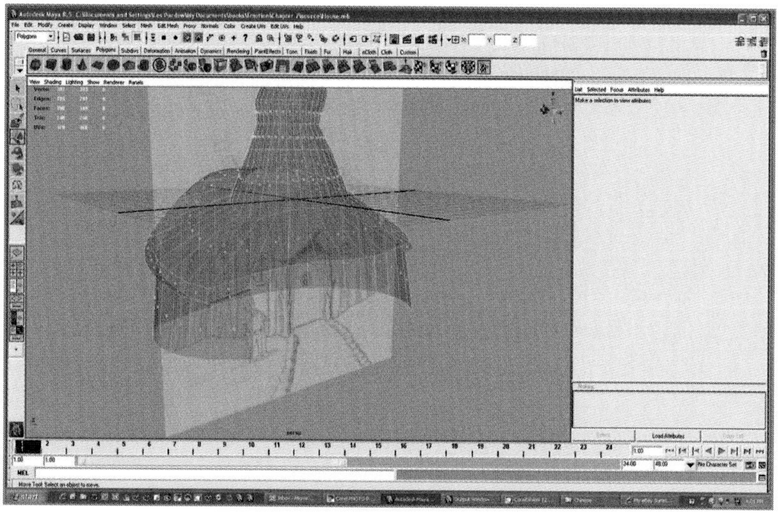

Figure 7.11 Delete the polygons on the back of the house.

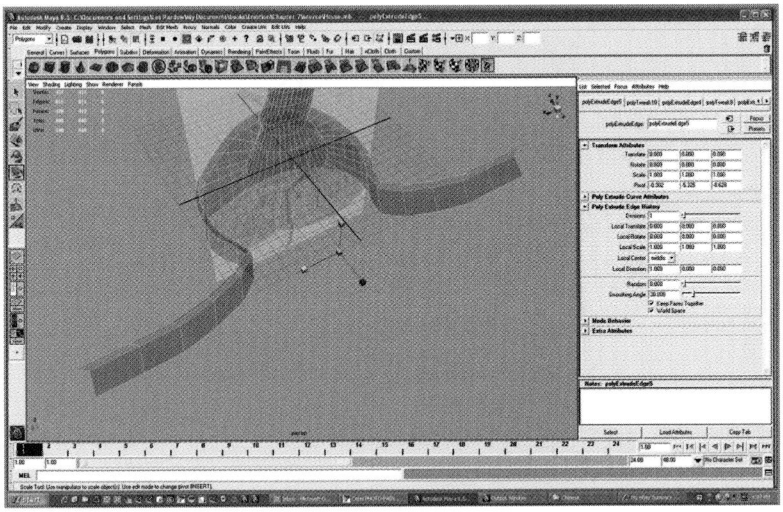

Figure 7.12 Create the embankment behind the house.

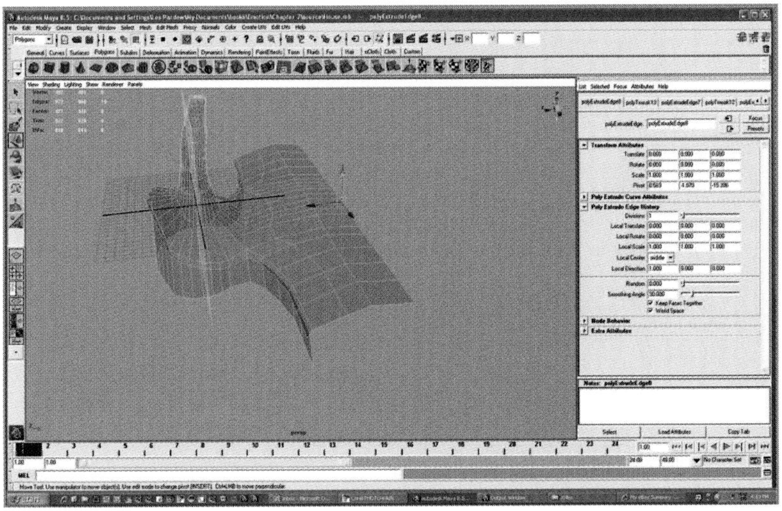

Figure 7.13 Create the ridge behind the house.

11

You don't want the ridge to look too mechanical so vary the height a little to make it look more natural, as shown in Figure 7.14.

12

Now we need to create the ground in front and to the sides of the house. Select all of the edges along the bottom of the house and embankment and extrude them out and forward, as shown in Figure 7.15.

13

You will need to go in and straighten out some of the polygons because the scaling tool will skew them to the sides. Adjust the vertices as shown in Figure 7.16. Merge the vertices in the corners as shown.

14

Now select the edges at the base of the house and extrude them out and down forming a little hill that our house will sit on, as shown in Figure 7.17.

15

Now you need to join the polygons around the house with those along the embankment. Snap the vertices of the hill to those of the embankment and then smooth them so they look more natural, as shown in Figure 7.18.

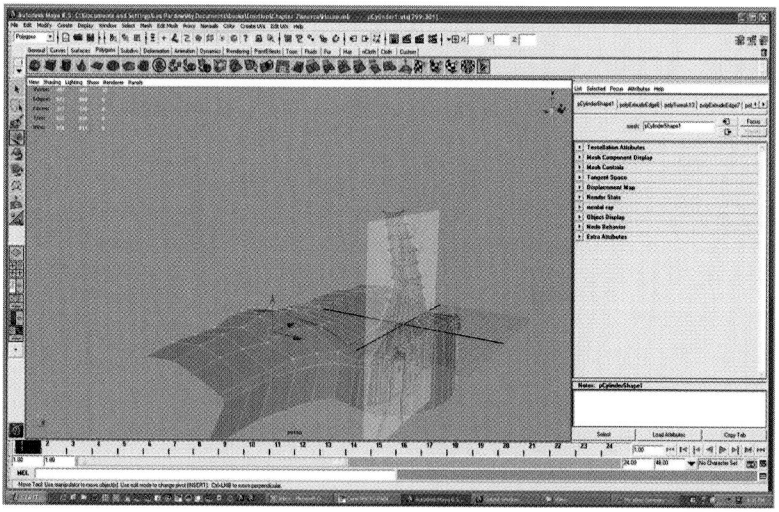

Figure 7.14
Move the vertices a little to make the ridge seem more natural.

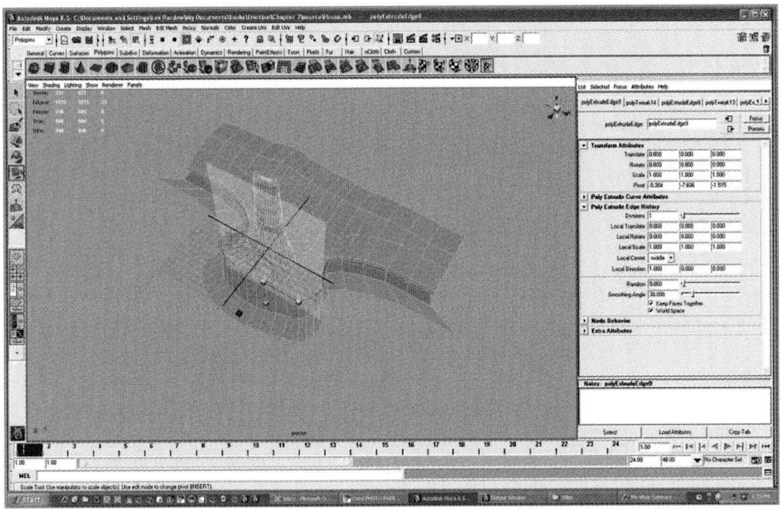

Figure 7.15
Extrude the polygons on the bottom of the model.

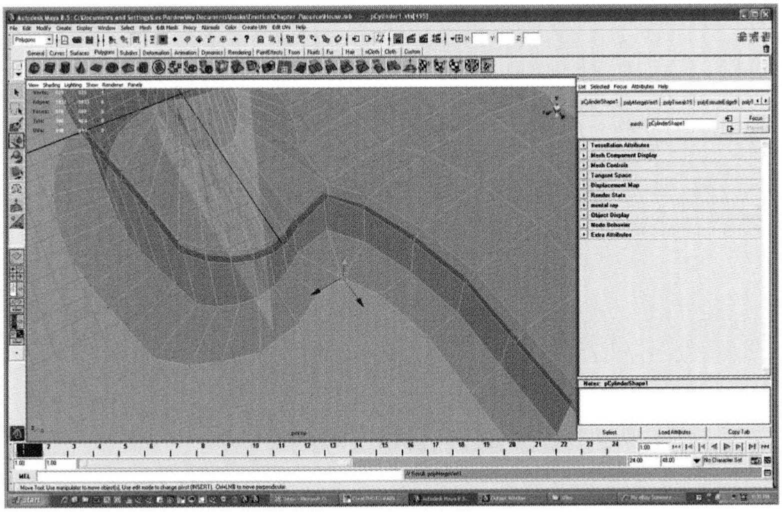

Figure 7.16
Merge the vertices in the corners.

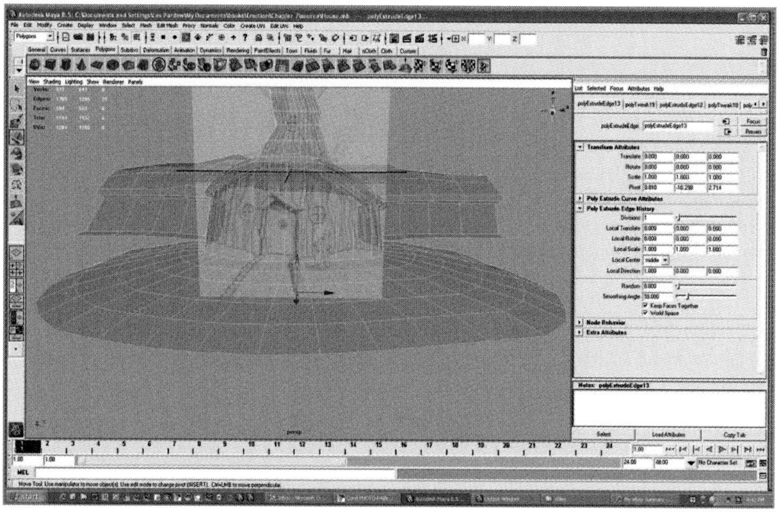

Figure 7.17
Create a hill for the house to sit on.

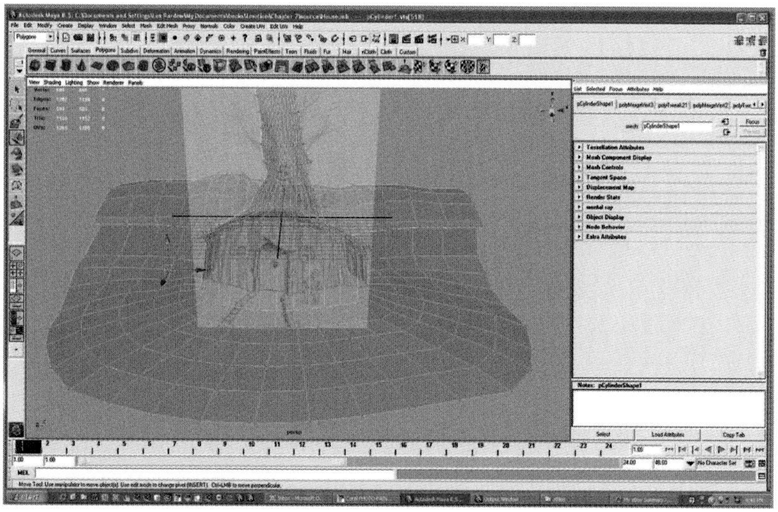

Figure 7.18
Join the hill to the embankment.

16

The house looks a little symmetrical. Go in and move a few of the vertices around to give it a more natural look, like that pictured in Figure 7.19.

17

Use the Split Polygon tool found in the Edit Polygons menu to create some roots extending from the tree, as shown in Figure 7.20. Once split you can then move the vertices to form the roots.

18

Now you need to add a few branches to your tree. Split the polygons in a circular pattern along the side of the tree where you want to place a branch and extrude the branch as shown in Figure 7.21.

> **NOTE**
>
> Remember when splitting polygons to only have four- or three-sided polygons. Although Maya will let you have more sides to your polygons, it is always a good practice to keep everything to three or four sides. Polygons with five or more sides can cause rendering, texturing, and surface problems later in the modeling process.

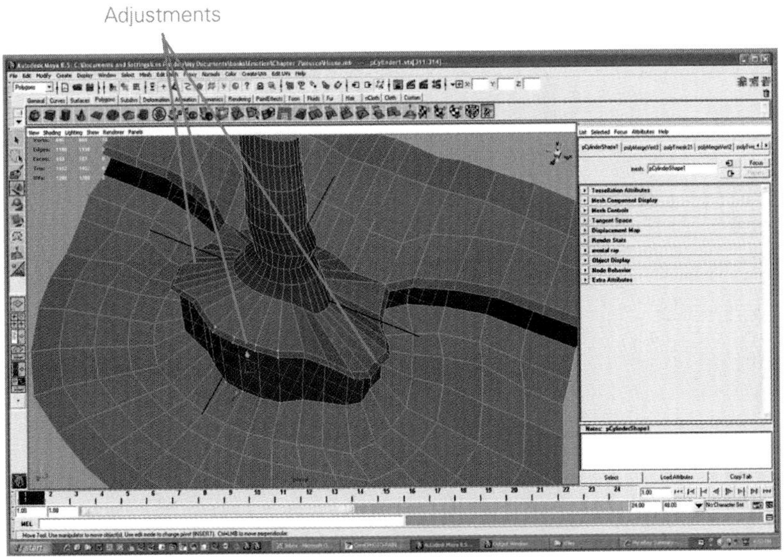

Figure 7.19
Make the house appear more natural by moving a few vertices.

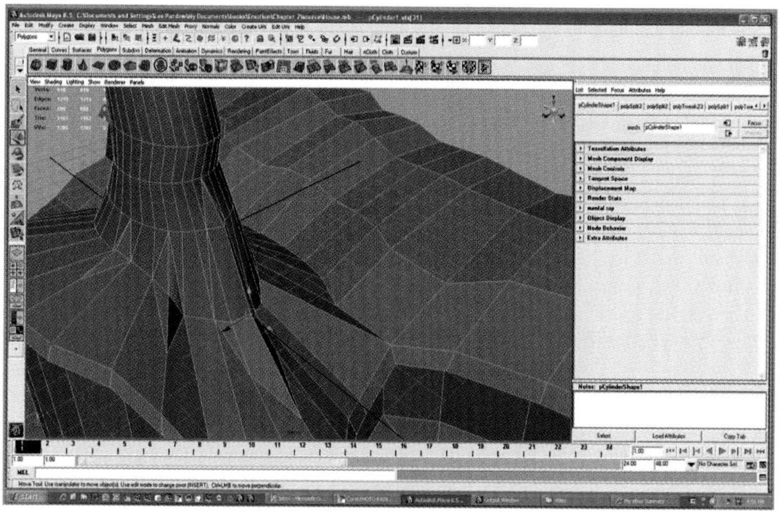

Figure 7.20 Build roots around the bottom of the tree.

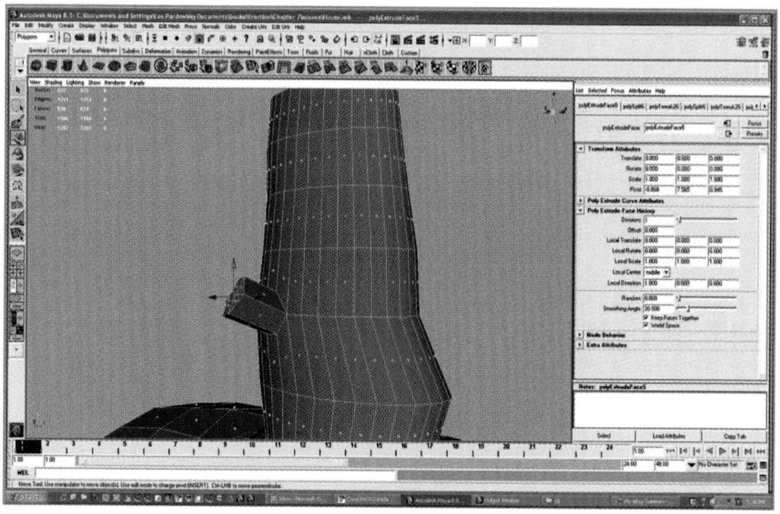

Figure 7.21 Extrude branches from the side of the tree.

19

Once you have the base for a branch you can continue to extrude to build the branch, as shown in Figure 7.22. You can split polygons along the branch as needed to extrude new branches.

20

Create the three branches shown in the drawing. When you are done, your house should look similar to Figure 7.23.

> **NOTE**
>
> The tree is flat on the top because it extends out of the picture frame in our setting. You are welcome to build a complete tree with all of its branches, but most of the time the set artist will only work on those areas that will be in frame in the show.

21

You are almost done. The model is beginning to look like the sketch. You just need to add a few more things to get it finished—like doors and windows. Let's begin with the door. Split some of the polygons around the front of the house so you can extrude the door, like the one shown in Figure 7.24.

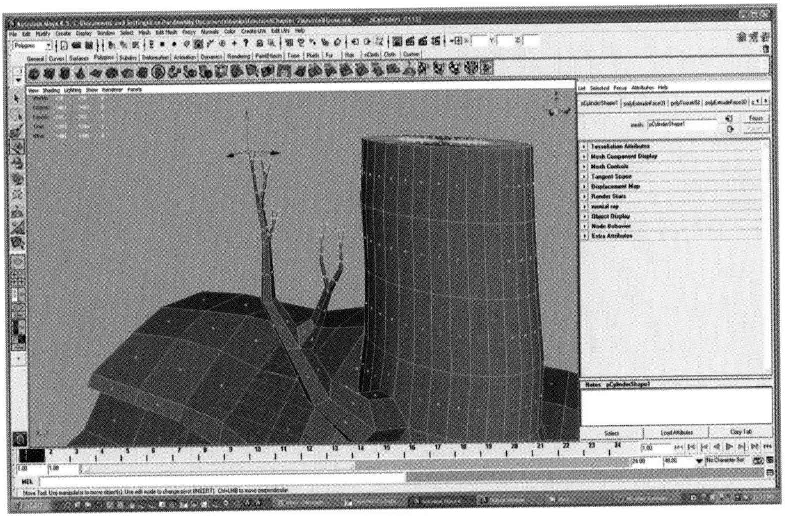

Figure 7.22
Extrude the branch and several smaller branches coming from it.

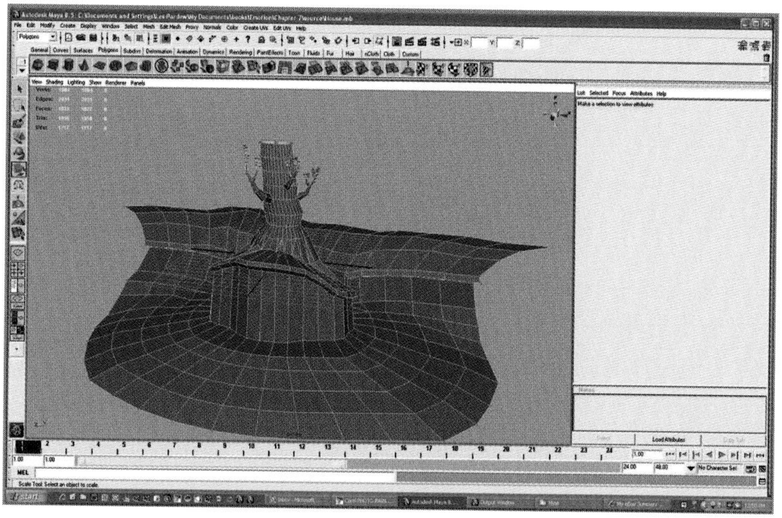

Figure 7.23
Add two more branches to the tree.

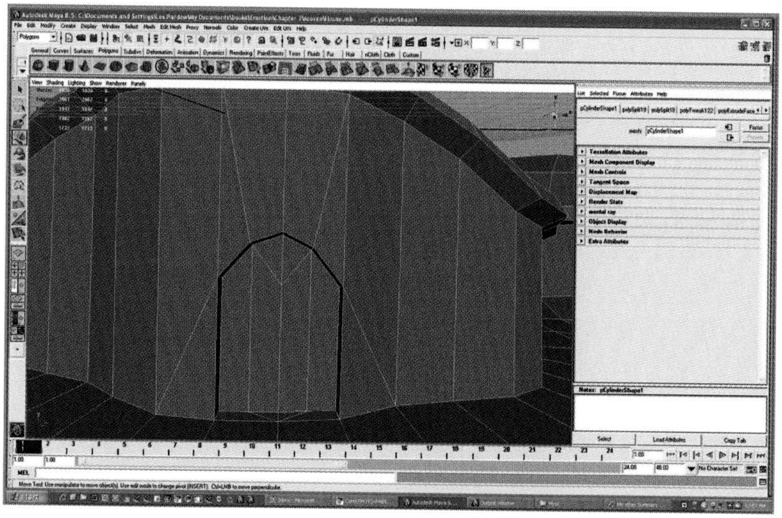

Figure 7.24
Build the door of the house.

Creating Background Objects

Instead of splitting polygons to create the windows and other elements of the scene, we will be making separate objects. It is a lot easier, for example, to create a circular object like the windows starting with a cylinder than it is trying to split polygons into a circle.

STEP-BY-STEP

1

Create a flat cylinder for the window that has 16 axis divisions and 3 cap divisions, as shown in Figure 7.25.

2

It is often easier to work on an object if the other geometry in the scene is not in the way. A simple way of getting rid of the extra geometry is to use the View Selected feature in the Show > Isolate Selected menus.

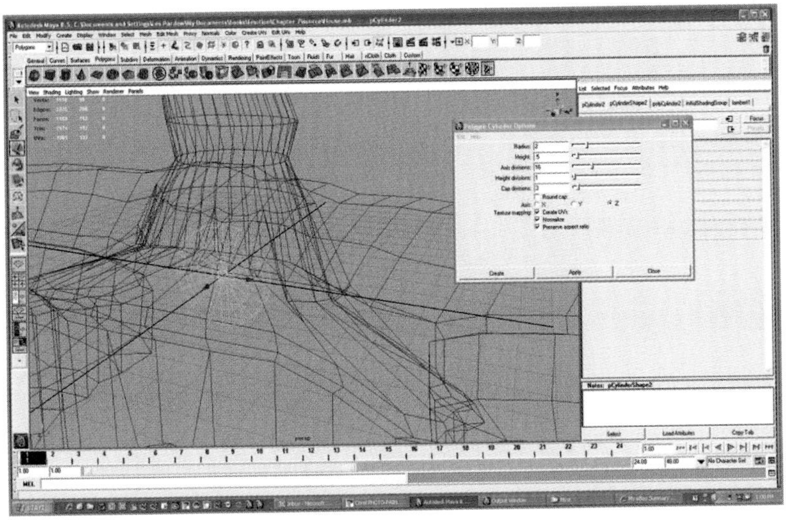

Figure 7.25
Create a cylinder for the window.

3

We will never see the backside of the windows so you can delete those polygons to make the modeling process easier.

4

The cap of the cylinder should have three rings of vertices. From the front view, scale the inside ring in and the middle ring out, as shown in Figure 7.26.

5

Move the vertices of the window as shown in Figure 7.27. This is where the window slats will feed into the center of the window.

6

Now you need to scale in the vertices of the slates so they are straight like the one shown in Figure 7.28.

7

You will need to make two extrusions, one for the windowpanes inward and one for the center and outside window molding outward, as shown in Figure 7.29.

8

Pull the vertices of the center forward to give the window a convex look, as shown in Figure 7.30.

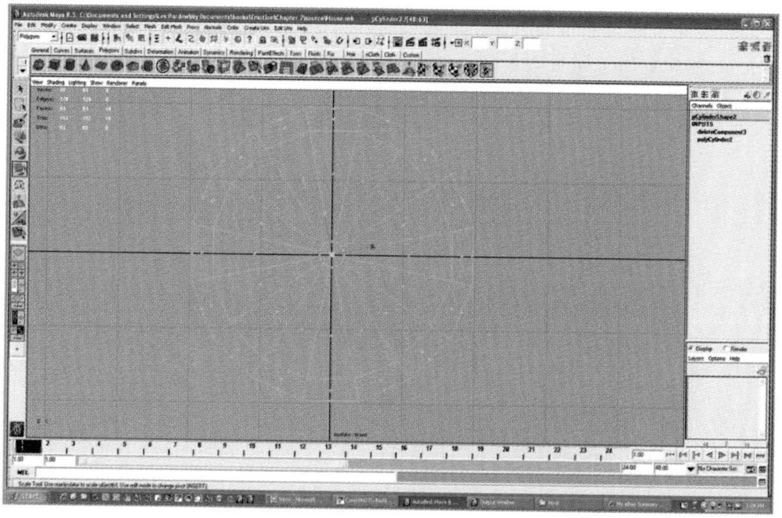

Figure 7.26
Adjust the front of the window.

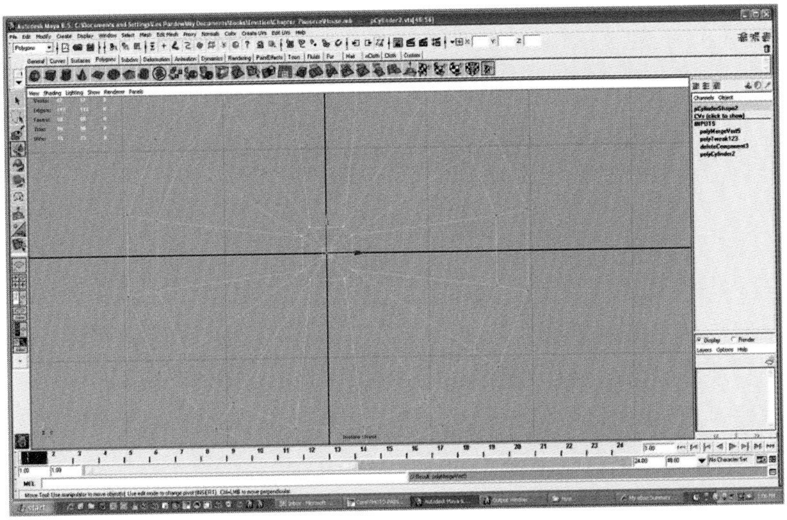

Figure 7.27 Move the vertices of the center.

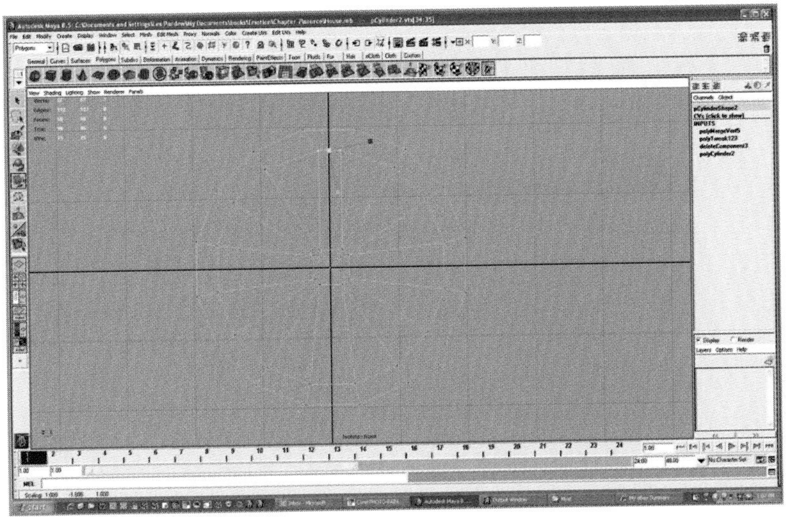

Figure 7.28 Move the vertices on the outside of the window slats.

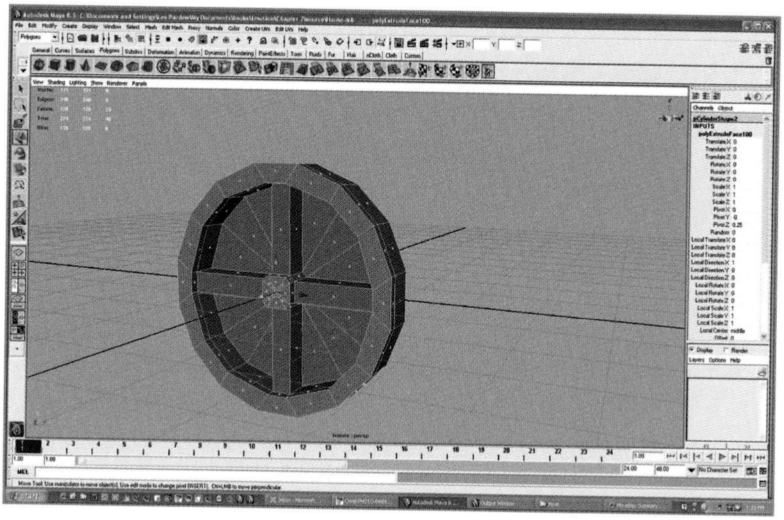

Figure 7.29
Extrude the windowpanes and molding.

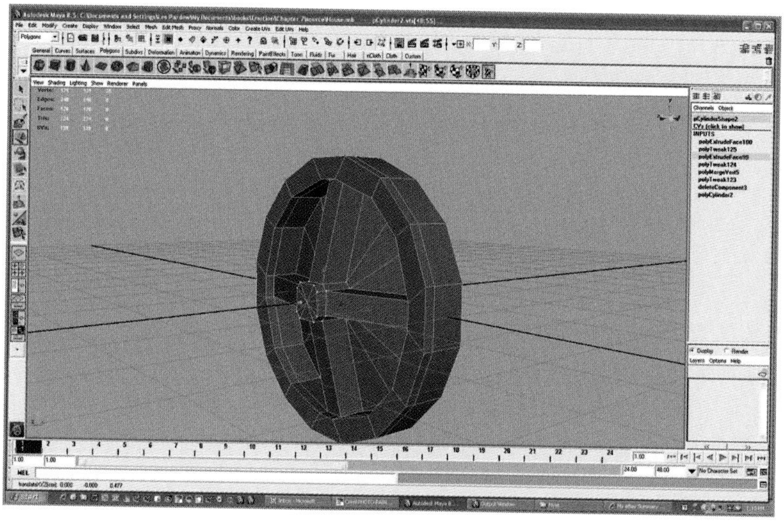

Figure 7.30
Make the window convex.

9

Now you can bring back the house model by exiting Isolation mode and place the windows in the tree and on the sides by the door. Pressing Ctrl+D on the keyboard will duplicate the model. The windows should protrude out from the house, as shown in Figure 7.31.

NOTE

You can remove the sketch template by hiding it any time it gets in the way. Just select the template and then select Hide in the Display menu. If you want it back you can select Show Last Hidden from the same menu.

10

Now let's create the porch roof. Start with a polygon cube with four polygon divisions in the width and two in height, as shown in Figure 7.32.

11

Peak the center of the cube and place it over the door so it looks similar to the porch roof shown in Figure 7.33.

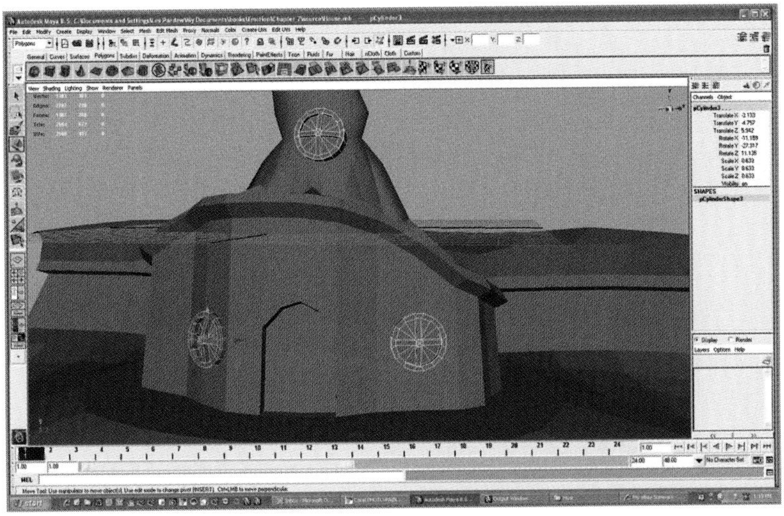

Figure 7.31
Place the windows on the house.

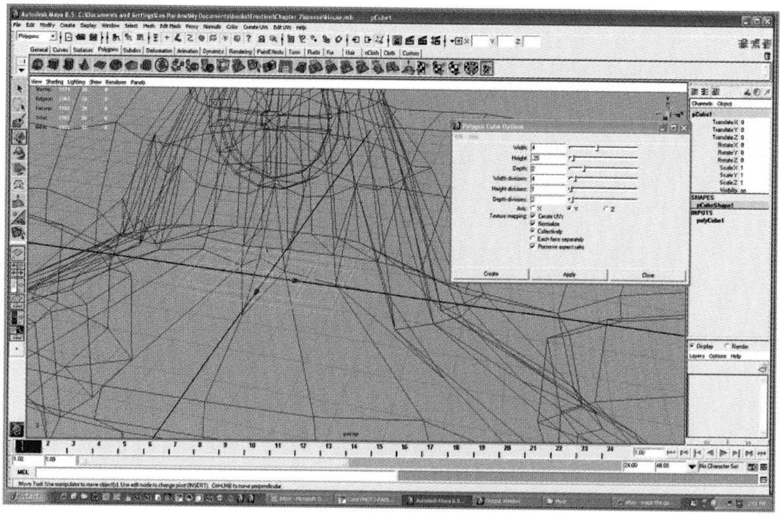

Figure 7.32
Use a polygon cube for creating the porch roof.

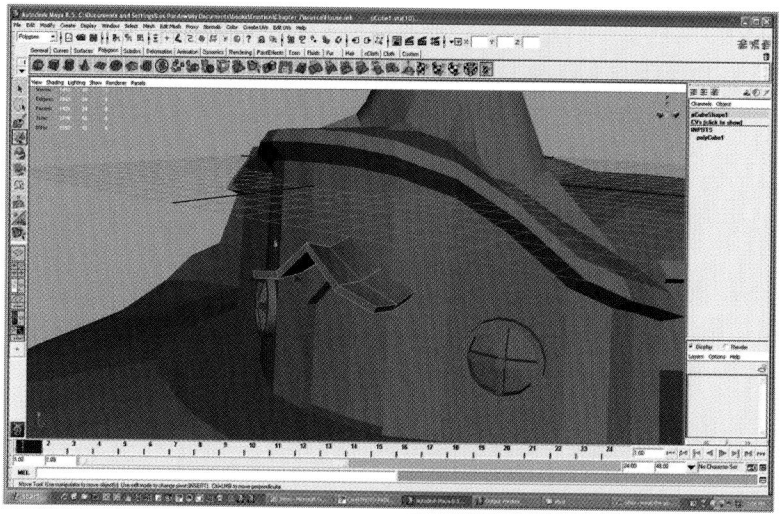

Figure 7.33
Place the porch roof just above the door.

12

Create a 16-sided cylinder for the porch roof supports with four divisions along the length, as shown in Figure 7.34.

13

Give the supports an organic look by modeling them similarly to the tree trunk with sawed off branches like those shown in Figure 7.35.

14

You need to create some beams under the porch roof. Use 16-sided polygon cylinders divided in the center so they can bend.

15

Place the beams under the roof in the middle and by the supports, as shown in Figure 7.36. You will need to bend them to get them to fit against the roof.

16

The set needs a path approaching the house lined with rocks on either side. To create this path, first line up the vertices of the polygons extending from the doorway so they are straight, as shown in Figure 7.37.

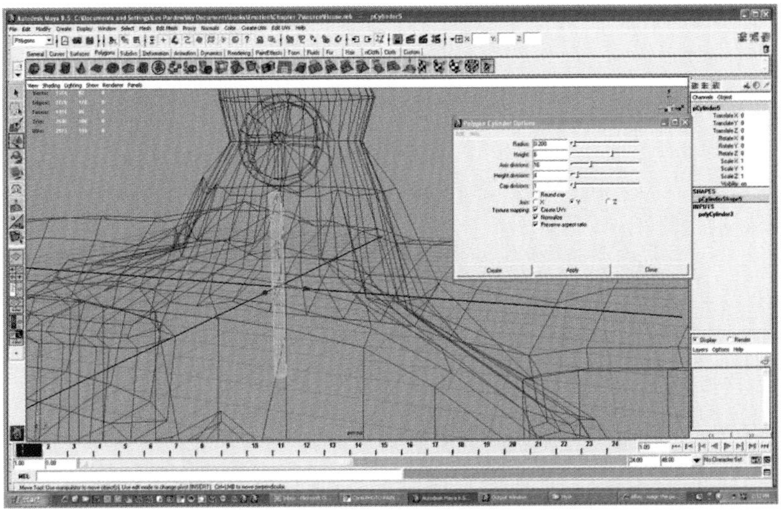

Figure 7.34 Use cylinders for the porch roof supports.

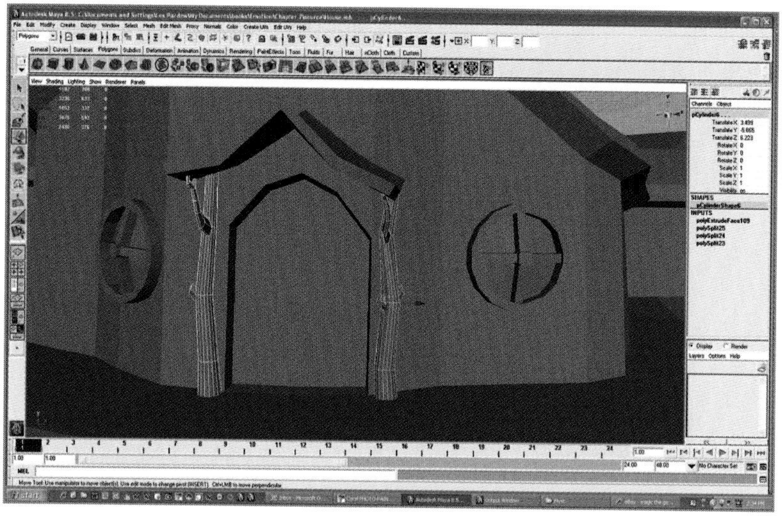

Figure 7.35 The roof supports should have an organic look.

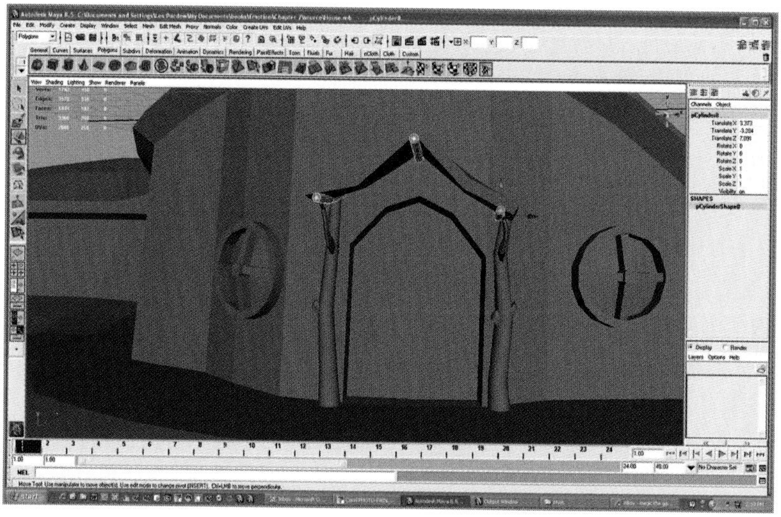

Figure 7.36 Add support beams to the porch roof.

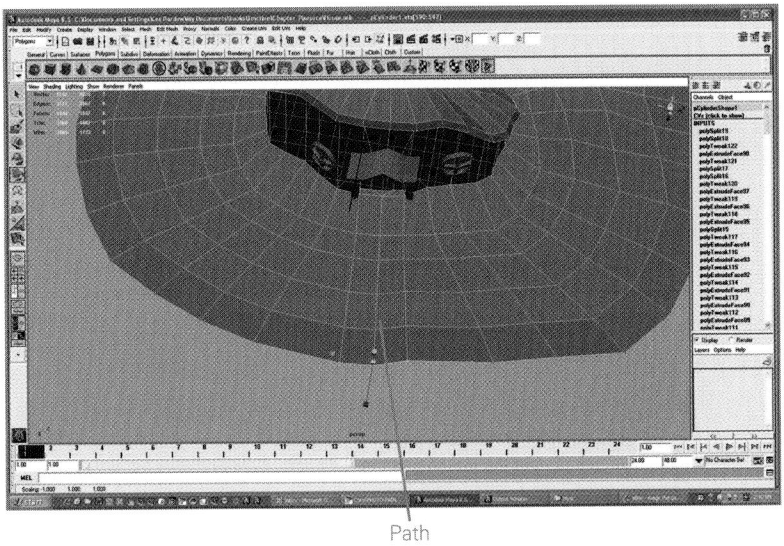

Figure 7.37
Line up the polygons of the path.

17

The rocks will be polygon spheres. Make sure you use as few polygons as possible when creating the rocks to avoid lengthy rendering times. Create a polygon sphere and scale it to look like a smooth river rock. Place the rock along the edge of the path.

18

Now duplicate the rock you just made and place the duplicate along the edge of the path. Use scale and rotate to make the duplicate a little different from the first rock. Continue the duplicating process until you have both sides of the path lined with rocks, as shown in Figure 7.38.

19

Just one more item to finish your model—the stovepipe. Create another 16-sided cylinder with 5 divisions along its length, as shown in Figure 7.39.

20

Bend the pipe and place it on top of the house, as shown in Figure 7.40.

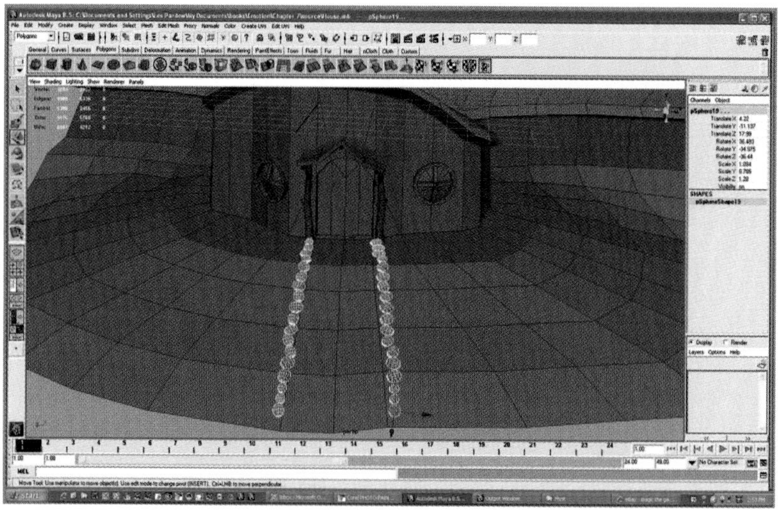

Figure 7.38
Line the path with rocks.

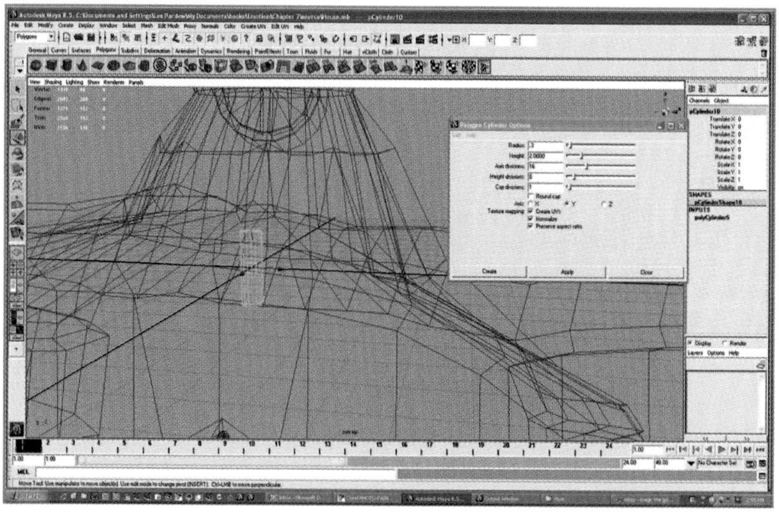

Figure 7.39
Create a cylinder for the stovepipe.

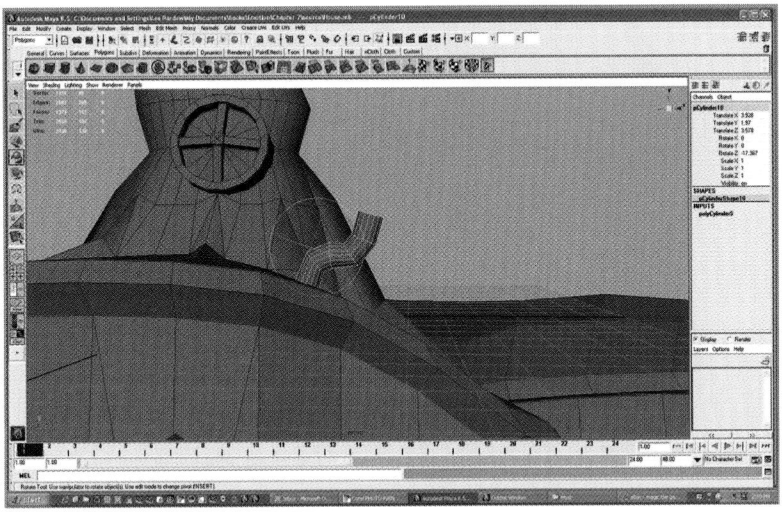

Figure 7.40
Place the bent stovepipe on top of the house.

The model is now complete. Now you need to move on to the texturing phase of the project.

Adding Textures

Before you can add the textures to the model, you need to prepare the model for texturing. The preparation process isn't hard; you just need to anticipate how you want to texture the model.

It is a lot easier to texture individual objects than it is to have multiple textures on a single object. The model of the house will require several textures like grass, dirt, tree bark, and the path. Before texturing these areas, you can simplify things greatly by making each texture area its own object. Use the Extract feature to isolate each area. It is located in the Mesh directory. It extracts selected faces from an object and makes them a separate object without moving any vertices. Figure 7.41 shows the embankment separated from the rest of the model.

The areas that you need to separate are the grass above and below the house, the embankment, the door, the tree, and the path. Once you have them all separated, you can start applying textures to the model.

Next you will be applying textures to the model. Textures are applied using a UV system. UVs are the texture coordinates used by Maya to apply 2D images to a 3D surface.

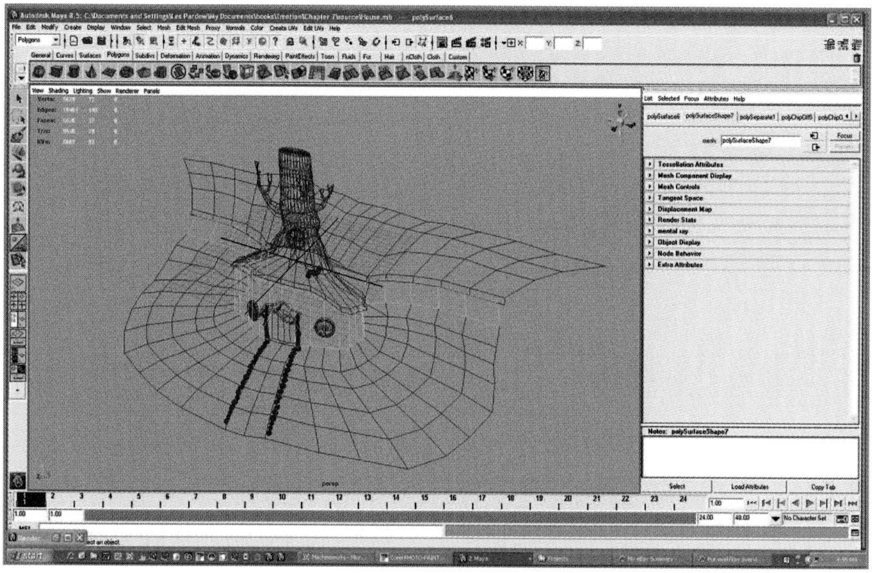

Figure 7.41
Separate embankment from the rest of the model.

STEP-BY-STEP

1

Select the areas that will be covered with grass, the land around the house not including the path, and the land above the house and use the Planar Mapping tool found in the Create UVs directory to map the area. Set the Planar Mapping tool to the Y axis so it projects straight down.

2

You will need to move some of the UVs because the ground above the house overlaps the ground around the house. Use the UV Editor panel to move the UVs, as shown in Figure 7.42.

3

Create a Lambert material and load the grass texture from the CD.

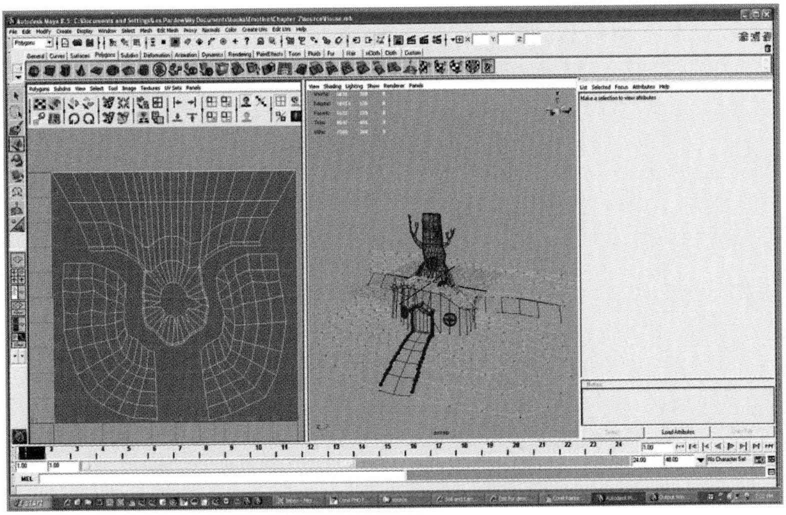

Figure 7.42 Scale the UVs of the grass sections so they don't overlap.

4

Apply the grass texture to the ground, as shown in Figure 7.43.

5

Maya Unlimited (not available in Maya Complete) has a great feature for creating grass. It is actually the Fur feature, but grass on the ground is similar to fur on an animal so it can be used for creating grass as well. In fact, they have a preset grass sample that we will use for this project. Click the Fur tab on the shelf to bring up the preset fur types. The seventh one from the left is the grass-preset type, shown in Figure 7.44.

6

All you have to do is select the object you want to have grass and then click the grass swatch. In Figure 7.45 I selected the ground above the house. Notice that once the grass is applied there will appear to be several strings coming out of the ground. These are real-time indicators that grass is placed on the ground.

7

To see how the grass will look in your scene when rendered, you need to render your scene. An easy way to do this is to click the Render icon at the top of your screen. This will render the image from the current view as shown in Figure 7.46. Notice that the grass is a little sparse.

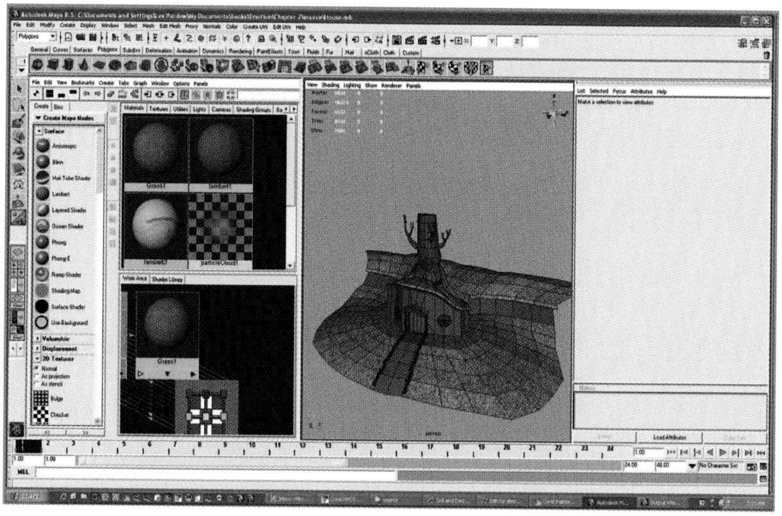

Figure 7.43
Give the ground a grass texture.

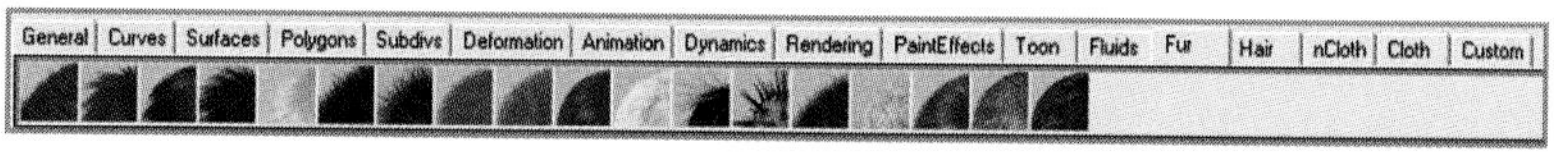

Figure 7.44
Grass is the seventh swatch from the left.

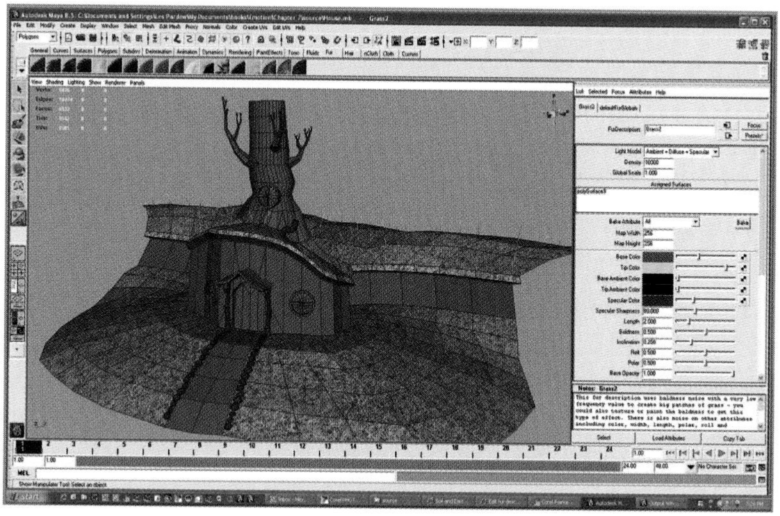

Figure 7.45
Apply grass to the ground above the house.

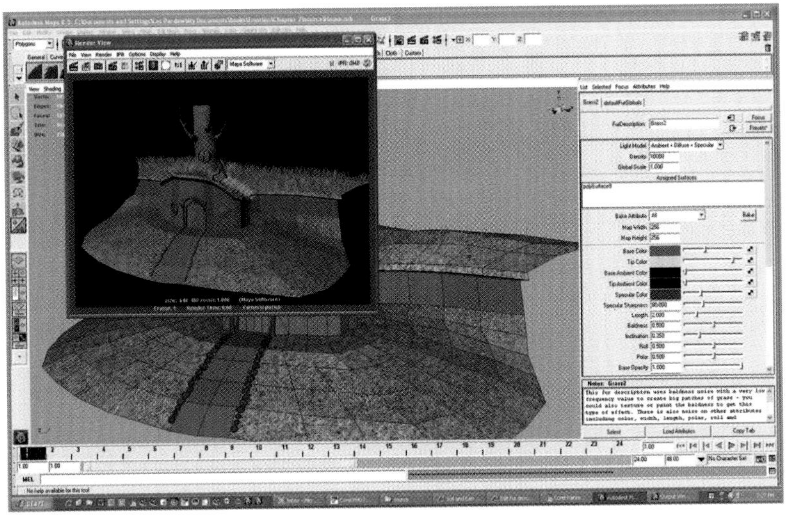

Figure 7.46
Render the scene.

8

Open your Attribute editor if it isn't already open and change the grass settings for Density to 50000 and Length to 2. Render the scene again. It should look similar to Figure 7.47. Now the grass looks thicker.

9

Repeat the procedure for applying grass to the other areas of the scene. This time, however, change the Height to .5 so the grass isn't as tall. See Figure 7.48.

10

The tree is a complicated object so a planar map will not work. If you want to have exact UV coordinates for the tree you can use cylindrical mapping and select the faces of each branch, but a quick way of setting up the UVs for the tree is to use Automatic Mapping found in the Create UVs directory. The results of the automatic mapping are shown in Figure 7.49.

11

Create a Lambert material and load the bark texture for the tree. Then select the tree and apply the texture found on the CD. When you render the scene, it should now look like Figure 7.50.

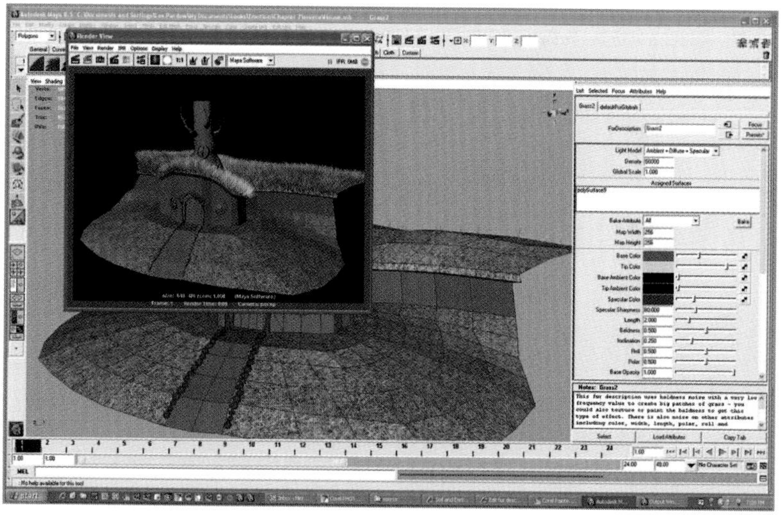

Figure 7.47 Thicken the grass in the scene.

Figure 7.48 Apply shorter grass to the area around the house.

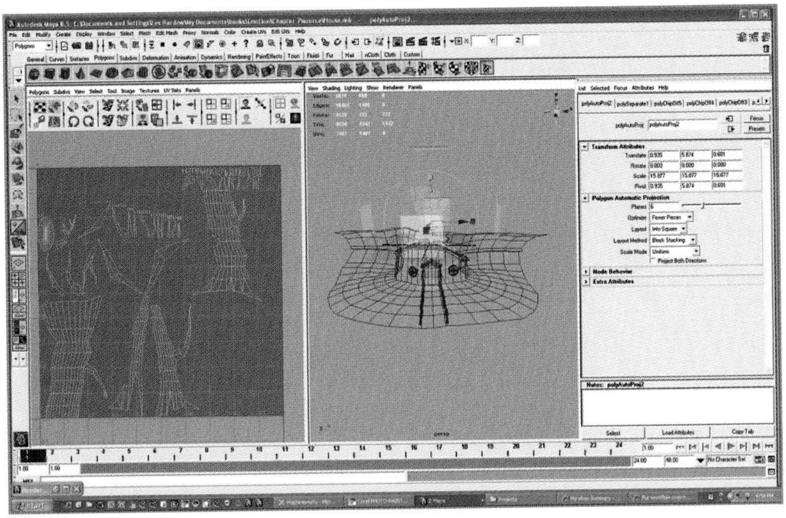

Figure 7.49
Map the UVs of the tree.

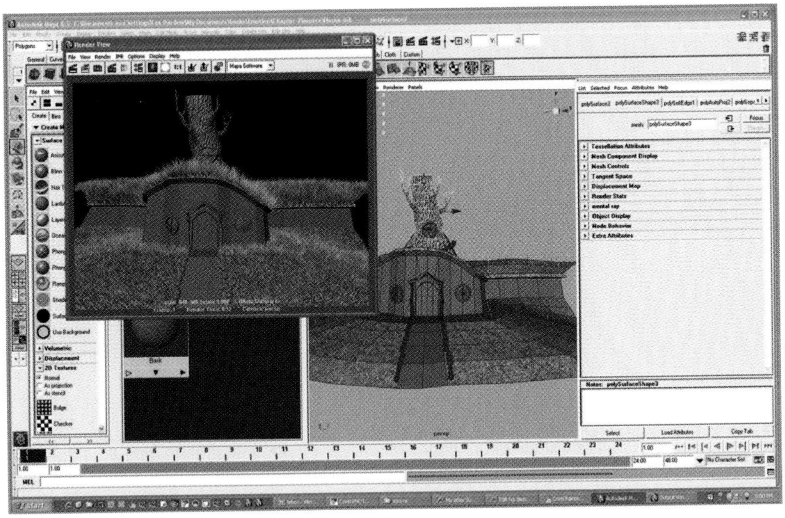

Figure 7.50
Apply a bark texture to the tree.

12

The dirt embankment texture is a little different from some of the other textures. It will require some individual UV adjustments. Go to the far-right side of the embankment and select the two polygons that make up the first section of the embankment. Use the Planar Mapping tool and apply a projection in the Z axis, as shown in Figure 7.51.

13

Repeat the mapping procedure around the embankment and across the house. When you get to the side of the house, you may want to select two or three polygon-wide sections because the texture is square and keeping each mapped section as square as possible is important.

14

When you get to the door, map the top of the door and the sides of the door with a single projection.

15

Now that all of the embankment polygons are mapped, you will need to line them up so they repeat without seams. You do this in the UV Editor. You should notice that when you click on the embankment object that all of the projected sections show up forming a lot of confusing white lines. To get rid of these lines, you need to take one section at a time. An easy way to isolate each section you mapped is to select the section's faces, then if you change the selection mode in the UV Editor to UVs, you can drag a bounding box around the

Figure 7.51
Apply the dirt embankment texture using the Planar Mapping tool.

UV area and it will only select the UVs of the selected faces. Move the selection to the area directly below the texture area and snap the edges to the corners as shown in Figure 7.52.

16

Continue to organize each section that you projected earlier. Some that are two or three polygons wide will need the inside UVs snapped within the texture block. Figure 7.53 shows the process just as I finished snapping the UVs of the door area. Because of the shape of the door, they are the most complicated area.

17

When you are finished with all of the UVs for the embankment, your scene and editor should look similar to Figure 7.54. Move the UVs from the lower section back up to the texture area.

18

The last section of the main model that we need to map is the path. Load the path texture into a Lambert material and apply it to the path.

19

Planar project the path in the Y axis for each four-polygon section.

20

Organize the UVs like you did for the embankment so the path lines up as shown in Figure 7.55.

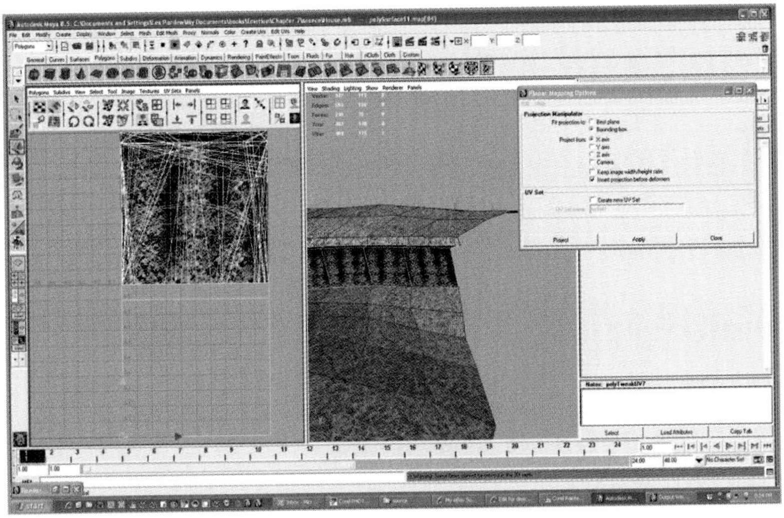

Figure 7.52
Organize the UVs of each projected section.

Figure 7.53 The door UVs are the most complicated.

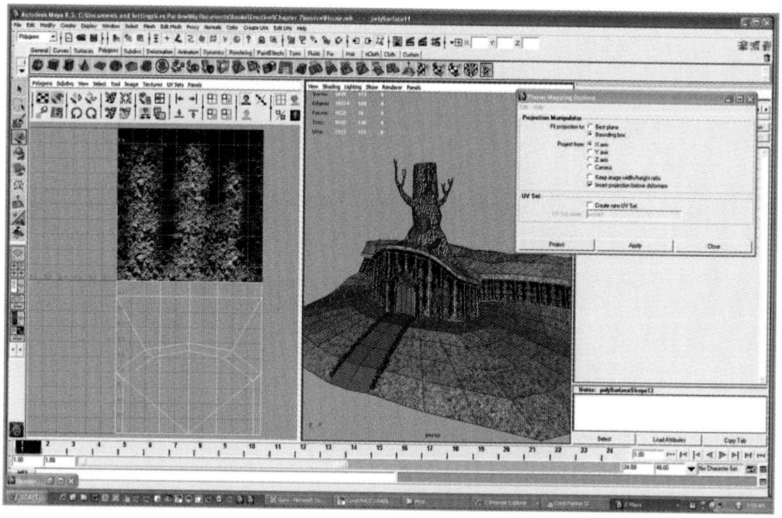

Figure 7.54 All of the UVs are organized.

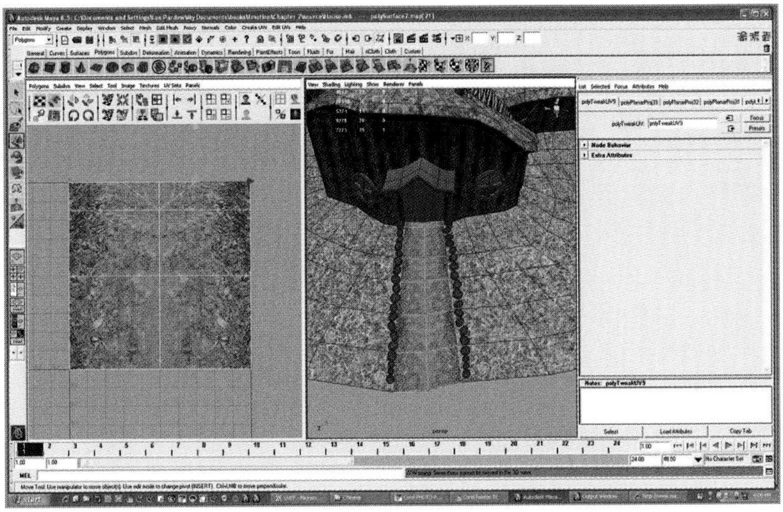

Figure 7.55 Apply the path texture to the path in the model.

Now the main model is textured and all you need to texture are the individual objects in the scene. We will tackle those in this next section.

Texturing Scene Objects

There are many reasons for creating objects as separate elements from the main scene model. The object might be movable in the scene, like a door or a rock. Maybe the object needs to be mapped separately. Another reason might just simply be that it was easier to model as a separate object. No matter what the reason, objects have to be texture mapped separately.

1

Let's start with an easy object—the rocks along the path. Load in the rock texture and apply it to one of the rocks. That is all you need to do. Now do it to the rest of the rocks, as shown in Figure 7.56.

2

Apply the thatch texture to the porch roof using the Planar Mapping tool. You will need to rotate the map to get it to go in the right direction. If you click the red corner of the projection, it will change to a universal manipulator that will allow you to rotate the projection as shown in Figure 7.57.

3

The front of the porch roof is also projected and then manipulated in the UV editor so it follows the grain of the texture. Figure 7.58 shows the UVs of the front of the porch roof.

4

The door is just a simple planar projection, as shown in Figure 7.59.

5

Use the bark texture and automatic mapping on the roof supports like you did with the tree. See Figure 7.60.

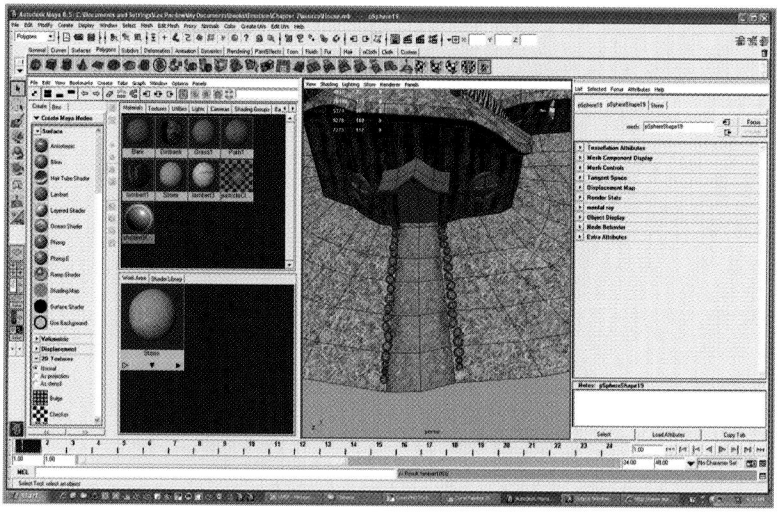

Figure 7.56
Give each rock a texture.

Figure 7.57
Apply the thatch texture to the porch roof.

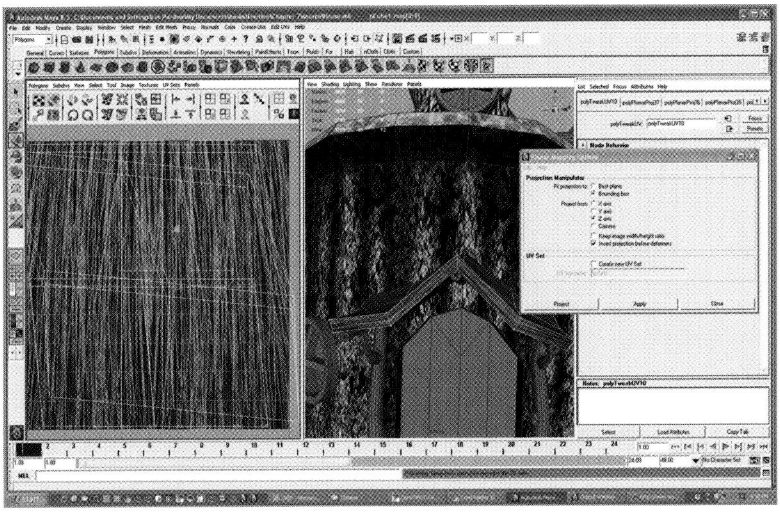

Figure 7.58
Have the front of the roof follow the grain of the texture.

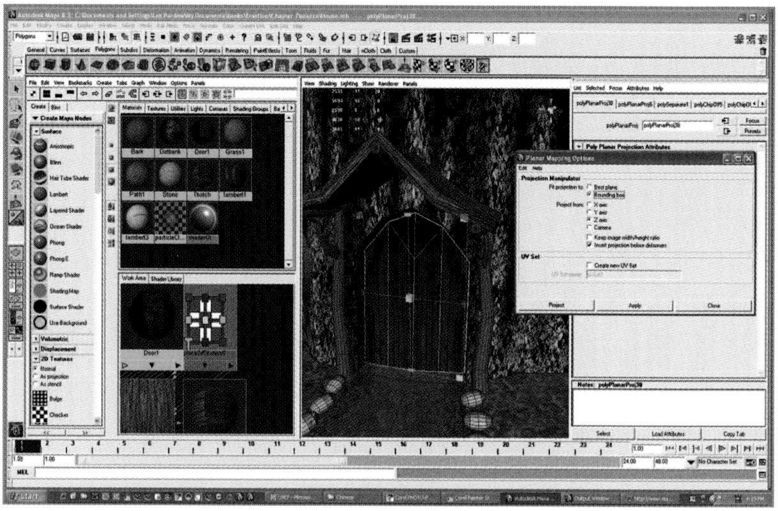

Figure 7.59
Use a planar map projection on the door.

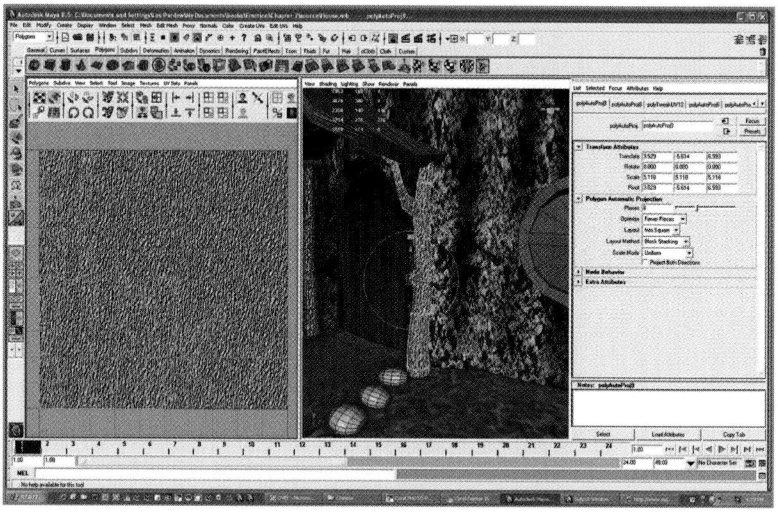

Figure 7.60
Apply the bark texture to the supports.

6

Use the Planar Mapping tool to apply the cut wood texture to the ends of the sawed-off branches on the supports, as shown in Figure 7.61.

7

Rather than using a texture map, the window will just use a color with a Blinn material. Create the material and change the color to a light gray-blue, as shown in Figure 7.62.

8

Apply a dark wood texture to the window molding, as shown in Figure 7.63.

9

The last item to texture in the scene is the stovepipe. Load that texture and apply it to the stovepipe object.

10

Because the original cylinder already has mapped UVs that are close to what we need, we will not use a projection on the pipe. Rather, organize the current UVs as shown in Figure 7.64.

Figure 7.61 Apply the sawed wood texture to the ends of the sawed-off branches.

Figure 7.62
Use a color for the window-panes.

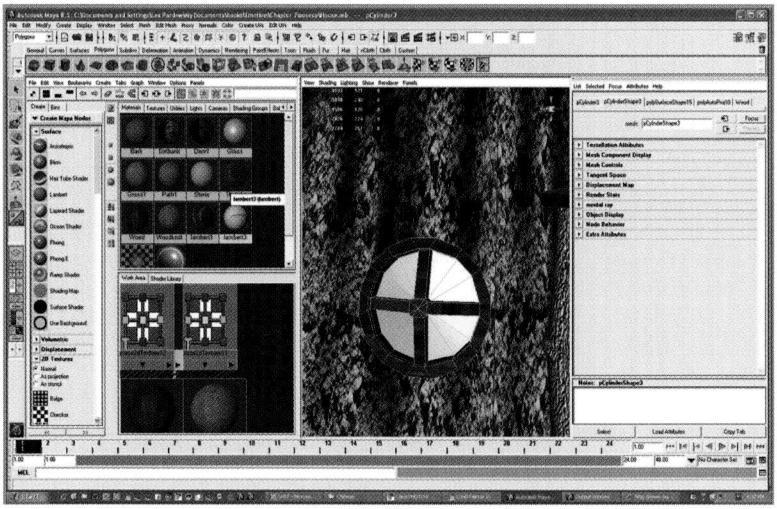

Figure 7.63
Use a wood texture for the window molding.

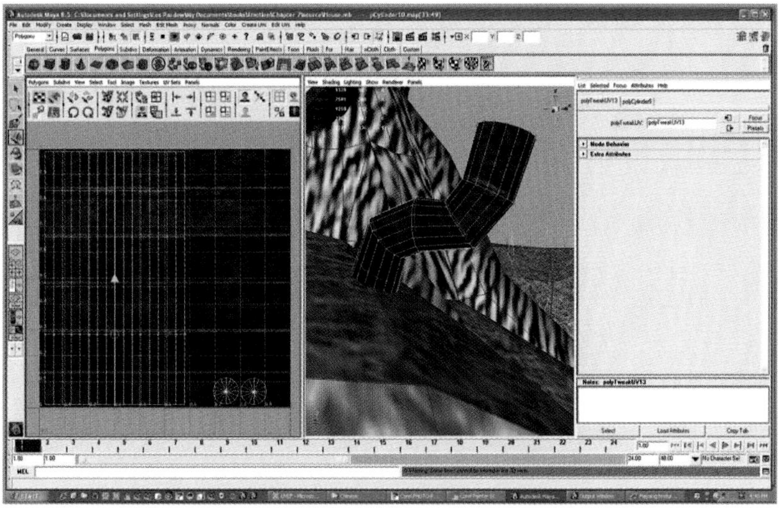

Figure 7.64
Apply the stovepipe texture to the stovepipe.

The set for the gnome's home is now complete. Your finished model should look similar to Figure 7.65.

You may notice that the embankment on the left side does not reach the side of the view. Because we will be using this view in the animation, that area needs to be fixed. In Figure 7.66 I have expanded the left side of the set. You should always test the camera angles you will be using in the production to make sure your set will look good from every angle.

Now I can render the set with a sky background, as shown in Figure 7.67 using the default lighting. The sky pictured here was added later in a 2D program.

The process for building a 3D set is a long one, but like other 3D assets, they last forever because they are digital and can be reused and changed whenever you want. This example was just a minor set. More complex sets will require more extensive modeling. This set is also still somewhat geometric in nature and not as organic as it could be. For a more truly organic look, you will need to use a lot more polygons. However, the example does give you a start in understanding how to build 3D sets for your animation.

I hope you have enjoyed learning about environments and how they affect emotions. The set you just built has some emotional qualities. Can you name a few of them? If you wanted to change the emotional quality of this set to something dark and sinister, what would you change?

Building sets can be fun and some artists specialize in doing this. Bringing emotional qualities to your production sets can help distinguish you from other set designers. A good set will always enhance the production if the set designer can bring the emotion of the scene to the audience.

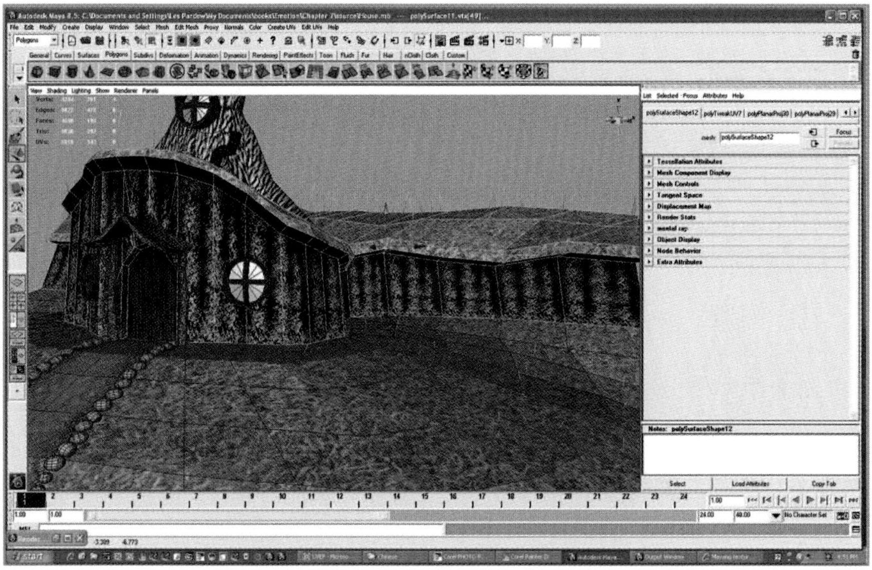

Figure 7.65 The set model is now finished.

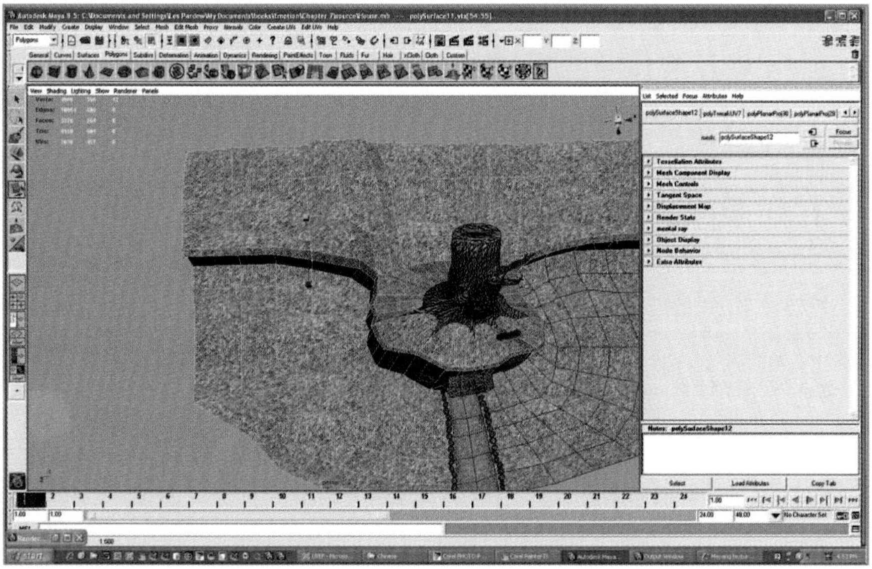

Figure 7.66 The left side needs to be wider.

Figure 7.67 The set is rendered.

CHAPTER 8

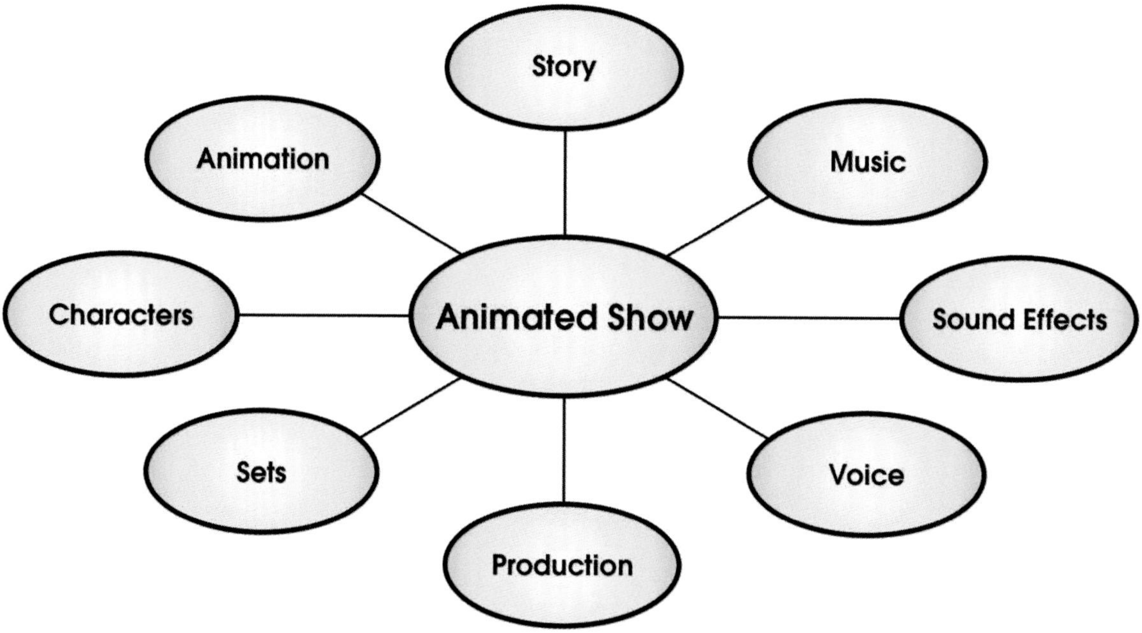
Story
Animation
Music
Characters
Animated Show
Sound Effects
Sets
Voice
Production

Bringing It All Together

So far in this book we have covered a lot about emotion in animation, from expressing emotion in characters to setting a mood in a scene. Hopefully you have picked up a few concepts that will help you with your animation. In this chapter, I want to tie everything together so you can see emotion in animation from a broader perspective.

The Audience

Learning how to have your characters express emotion is important, but it isn't the most important emotion in your animated show. The most important emotion expressed will be that experienced by your audience. Too often animators, particularly beginning animators, will focus so much on their characters and working on their animation technique that they often don't keep the most important aspect of animation at the forefront of their production. The most important aspect for any animator is the audience's experience.

The common path of development for any animator will likely involve three phases.

STEP-BY-STEP

1

The first phase an animator goes through is that of learning how to get characters and objects to move on-screen. The animator struggles with creating walk cycles, timing movements, and other basic elements of learning how to animate.

2

The second phase an animator goes through is that of learning how to go beyond simple movements and adding personality to a character's actions. The animator no longer has to worry about how to get a character to move but has moved on to learning how to make the move express a feeling. At this stage, the animator is a competent artist who could work at any number of animation houses across the country. However, mastering this second stage is not the end of an animator's development.

3

The third phase of an animator's development is that of learning how to connect and understand the audience. It is at this stage the animator is no longer satisfied with just knowing how something animates but has moved on to how the animation affects those who watch it. Just like a great actor, a great animator must connect with the audience. The animator has to know what the audience is feeling during the show and how to direct those feelings as the show progresses.

The animator's task of connecting with the audience is a lot more difficult than the theatrical stage performer who can read the audience while acting or even the movie actor who gets an immediate response from the show's director. The animator has to project himself into the role of the audience, visualizing how the scene will appear and how each character and element of the scene will unfold long before the characters and settings have been created. This type of projection requires that the animator become a student of the audience. This starts with the animator's own emotional reaction when viewing a show. Before you can understand other's emotions, you need to understand your own.

Here is a simple exercise you might want to try the next time you go to see a movie, theater, TV show, or any other form of entertainment. Bring a notepad with you and keep track of the feelings you experience while watching. This may seem to distract from the show but it is important. With each emotion think about what happened in the show that caused you to feel that emotion. Why did you laugh when you did? What caused you to feel sad? Why were you angry when you were? With each emotion, you need to re-create in your mind all of the elements that came together to cause you to feel that emotion.

Behind every emotion there are two factors that come together to cause that emotion. The first factor is personal circumstance and the second factor is a triggering event. While you may not have much control over anyone's personal circumstances, your animation can be a triggering event.

With most audiences there is really no way for you to know each individual's personal circumstances so it is best to work with those that are common among most people, like feeling love for family members or being upset when someone is unfairly punished. However, even directors of major motion pictures do everything they can to define their audiences before they start developing the script. Rather than thinking almost anyone can walk into a movie, they consider who will likely come to see their show. For example, I recently went with my wife to see a Nancy Drew movie. After the show I noticed that I was the only male in the entire theater. On the other hand, when I went to see a Disney animated movie a week later, there were a lot of males but they were mostly with their families and not by themselves. Both of these shows had target audiences and are useful studies in demographics. A target audience is a demographic group of people that the movie director and producer want their movie to appeal to.

Defining Your Audience

You are more likely to be successful appealing to an audience that you can define as having common personal circumstances than you are trying to appeal to everyone. Similar personal circumstances give you common experiences that you can work with in bringing emotion to your audience. For example, a show about an unfair teacher may bring indignation in a number of audiences, but it is likely that greater emotional response will come from those who have experienced an unfair teacher and even greater will be those who are dealing with an unfair teacher when they see the show. Therefore, a good target audience would be students who are currently attending classes because they are more likely to be having problems with teachers.

Defining your audience means that you determine what groups are likely to attend your show and search for common attributes among them. This will require you to think about to whom your show will appeal. It will also require you to think about what appeals to specific audiences. For example, what audience would a horror show appeal to? Going in the other direction, the question might be what type of show appeals to a teenage male audience?

A lot of defining an audience is common sense. Just thinking for a few minutes can narrow your target audience quite a bit. To illustrate this, let's look at the following audiences on the left and match them with a type of movie they are likely to see on the right:

Teenage Males 14-18	Classic movie remake
Teenage Females 14-18	Action racing movie
Parents of young children	Romantic comedy
Retired people 65 and older	Teen romance
Couples between 24 and 35	Animated fantasy

As you can see, it isn't hard to narrow your audience. For most beginning animators this type of common sense approach will probably be enough to get the job done. For more experienced animation directors with multi-million dollar budgets where a mistake can bring financial ruin, the common sense approach will likely not be enough.

A lot of research goes into defining audience demographics, which, unless you are a major motion picture executive, you may not have access to. However, this type of information appears quite often in the press.

A few good sources for getting specific research on audience demographics are listed here:

- http://www.medialifemagazine.com
- http://www.businessweek.com
- http://www.variety.com
- http://www.hollywoodreporter.com/hr/index.jsp
- http://www.showbizdata.com/

Understanding your audience is the mark of a great animator. Some animators come by it naturally and consider the audience in every aspect of their animation. Other animators have to work at it. Regardless of whether you are comfortable with remembering your audience while you develop your animation, it is a vital part of the animation process and should be top of mind during the development of the animation.

For larger animation studios, defining the audience in the minds of everyone on the team is critical and the job of the animation director. For smaller studios or individual animators, it is the job of all who are involved in the development of the production.

Total Production

Good animation of characters by itself does not make a great animated movie. It is only part of the many elements that must come together. You need to think of your productions as a total experience for your audiences. The diagram shown in Figure 8.1 shows eight important elements that are all part of the total experience.

For your animated production to be the very best possible, you need to pay attention to each element of the production.

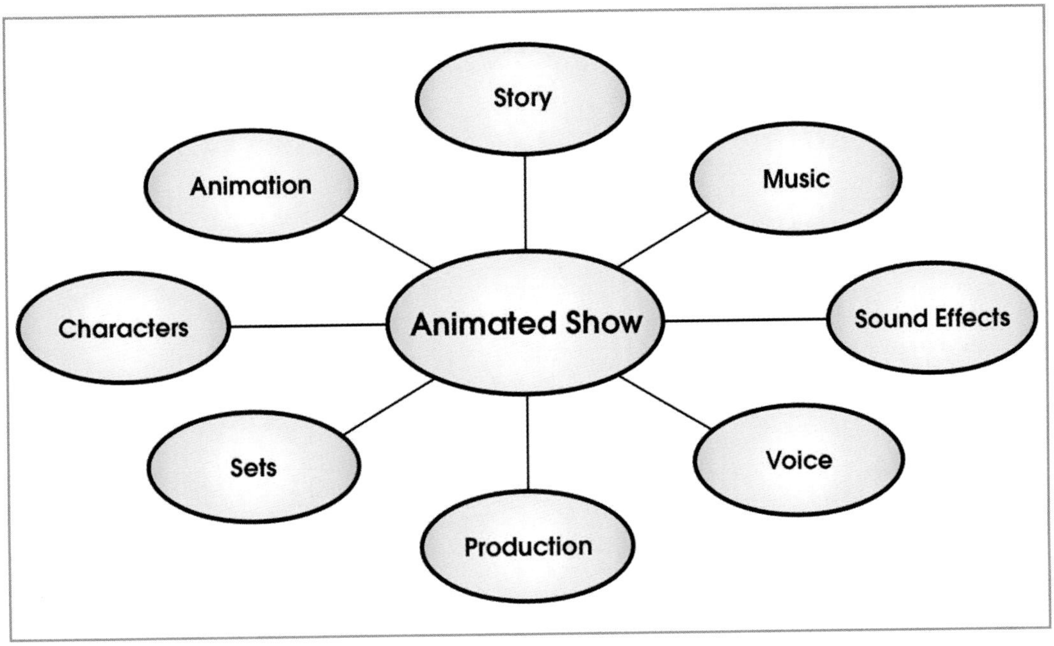

Figure 8.1 Each of these eight elements is important to the animated production.

Story

At the foundation of any animated movie is a story. For an animated project to begin it has to have a story. The story guides the rest of the production. Without a great story even the most inspiring of animation or visual effects will fall short of its full potential. Great care should be taken up-front to ensure that the story is compelling and well written. Money and effort invested early to ensure a great story will pay big dividends during the entire project.

Once you have a great story, you need to make sure that everyone on the animation team understands the story and their role in bringing the story to life.

Animation

Animation here means anything that moves on the screen whether it is an animated character or a visual effect. Every day the expectations of audiences with regard to animation are increasing. The quality of the animator's work is scrutinized more than ever before. If you want your movie to have a positive impact on the audience, then the visual quality of your animation needs to be of the highest standard you can achieve. The motion needs to look believable, the timing needs to be exact, the colors have to work, and the effects have to be convincing.

Music

A bad musical score or music that doesn't fit the show will greatly harm an animated production. Don't wait until the last minute when your budget is short to design the music for your movie. If you notice the music shelves in your local music stores, you will notice that many of those CDs are soundtracks from motion pictures. The motion picture industry learned years ago that great music has a dramatic impact on the perception of their movies. Make sure you get the very best music you can for your show.

Characters

Great character design can have a big influence on the quality of the production. The audience is most likely to identify with the character element than any other. You need to plan and develop your characters so they not only fill their assigned role but they also have qualities that resonate with the audience. Things like personality traits, idiosyncrasies, along with visual design are all important in getting that great character.

Once you've developed some of your characters, you need to put them together to see if they will work well with each other. Every character needs to fill its role. You don't want your main character overshadowed by one of the minor characters. Characters should be designed as a group so they interact well with each other. This includes not just visually but also their personalities and other character traits.

Sound Effects

Good sound effects can help a movie on several levels. To begin with, they bring believability to the animated world. We have sound around us all the time. Stop and listen and you will hear sound, most of which is unnoticed consciously but does register in our subconscious.

Sound effects can direct attention or build anticipation. The sound of approaching footsteps, for instance, will help the audience anticipate the appearance of a character.

Sound effects can be used in conjunction with the visuals in the production to progress the story and build emotion. A sequence of several odd or strange sounds in a spooky house can go a long way to setting the mood for a scene.

Sets

Sets are important to the total feeling of an animation. The set is the background on which the animation takes place. It may have ambient animation, but usually it is static art for 2D animation and a static 3D model for 3D animation. For this reason the audience typically will see it for extended periods of time without major changes. Thus, the quality of the background can make or break a show. The more time characters spend on any given set the more time the audience has to look for flaws or inconsistencies.

A good background will enhance the emotional mood of the scene while not overpowering the characters.

Voice

Voice talent will dictate much of what an animated show will become. Most of the time the voice is recorded before the characters are animated. The animator then uses the voice track to help work out the timing for the scene. The voice actors, therefore, have a huge impact on the total production.

Voice talent is critical to the emotional quality of the movie. For an expressed emotion to seem believable to the audience the voice and action need to work together. For example, if a character is to be surprised in a scene and the animator does a great job of creating a good surprise animation but the voice doesn't sound surprised, the scene will fall apart. Incongruent voice and action might work as a humorous effect, but most of the time it just feels like shoddy production to the audience.

Production

The production includes all aspects of the development of the animation, from the materials and equipment used to create the animation to the talents of the people involved in the development of the show. It is the backroom development that the audiences don't see directly, but it has a direct impact on the quality of the work produced. In a nutshell, better tools and better talent generally make better products. Every production has limited resources. The animation director is placed in the position of choosing what resources will do the job while staying within budget.

If I had a choice on any production I would choose talent over equipment. A great artist can create amazing things with a stick and mud, while great equipment without good talent to operate it will never reach its full potential. Even a great artist will need good tools to create to his or her full potential, but when the animation director has to get the most possible from a limited budget, the best option to me is to look for talent first.

Bringing It Together

I have watched and worked on a number of animated productions. Those that are truly good will excel in a few of the major elements of animation, but they are also very good in all of the others as well. If you are looking to create animation and you want to have the greatest possible emotional impact on your audience, then you have to balance all aspects and be as good as possible in each one. Think of the show as a total experience and not just characters moving on the screen.

I hope this book has helped you to better understand how to incorporate emotion into your animated productions. Emotion in animation is more than getting your characters to express emotion, it is emotion in music, sound, lighting, scenery, and most important, it is the emotion that the audience feels while viewing the animation. Keep that in mind as you develop your animation and you will be able to produce animation emotion that the audience will feel and understand.

52

APPENDIX A

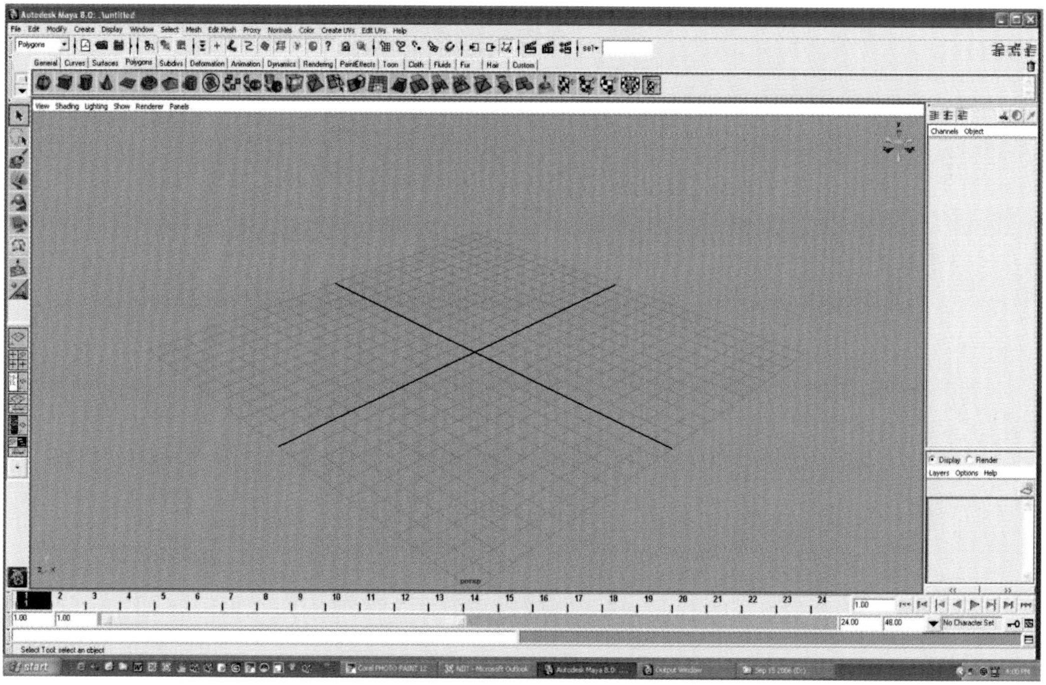

Autodesk Maya 8.0: ..\untitled
File Edit Modify Create Display Window Select Mesh Edit Mesh Proxy Normals Color Create UVs Edit UVs Help
Polygons
General Curves Surfaces Polygons Subdivs Deformation Animation Dynamics Rendering PaintEffects Toon Cloth Fluids Fur Hair Custom
View Shading Lighting Show Renderer Panels
Channels Object
Display Render
Layers Options Help
No Character Set
Select Tool: select an object

Maya Tutorial

The Maya Screen

The first look at the Maya interface can be a little overwhelming. The sheer number of menus and icons seems endless, and it would take volumes of books to explain every feature in Maya. Don't worry right now about learning every feature. The step-by-step instructions in this appendix are designed to help you understand the features of the program that are needed to create each project. As you work with Maya, you will become accustomed to the features.

Like moving to a new city, the first thing that you need to know about Maya is how the program is set up and where the essential tools are located. From there, you can move forward in creating 3D digital art. The more you use Maya, the more accustomed you will become to the tools.

Figure A.1 shows the Maya interface screen as it comes up for the first time.

The interface screen can be broken down into several component parts to help give clarity to how the program works. To help you better understand the different elements of the screen, we will go over each in detail.

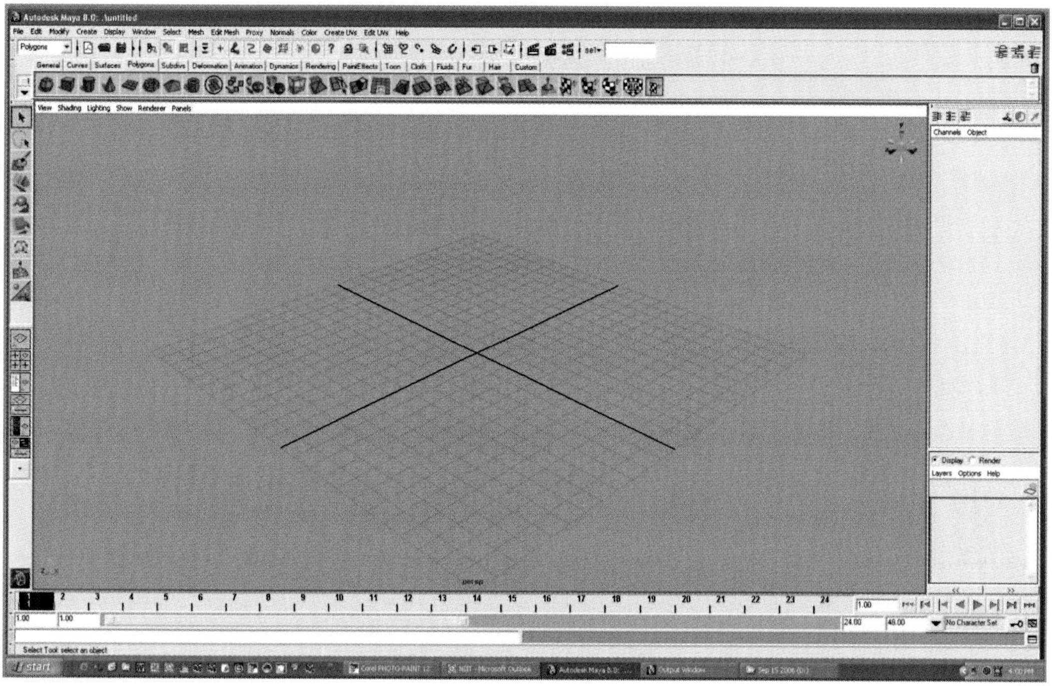

Figure A.1 The Maya interface screen has many features and options.

The Workspace

The Workspace is where most of your work will take place. It is where you will build the model, animate your characters, apply textures, and do almost everything else. Notice that it has its own menu in the upper-left corner. This menu is called the Panels menu. Figure A.2 shows the area of the screen called the Workspace.

There are a few important elements of the Workspace that you should know about. The Panels menu is used to control functions and features specific to the Workspace.

Within the Workspace is a grid with two intersecting dark lines. The point at which these two lines intersect is called the *origin*. The origin is the zero point of the X, Y, and Z axes.

In the upper-right and lower-left of the screen, there are two helpful little indicators. These are the Axis Direction Indicators.

In the bottom-center of the Workspace is the name of the camera. In Maya, you view a scene through a camera. It isn't a real camera; rather, it is a virtual camera. Imagine a director shooting a

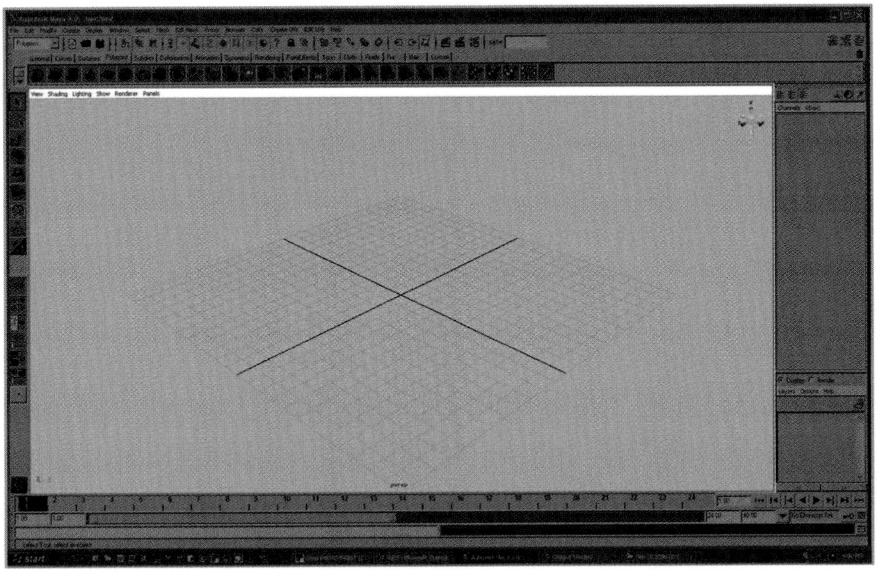

Figure A.2 The Workspace is the work area of the interface.

movie with multiple cameras looking at the scene from several different angles. The scene will look different from one camera to another, even though they may all be pointed at the same scene. Maya also has several cameras, which are called *camera views*, or just *views* for short.

Currently the Workspace has only one view. You can lay out the Workspace to have a single view or many views. Go to Layouts in the Panels menu, as shown in Figure A.3.

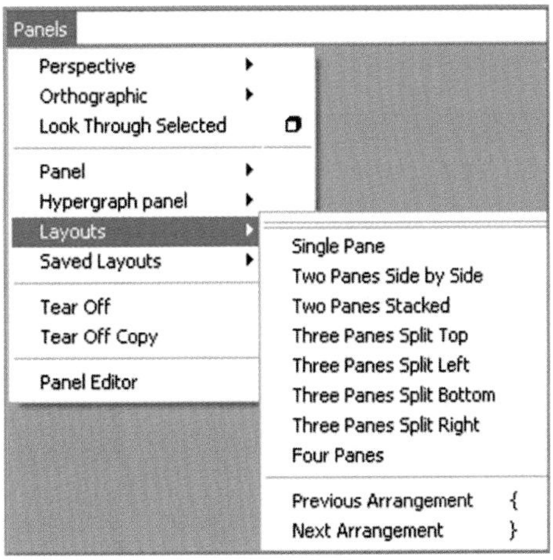

Figure A.3 There are several preset panel layouts in Maya.

Choose the layout titled Two Panes Side by Side. Notice that the Workspace now has two views, or, as they are called in Maya, *panes* (as in window panes). Experiment with some of the different layouts to see what they look like. When you are finished, go back to the Single Pane view.

Next we'll take a look at what can go in a pane. Take a look at the Panels menu, as shown in Figure A.4. Notice that the first two menu items are Perspective and Orthographic. Each menu item has a submenu. Go to Orthographic > Front. Orthographic views are like drafting views. They show the model straight on with no perspective. The Perspective views, on the other hand, show objects as if you were looking at them in real life, with perspective.

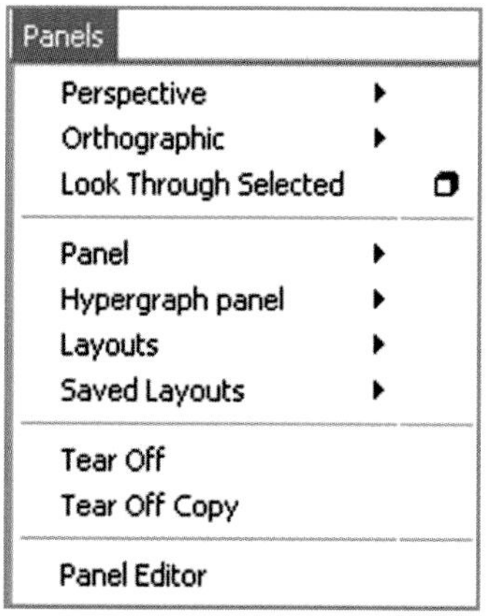

Figure A.4 Perspective and Orthographic are the two types of views at the top of the menu.

Let's create an object so you can better see how these views work. Go to the main menu (it is the one at the very top of the screen) and bring up the Create menu by clicking on it. Under Polygon Primitive, select Torus. Now change the layout to four panes, as shown in Figure A.5.

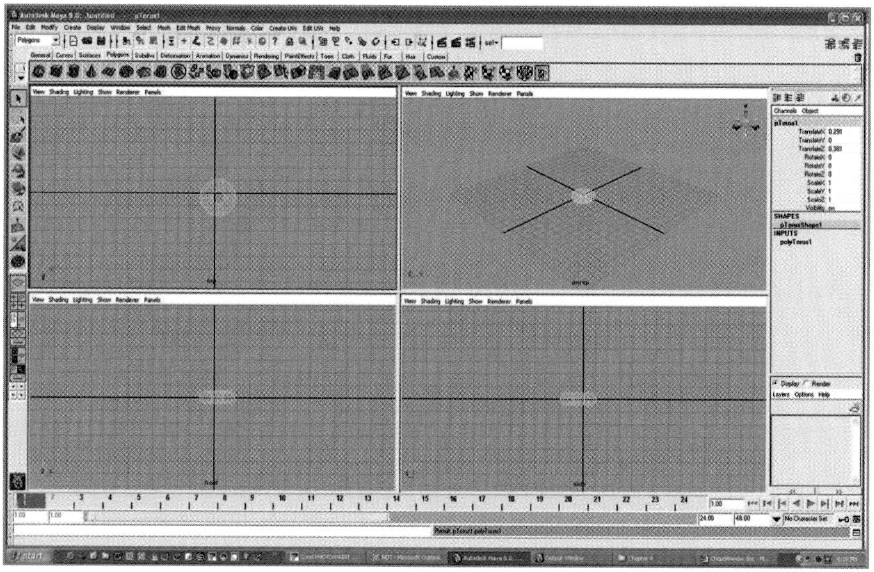

Figure A.5 Change the Workspace to four panes.

> **NOTE**
>
> When you change the Workspace to four panes, whatever view you started from will be in the upper-left pane. Because you started from the Front view, you currently have two Front views. You can change any pane to a new view from the Panels menu. There is a Panels menu for each pane.

Now that you know how to change views and layouts, let's take a look at navigating within the Workspace. Go back to the single-pane Perspective view.

Maya uses the Alt key for navigation. Press the Alt key, and then hold down the left mouse button. You will see the cursor change to two arrows, making a circle. Move the mouse around a little. Notice how easy it is to look at the torus from almost any angle. In Maya, this action is called *tumbling*.

Now press on the Alt key and hold down on the center mouse button or, if you have a wheel mouse, press and hold down the wheel. The cursor will change to a circle with four arrows extending from it. Move the mouse around. Notice that the view is now panning. In Maya, this is called *tracking*.

In addition to tumbling and tracking in the Workspace, you can also dolly. *Dolly* is an old cinematic term from when cameras were mounted on tripods with wheels so that the camera could be moved in and out of a scene. Press the Alt key and the right mouse button. Moving the mouse down or to the right will move the view into the scene, and moving the mouse up or to the left will pull back from the scene.

The Toolbox and Quick Layout Buttons

Figure A.6 highlights the area to the far left of the screen. This area houses the Toolbox and the Quick Layout buttons. The Toolbox is in the upper section of the area, and it contains model manipulation tools. An icon represents each tool.

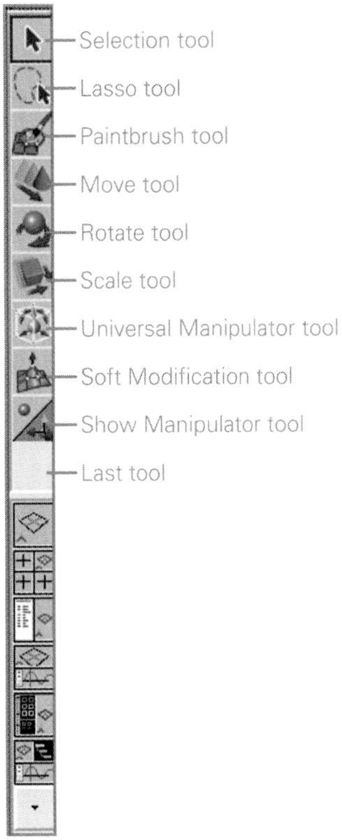

Figure A.6 This area contains the Toolbox and the Quick Layout buttons.

The lower part of the area has icons that are used to change the view layout of the Workspace.

There are 10 tools in the Toolbox; each is used to either select or modify an object or part of an object. The tools going from top to bottom are as follows:

- **Selection tool.** Use this tool to create a selection by clicking or by drawing a bounding box.
- **Lasso tool.** Use this tool to create a selection by drawing a defined area.
- **Paint Selection tool.** Use this tool to select parts of an object by painting on the object.
- **Move tool.** Use this tool to move or translate a selected object or component in the scene. In Maya, the word "translate" is used to describe the movement of an object from one location to another.
- **Rotate tool.** Use this tool to rotate a selected object or component in a scene.
- **Scale tool.** Use this tool to scale up or down in size a selected object or component.
- **Universal Manipulator tool.** This tool combines the Move, Rotate, and Scale tools into a single tool.
- **Soft Modification tool.** This tool is used to soft-modify an object. Soft modification adjusts vertices in an object similar to how a sculptor modifies a lump of clay.
- **Show Manipulator tool.** Some elements, such as lights, have their own manipulators. Clicking this tool activates the manipulator for an element.
- **Last tool.** The last tool in the Toolbox is not really a tool; rather, it holds the last tool or function used. This becomes very handy when you have a repeating function.

Below the Toolbox are the Quick Layout buttons. You can change the Workspace layout to a few widely used configurations by simply clicking on one of these buttons.

Main Menu

Figure A.7 shows the main menu. This is where many of Maya's features are located. Almost every function or tool can be found in the main menu or one of its submenus. There are several configurations of the main menu, depending on the type of work being performed. We will go over how to change the menu configuration in the next section. The first menu items are common to all menu configurations and do not change. The remaining menu items change.

Figure A.7 Many of Maya's features are located in the main menu.

Status Line

Figure A.8 shows the status line, which contains many buttons. On the far-left side of the status line is a drop-down list that you can use to configure the main menu. The available configurations are as follows:

- **Animation.** This brings up the Animation submenu.
- **Polygons.** This brings up the Polygons submenu.
- **Surfaces.** This brings up the Surfaces submenu.
- **Dynamics.** This brings up the Dynamics submenu.
- **Rendering.** This brings up the Rendering submenu.
- **Cloth.** This brings up the Cloth submenu.
- **Customize.** This allows the user to customize the menus.

The status line also contains many common functions. If you hover the cursor over any icon on the status line, a window will appear, identifying the icon. These functions are split into groups, as follows, from left to right:

- **Scene buttons.** These are used to bring up new scenes or to save and load scenes.
- **Selection Mask drop-down list.** This is used to change the selection mask so that it is easier to select a specific element in the scene.
- **Selection Mask buttons.** These are used to help with selections by masking objects of components.
- **Snap Mode buttons.** These are used for selecting different modes of snapping.
- **History buttons.** These are used to enable, disable, and access the construction history.
- **Render buttons.** These are used to render the scene and set rendering parameters.
- **Set Field Entry Mode buttons.** These are used to change the field entry.
- **Show/Hide Editors buttons.** These are used to show or hide editors and tools used to modify or manipulate objects or parts of objects. These editors appear in what is called the *sidebar*, which is the area directly to the right of the Workspace.

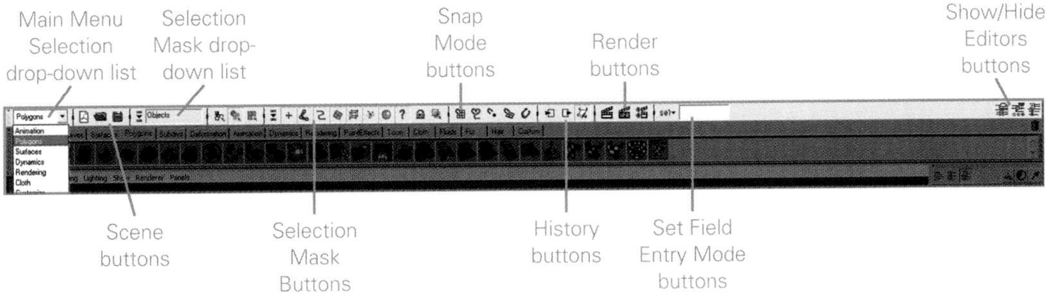

Figure A.8 The status line is directly below the main menu.

Shelves

The area shown in Figure A.9 directly below the status line is called the *shelves*. The shelves contain icons and tabs. Each tab has different icons, and each icon has a different function in Maya. The tabs are used to group functions for specific tasks.

The current tab shown in Figure A.9 is the Polygon tab. Click on a few other tabs to see how they look. You can build your own shelf if you want to. On the far left of the screen is a black down arrow. This arrow brings up several editing functions for the shelves, including the Shelf Editor.

Sidebar

Figure A.10 shows the area of the screen called the *sidebar*. This area contains several editor elements and consists of two parts. The top part is the Channel box, which is used to edit object attributes. The bottom part is the Layer Editor, which is used to edit display and render layers.

The Channel box is used often in modeling and animating 3D models. It contains entries for a number of attributes for a selected object. These attributes can be modified numerically in the Channel box. This is very helpful when you need an attribute to be a specific number. Below the attribute list in the Channel box is a history. The history contains a list of all modifications made to the object.

The Layer Editor is used to organize scene elements. It is very useful in complex scenes. For example, a city scene might be organized into roads, buildings, foliage, and vehicles. Each type of scene element is put on a different layer so the artist can make them visible or invisible by turning on or off the layer.

The Channel box and Layer Editor are not the only sidebar configurations. As stated earlier, on the right side of the status line are three icons. These three icons control the sidebar configuration. The Channel box is the icon on the right. The middle icon shows and hides the tool options, and the icon on the left shows and hides the Attribute Editor.

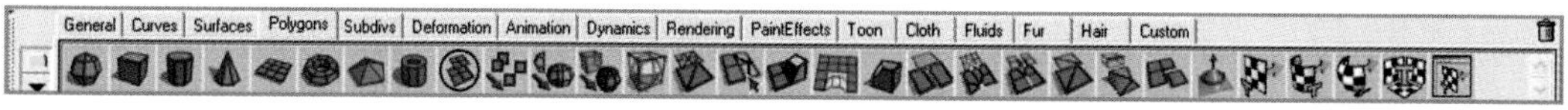

Figure A.9 The shelves contain icons that call up specific functions.

Figure A.10 The Channel box and Layer Editor are part of the sidebar.

Animation Tools

Figure A.11 highlights the lower part of the Maya screen. This is where Maya's animation tools are located. It includes the Time slider on the upper portion of the highlighted area and the Range slider on the lower portion of the highlighted area. The right side of the highlighted area contains several tools for playing and viewing animations.

Command and Message Boxes

At the bottom of the screen shown in Figure A.12 are three text windows. The one on the upper-left side of the highlighted area is the command line. This is where special scripts can be entered. The text window directly to the left of the command line is the area that shows the results of each command. Below the command line is the help line. This window is used for help messages. On the far right is an icon that brings up the Script Editor.

See, that wasn't so bad. Now that you know the basic parts of the Maya screen, it's time to put some of that knowledge to work. Click on the New Scene icon on the status line to reset the scene.

Figure A.11 Maya's animation tools are located in the lower part of the screen.

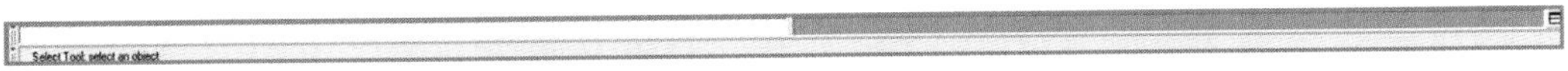

Figure A.12 The command and help lines are located at the bottom of the screen.

Having a Ball

This section is very basic, so if you have experience with 3D programs, you may want to skip it. If, however, you are new to Maya, this section will help you get started. In this section, you will learn to create a simple 3D ball.

STEP-BY-STEP

1

Create a polygonal sphere, as shown in Figure A.13. To do so, open the Create menu, choose Polygon Primitive, and click the box next to the Sphere command.

> **NOTE**
>
> The box next to the Sphere menu entry indicates that there is a dialog box associated with the function. Dialog boxes are used to change attributes or settings for the function.

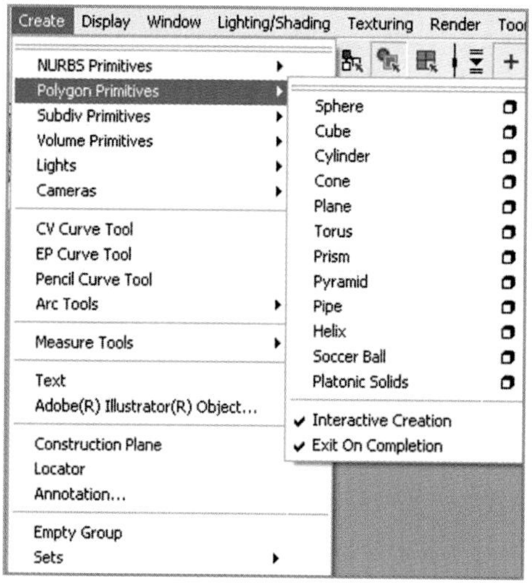

Figure A.13 Select the box next to the Sphere option.

2

The Polygon Sphere Options dialog panel will open. Change the Radius setting to 10.

3

Change the Subdivisions Around Axis and Subdivisions Along Height settings to 20.

4

Change the Axis setting to Y.

5

Change the Texture setting to Saw Tooth at Poles. The dialog box should match the one in Figure A.14.

6

Click the Create button to create the sphere; the results are shown in Figure A.15.

7

The 4, 5, and 6 keys on the keyboard control the view modes in Maya. The 4 key changes the view mode to Wire Frame; the 5 key changes the view mode to Flat Shaded; and the 6 key changes the view mode to Smooth Shaded. (The view modes can also be controlled using the View option in the Panels menu.) Press the 6 key on the keyboard to change to Smooth Shaded view; Figure A.16 shows the result.

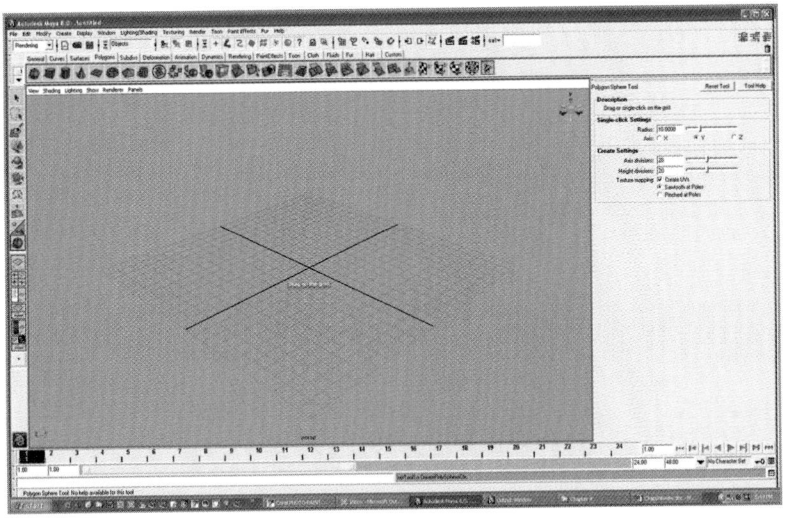

Figure A.14
Use this dialog box to set the options for creating a polygonal sphere.

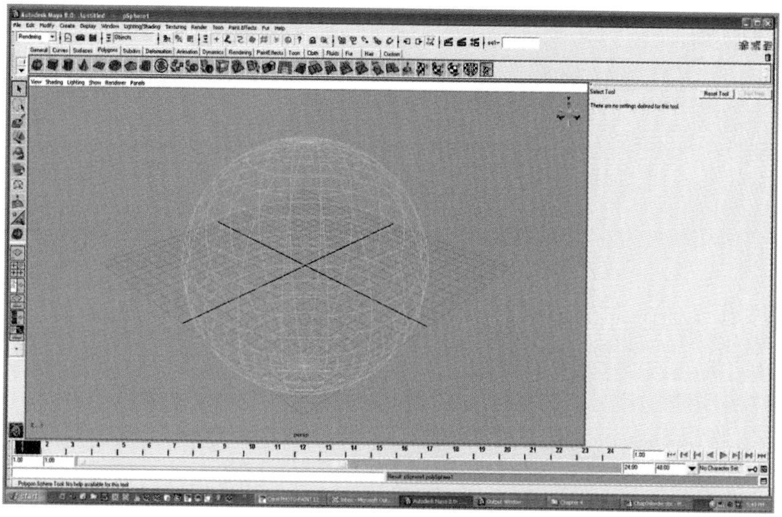

Figure A.15 The new polygonal object is now in the work area.

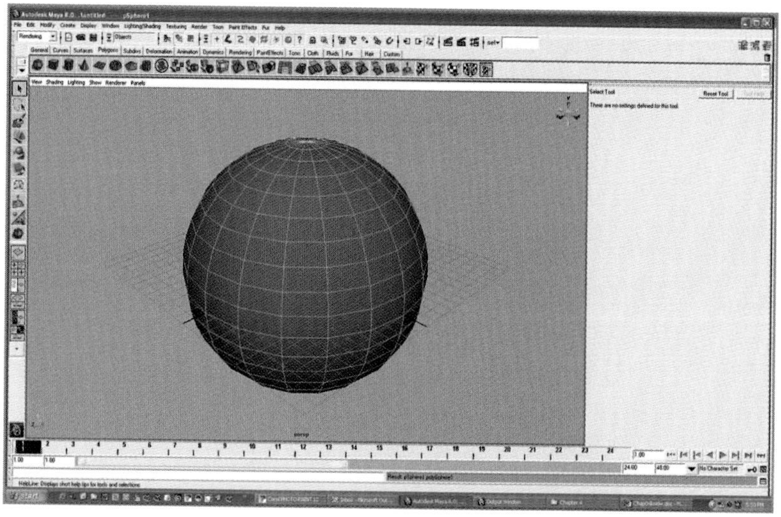

Figure A.16 Change the view mode to Smooth Shaded.

8

The next step is to change the surface of the sphere. Maya has a tool called Hypershade that is used to change the surfaces of objects. To access this tool, open the Window menu, choose Rendering Editors, and select Hypershade, as shown in Figure A.17.

9

In the Hypershade window, open the Create menu, choose Materials, and select Blinn, as shown in Figure A.18.

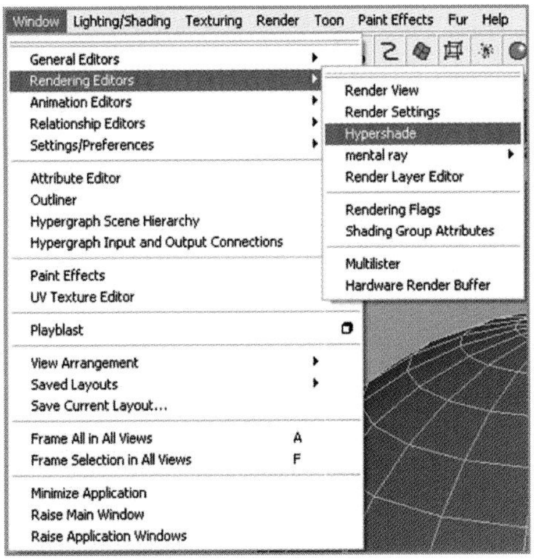

Figure A.17 Hypershade is one of the options in the Rendering Editors submenu.

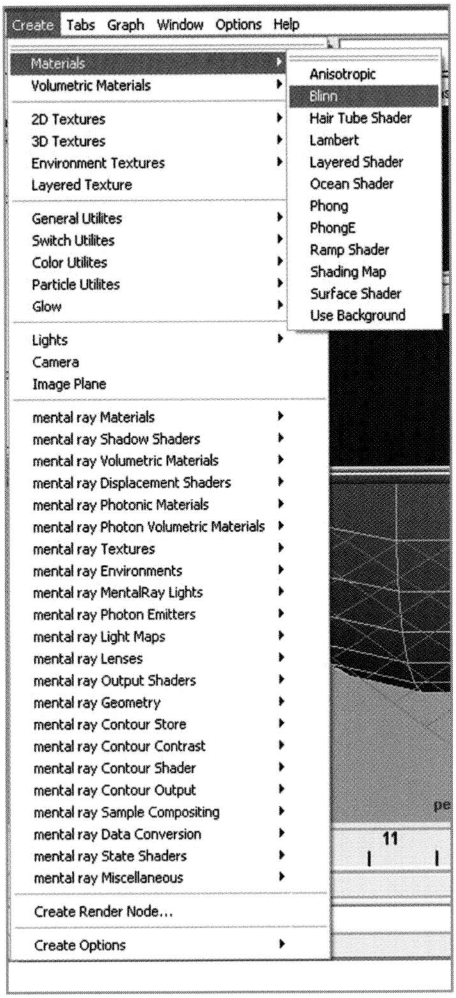

Figure A.18 Create a Blinn material.

10

Blinn materials have a number of attributes that can be adjusted to create sophisticated surfaces on 3D objects. To do so, you use the Attribute Editor. To launch the Attribute Editor, click the Attribute Editor button in the status line (it's the third button from the end). The Attribute Editor will open in the sidebar, as shown in Figure A.19.

11

Click the checkered button to the right of the Color setting in the Attribute Editor to open the Create Render Node window, as shown in Figure A.20.

12

The Create Render Node window features many choices for changing the color and texture of a material; click the Checker button. The material in the Hypershade window will assume a checkered pattern.

13

Apply the material to the sphere. To do so, select the sphere in the Workspace, right-click the new material in Hypershade to open the marking menu, and choose Apply Material to Object. The sphere now has a checkered pattern, as shown in Figure A.21.

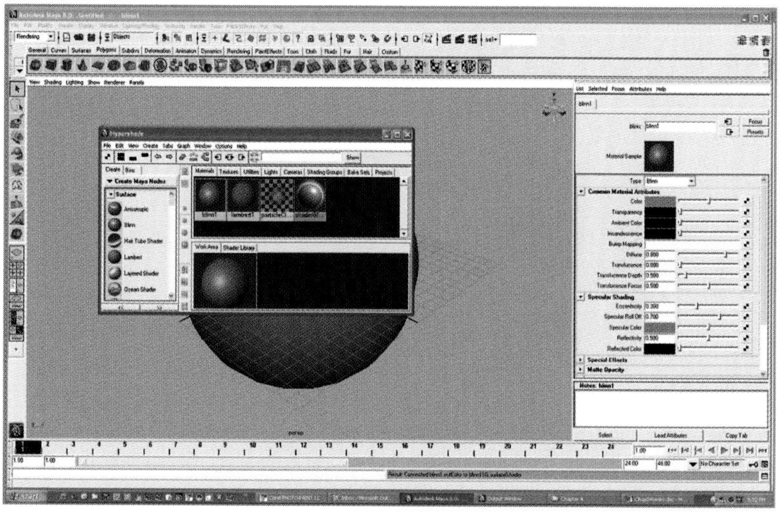

Figure A.19
Open the material's Attribute Editor.

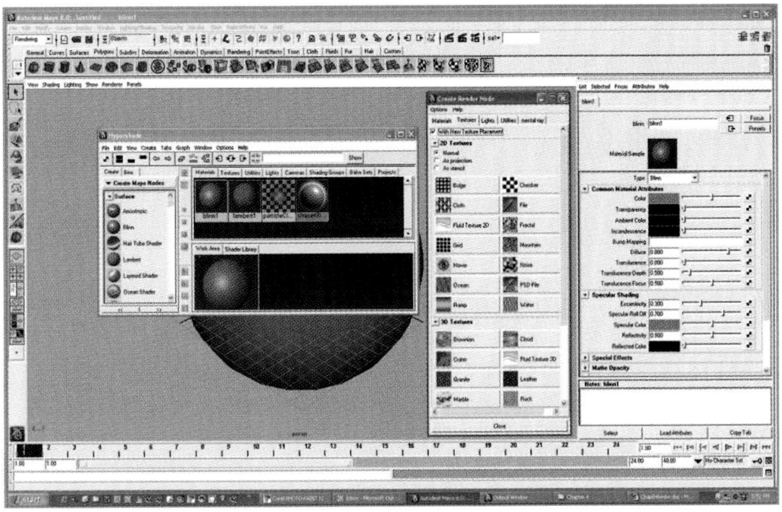

Figure A.20 Launch the Create Render Node window.

Figure A.21 Apply a new material to the sphere.

NOTE

Marking menus are floating menus in Maya that are used for quick access to common functions. You access marking menus by selecting an item and then right-clicking it. When the marking menu appears, simply drag the cursor over the desired menu item and release the mouse button.

14

Click the red X button in the upper-right corner of the Hypershade window to close it.

15

Before you progress to the next section, you need to clear the scene. To do so, click the New Scene button in the status line.

There you have it; you have created and textured your first model in Maya. That wasn't so hard, was it?

Menus

Although there are many buttons on the Maya interface, really understanding how to use the program will require an understanding of the layout of Maya's menus. This section shows how Maya's menus are arranged and how to use them. It also shows their main purposes. Because covering all the menu items in detail would be excessively boring, not all of them are covered here. Instead, you'll learn how to use Maya's menus by using them in animation projects throughout the book. In the meantime, take a moment to explore Maya's menus to get a sense of where everything is.

NOTE

If you are new to Maya, you might feel a little lost as you explore the menus because they contain many terms that may be unfamiliar. Don't worry too much about not knowing everything right now. Just use this section as a reference. You will learn most of the terms associated with the menus through the projects in the book.

Menu Layout

Grouping menu items helps to define related functions. For this reason, each menu in Maya contains groups of commands separated by lines. In the File menu (see Figure A.22), the first group contains two menu items: New Scene and Open Scene. Both are used to start a session in Maya, one by starting a new scene and the other by loading a saved scene.

> **NOTE**
>
> Notice the double line at the top of the File menu. This double line indicates that the menu is detachable. If you click this line, Maya copies the functions to a separate menu that you can place anywhere on the screen for easy access.

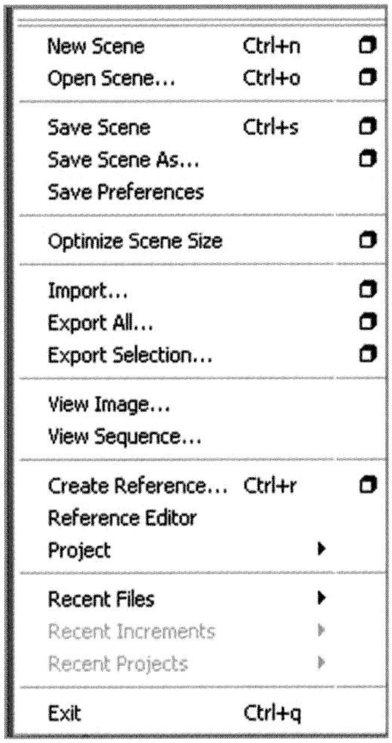

Figure A.22 The File menu is the first menu in the main menu.

Menus in Maya have four columns:

- The first column, starting from the left, is the name of the menu item.
- The second column gives a keyboard shortcut for the menu item. The keyboard shortcut, or *hotkey*, enables you to access the function through the keyboard. You can see from the File menu that Ctrl+N is the keyboard shortcut for the New Scene command. This means that instead of clicking the New Scene button or selecting New Scene from the File menu, you can simply press Ctrl+N to create a new scene.
- The third column contains arrows. These indicate that if you select the menu item, a submenu will appear. For example, selecting the Project menu item from the File menu reveals a submenu. You can then slide your cursor over the submenu and select one of the items it contains.

✎ The fourth column indicates whether the menu item has a dialog box associated with it. If a box icon is present in this column, it means that selecting the box will launch a dialog box or panel, which you use to adjust settings for the menu function. For example, click the box icon next to the New Scene menu item, and the dialog box shown in Figure A.23 will appear. As shown, the settings in this dialog box relate to setting up new scenes.

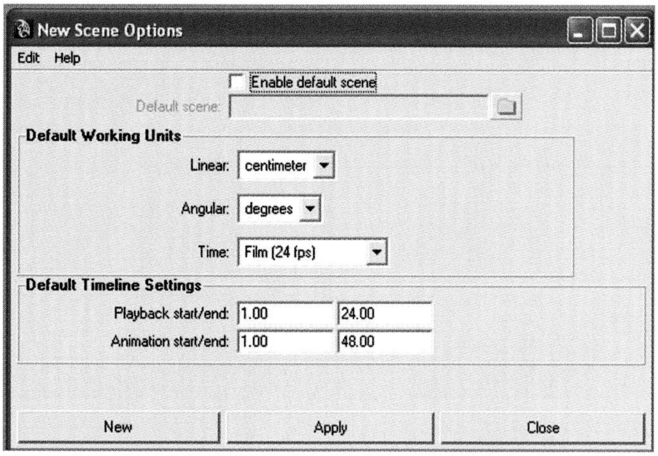

Figure A.23 The New Scene dialog box.

Many dialog boxes, including the New Scene dialog box, are divided into sections. For example, the first section of the New Scene dialog box is for setting up custom new scenes. This is useful if you want to start every new scene with specific settings, such as a particular background or specialized geometry. The second section of the New Scene dialog box lets you customize your default working units. By default, centimeters are used, which is fine for small objects but becomes a problem if you are building, say, a diesel truck. Angles can be set to degrees or radian. The Time setting relates to animation and has a long list of options depending on the end target for your scene. Currently Time is set for film animation. The third section of the New Scene dialog box lets you customize the length of the playback and the total number of frames in the animation. At the bottom of most dialog boxes, including the New Scene dialog box, are three buttons: Now, Apply, and Close. Clicking the Now button activates the function with the current settings and closes the dialog box. Clicking the Apply button activates the function with the current settings, but leaves the dialog box open, which is useful if you need to apply the function multiple times. The Close button closes the dialog box without activating the function. For now, close the New Scene dialog box, and let's continue our tour of the menus.

NOTE

Dialog boxes are available via the menu, but not via hotkeys or onscreen buttons. Hotkeys and buttons are useful if you want to perform a function, but you don't need to change any settings first.

Common Main Menu Options

As shown in Figure A.24, there are seven common menus in the main menu, plus a series of menus that vary depending on which option is selected in the drop-down list on the status line.

> **NOTE**
>
> Some menu items that follow may not appear on the Maya PLE version. This is because these menu items are only in the Maya Unlimited version of the software. They are included here to give you an idea of the full capabilities of the software.

From left to right, these common menus are as follows:

- **File.** The File menu contains functions dealing with files, projects, importing, and exporting.
- **Edit.** The Edit menu contains functions dealing with basic editing, selecting, grouping, and parenting operations.
- **Modify.** The Modify menu contains functions dealing with modifying geometry or other scene elements.
- **Create.** The Create menu contains functions dealing with the creation of scene elements, such as geometry, lights, curves, and text.
- **Display.** The Display menu contains functions dealing with on-screen display elements, including objects, components, and interfaces.
- **Window.** The Window menu contains functions dealing with the many editors and tools in Maya.
- **Help.** The Help menu contains functions dealing with online help, tutorials, references, and product information.

Figure A.24 The common menus in the main menu.

The Animation Menu Options

When Animation is selected from the drop-down list on the status line, the main menu features six Animation menu items (see Figure A.25).

From left to right, they are as follows:

- **Animate.** The Animate menu contains functions dealing with keys, clips, and paths.
- **Deform.** The Deform menu contains functions dealing with high-level tools used to manipulate low-level components.
- **Skeleton.** The Skeleton menu contains functions dealing with the creation and editing of joints, as well as animation helpers.
- **Skin.** The Skin menu contains functions dealing with attaching geometry to skeletal systems.
- **Constrain.** The Constrain menu contains functions dealing with setting limits or constraints on animated objects.
- **Character.** The Character menu contains functions dealing with the creation and editing of characters.

The Polygon Menu Options

When Polygons is selected from the drop-down list on the status line, the main menu features eight Polygons menu items (see Figure A.26).

From left to right, they are as follows:

- **Select.** The Select menu deals with selection options for polygon objects and components.
- **Mesh.** The Mesh menu deals with modifying polygon objects.
- **Edit Mesh.** The Edit Mesh menu deals with editing polygon object components.

Figure A.25 The Animation menu set includes six menu items.

Figure A.26 The Polygons menu set includes eight menu items.

- **Proxy.** The Proxy menu is for creating and editing a polygon proxy for subdivision surface models.
- **Normals.** The Normals menu is used for editing polygon normals.
- **Color.** The Color menu is used to edit vertex color on polygon objects.
- **Create UVs.** The Create UVs menu contains functions for applying and editing UVs on polygon objects.
- **Edit UVs.** The Edit UVs menu contains functions for editing UVs once they have been placed on an object.

The Surfaces Menu Options

Surface menu options control the building of objects using NURBS and subdivision surfaces. There are four main menu items in the Surfaces submenu, as shown in Figure A.27.

From left to right, they are as follows:

- **Edit Curves.** The Edit Curves menu contains functions dealing with editing and modifying curves
- **Surfaces.** The Surfaces menu contains functions dealing with creating and editing surfaces.
- **Edit NURBS.** The Edit NURBS menu contains functions dealing with NURBS modeling and NURBS editing.
- **Subdiv Surfaces.** The Subdiv Surfaces menu deals with building and editing subdivision surfaces.

The Dynamics Menu Options

When Dynamics is selected from the drop-down list on the status line, the main menu features seven Dynamics menu items (see Figure A.28).

From left to right, they are as follows:

- **Particles.** The Particles menu contains functions dealing with the creation and editing of particles
- **Fluid Effects.** The Fluid Effects menu contains functions for creating and editing fluid effects.
- **Fields.** The Fields menu contains functions dealing with the creation of fields.
- **Soft/Rigid Bodies.** The Soft/Rigid Bodies menu contains functions dealing with the creation and editing of soft and rigid body objects.

Figure A.27 The Surfaces menu set includes four menu items.

Figure A.28 The Dynamics menu set includes seven menu items.

- **Effects.** The Effects menu contains functions dealing with the creation of specialized effects, such as fire or lightning.
- **Solvers.** The Solvers menu contains functions dealing with a collection of specialized solutions for dynamics animation.
- **Hair.** The Hair menu contains functions for creating and editing hair effects.

The Rendering Menu Options

When Rendering is selected from the drop-down list on the status line, the main menu features six Rendering menu items (see Figure A.29).

From left to right, they are as follows:

- **Lighting/Shading.** The Lighting/Shading menu contains functions dealing with editing materials and lights.
- **Texturing.** The Texturing menu contains functions dealing with 3D paint, PSD, texture referencing, and NURBS texture application.
- **Render.** The Render menu contains functions dealing with the rendering of scenes.
- **Toon.** The Toon menu contains functions dealing with Maya's Toon Shader.
- **Paint Effects.** The Paint Effects menu contains functions dealing with creating paint effects.
- **Fur.** The Fur menu contains functions for creating and editing fur.

Figure A.29 The Rendering menu set includes six menu items.

The Cloth Menu Options

The Cloth menu set, as shown in Figure A.30, is used for controlling cloth effects in Maya. Cloth is an advanced feature only available in Maya Unlimited.

The Cloth menu contains three menu items, listed from left to right as follows:

- **Cloth.** The Cloth menu contains functions for creating and defining cloth objects.
- **Constraints.** The Constraints menu contains menu items used to constrain the movement and reaction of cloth objects.
- **Simulation.** The Simulation menu contains solvers and other tools for simulating the effects of cloth objects.

Figure A.30 The Cloth menu set includes three menu items.

APPENDIX B

Image Gallery

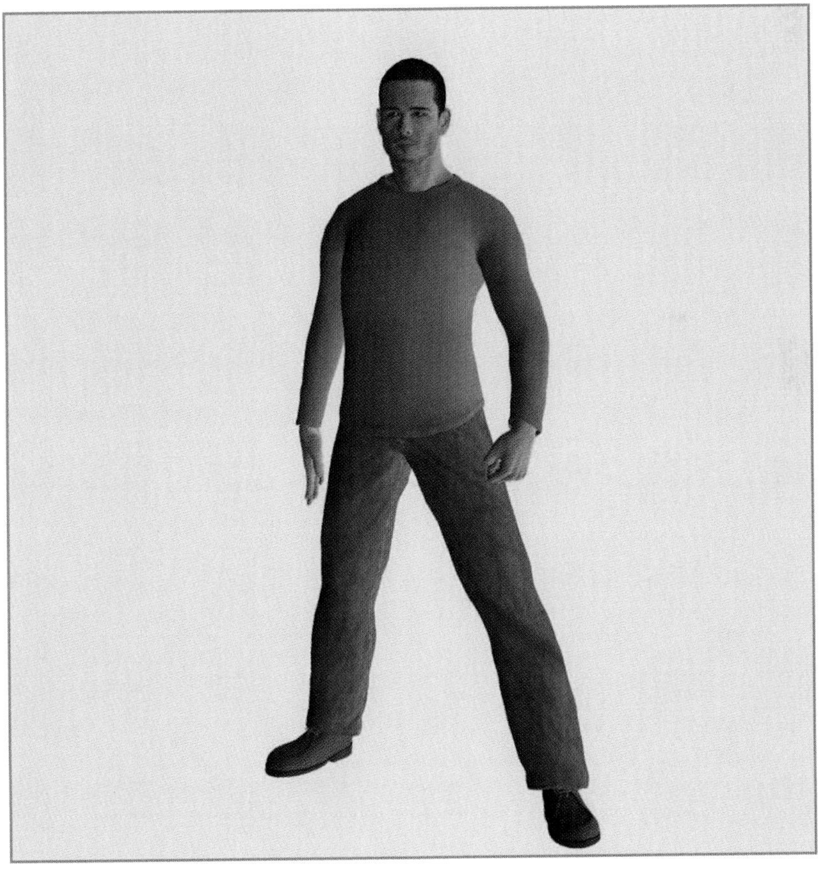

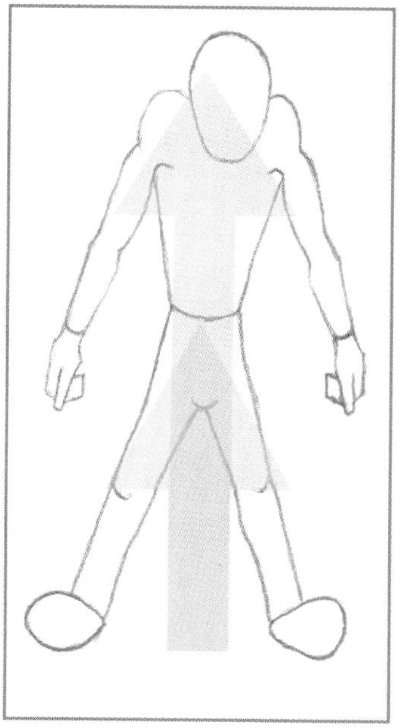

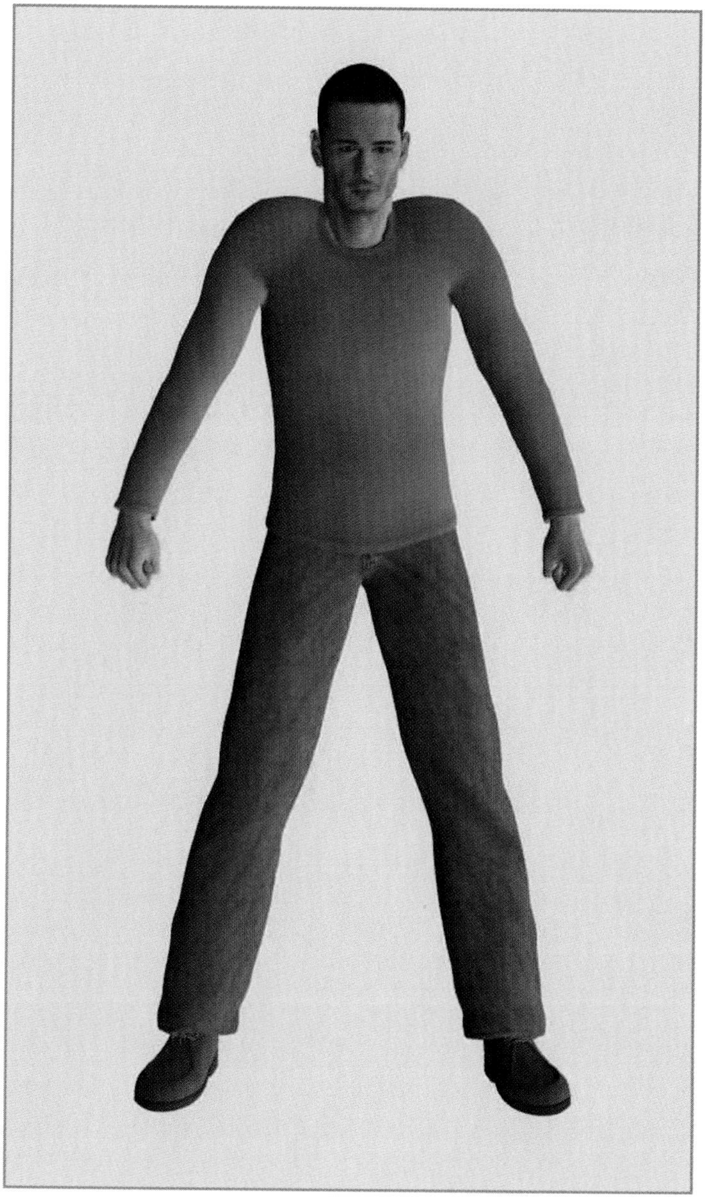

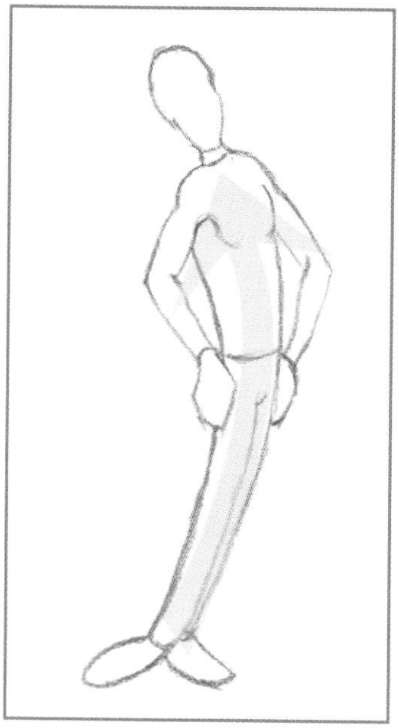

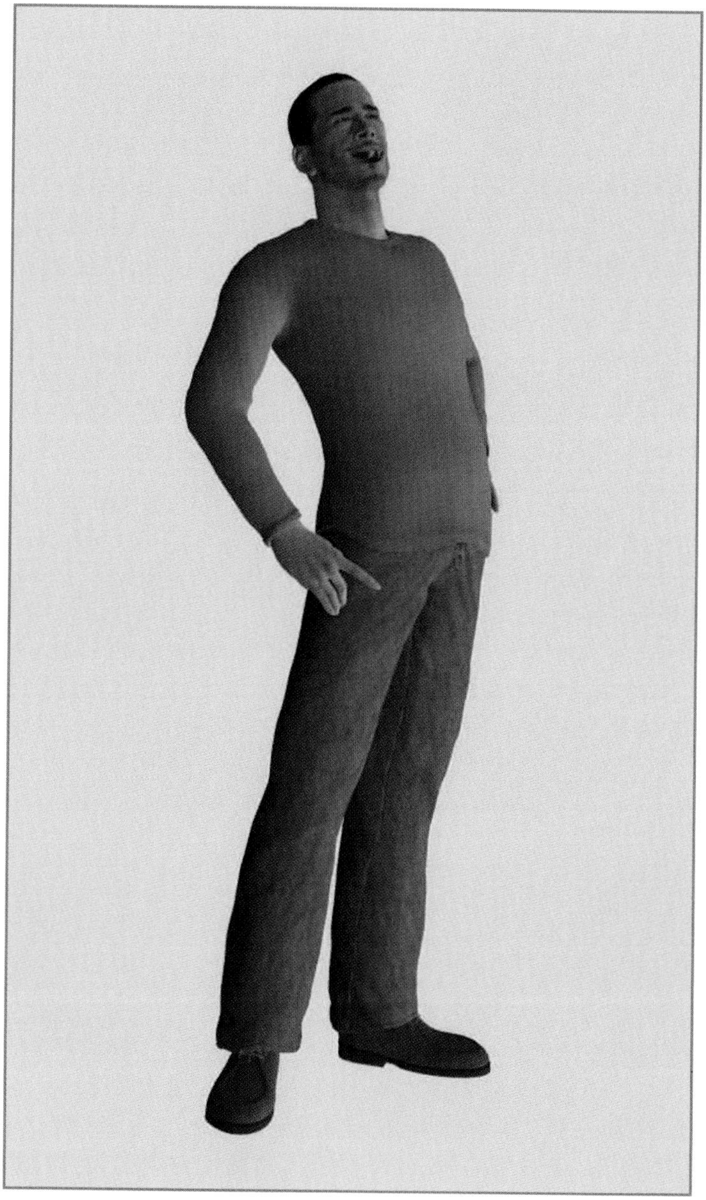

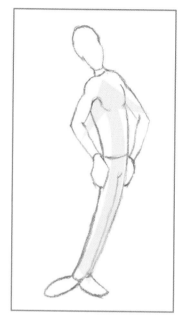

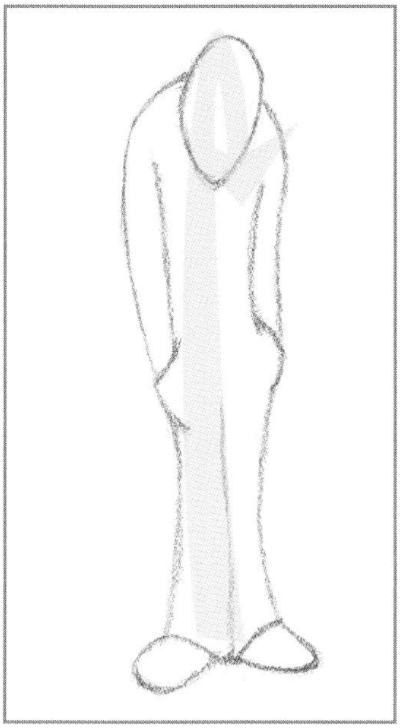

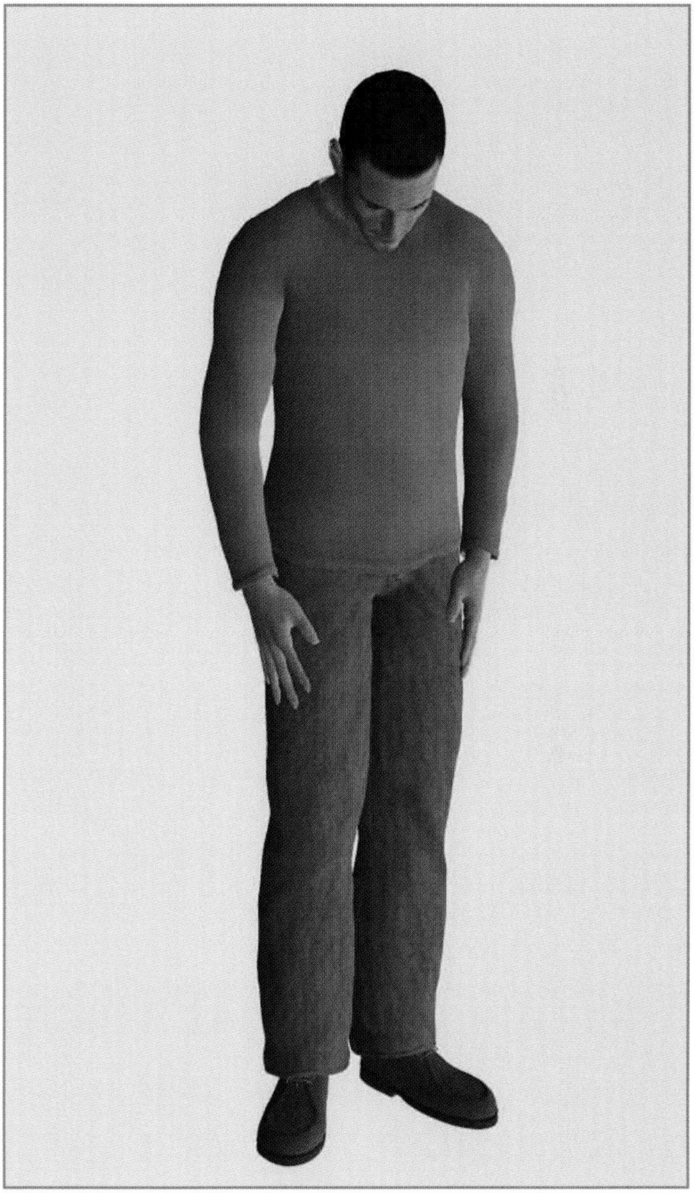

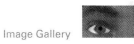

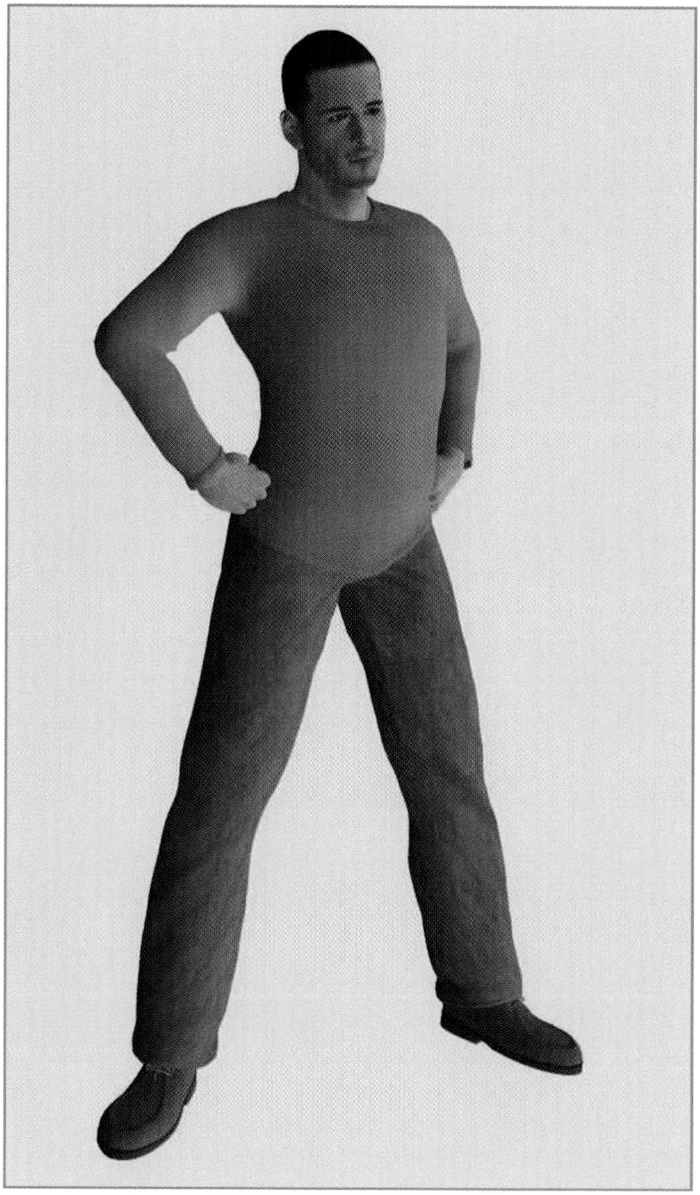

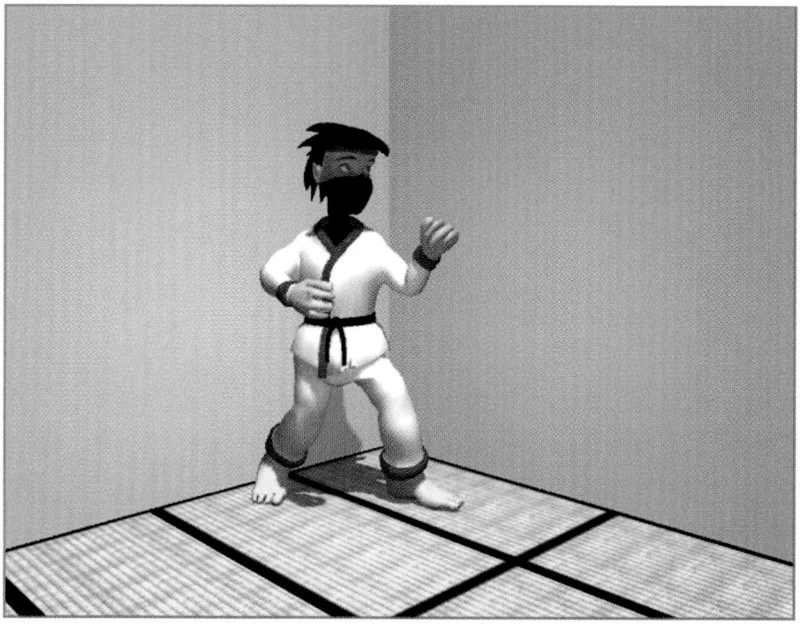

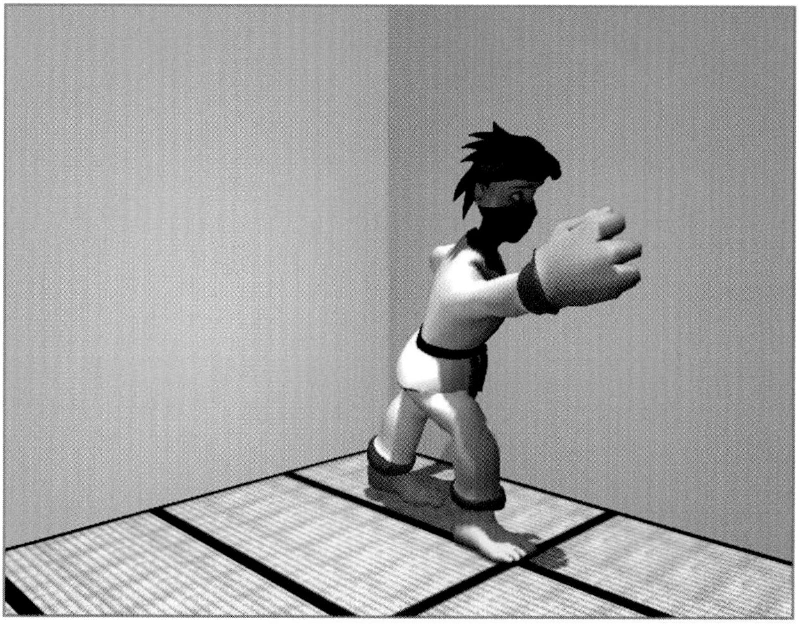

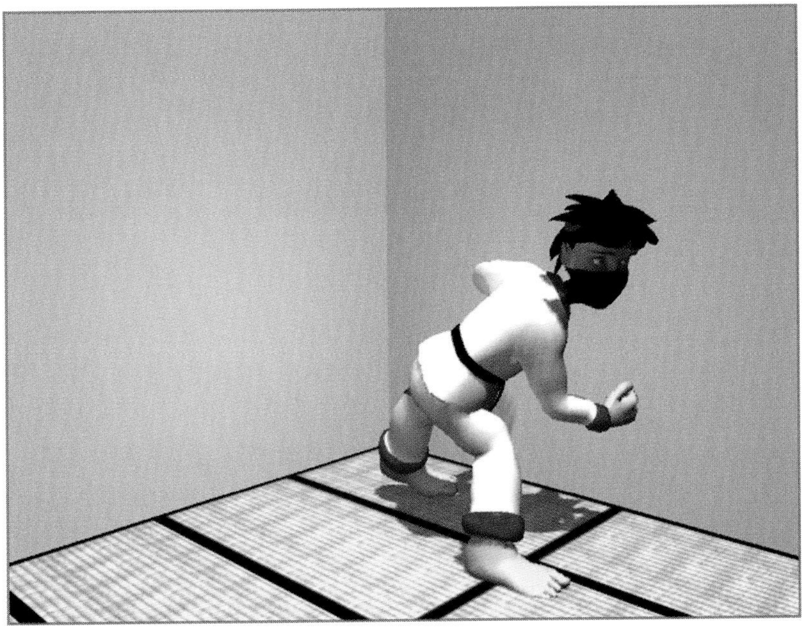

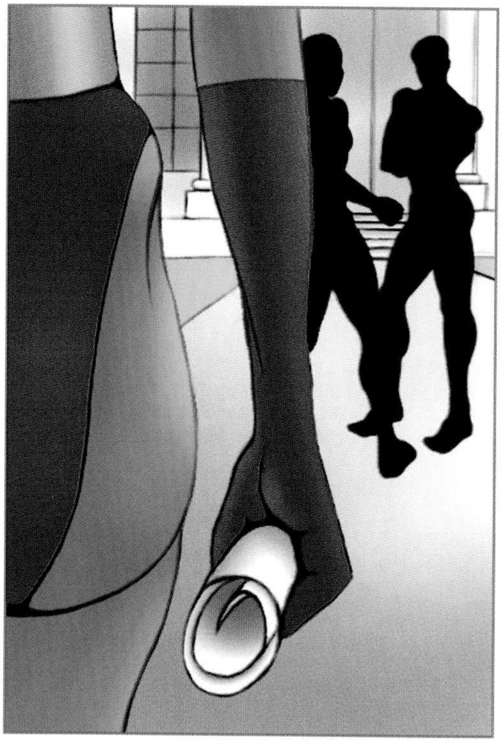

52

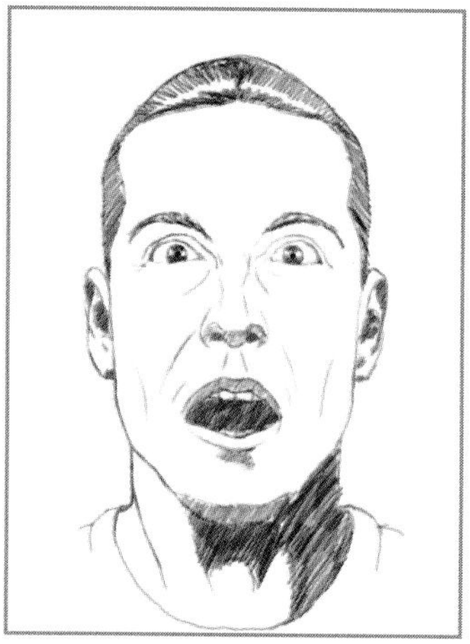

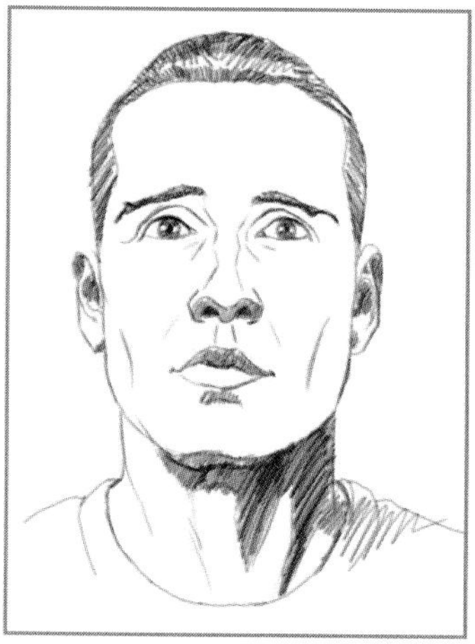

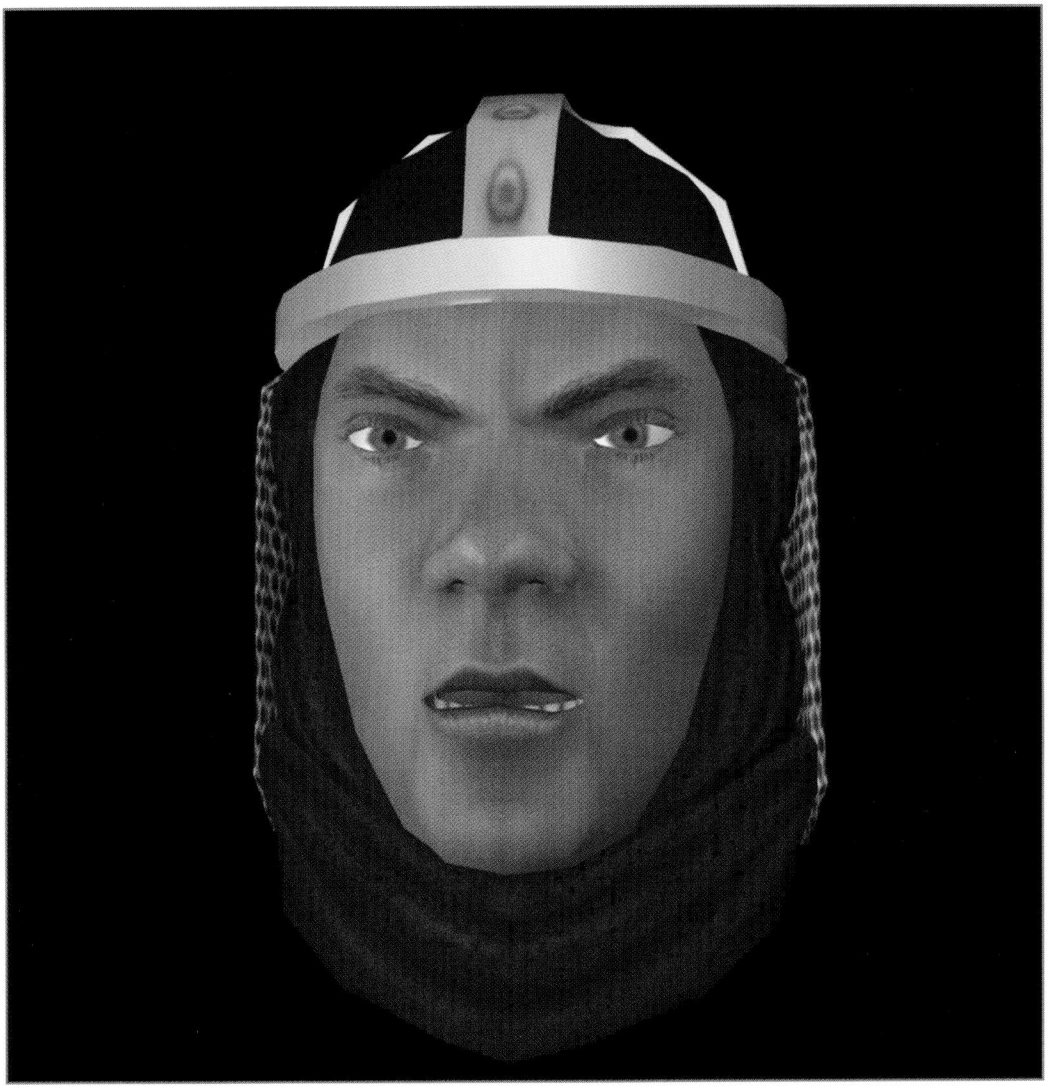

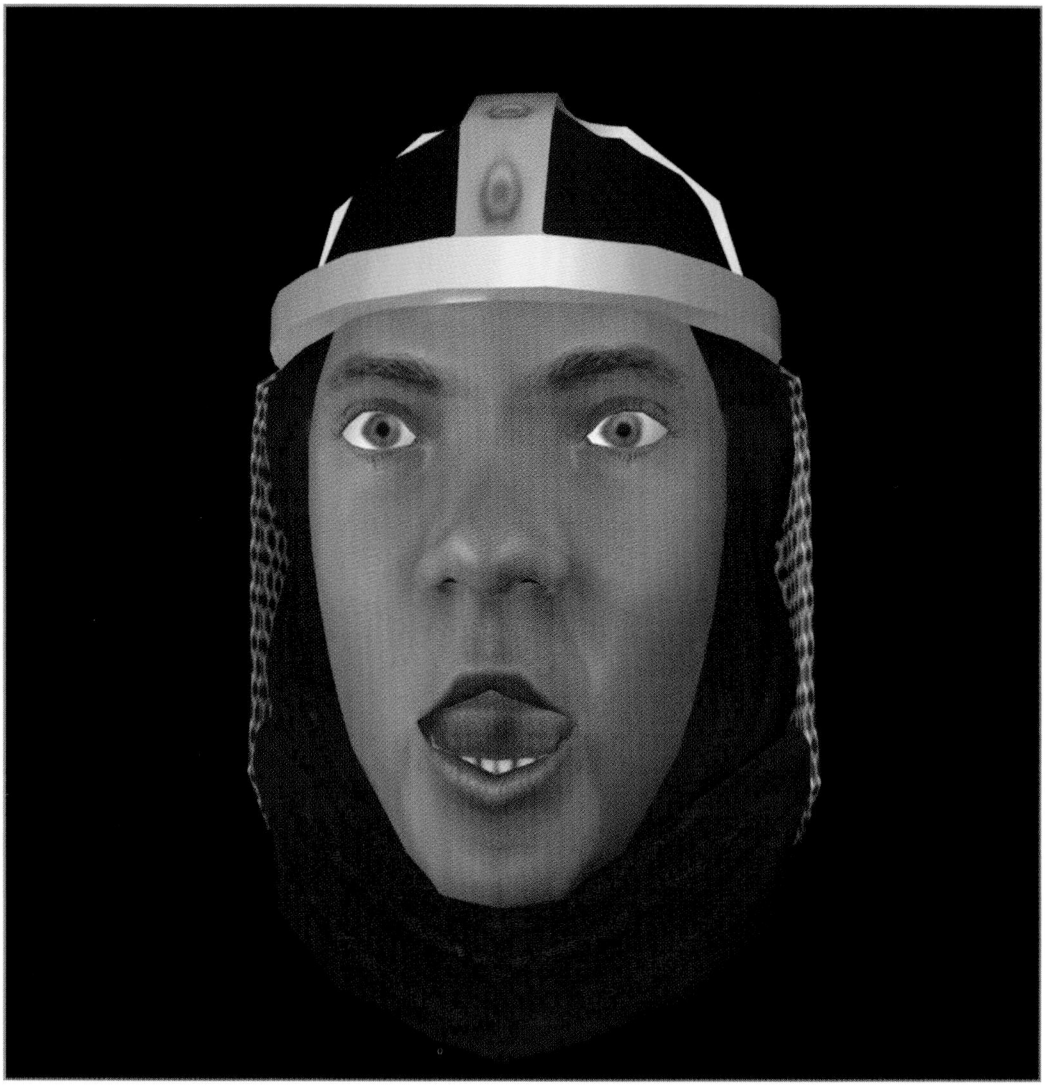

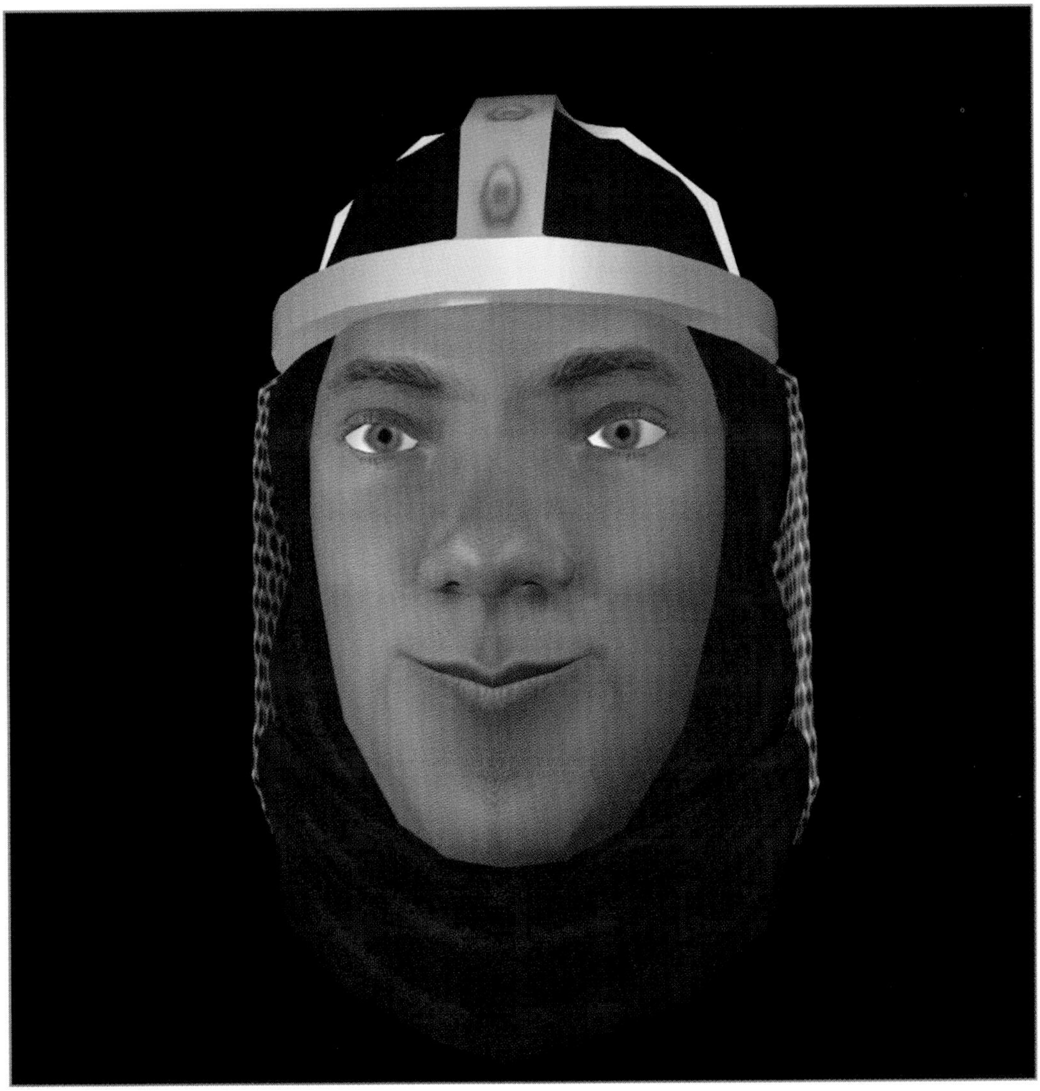

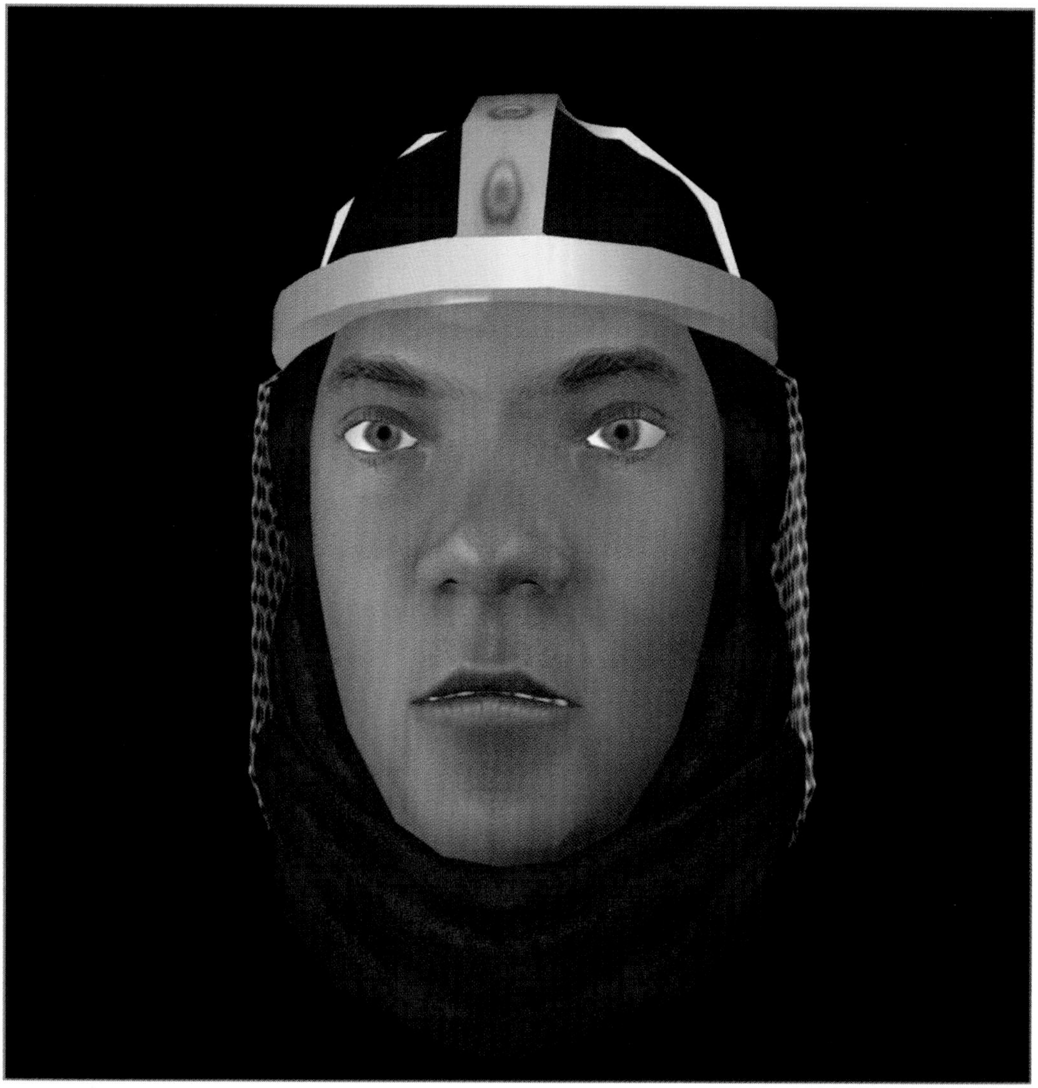

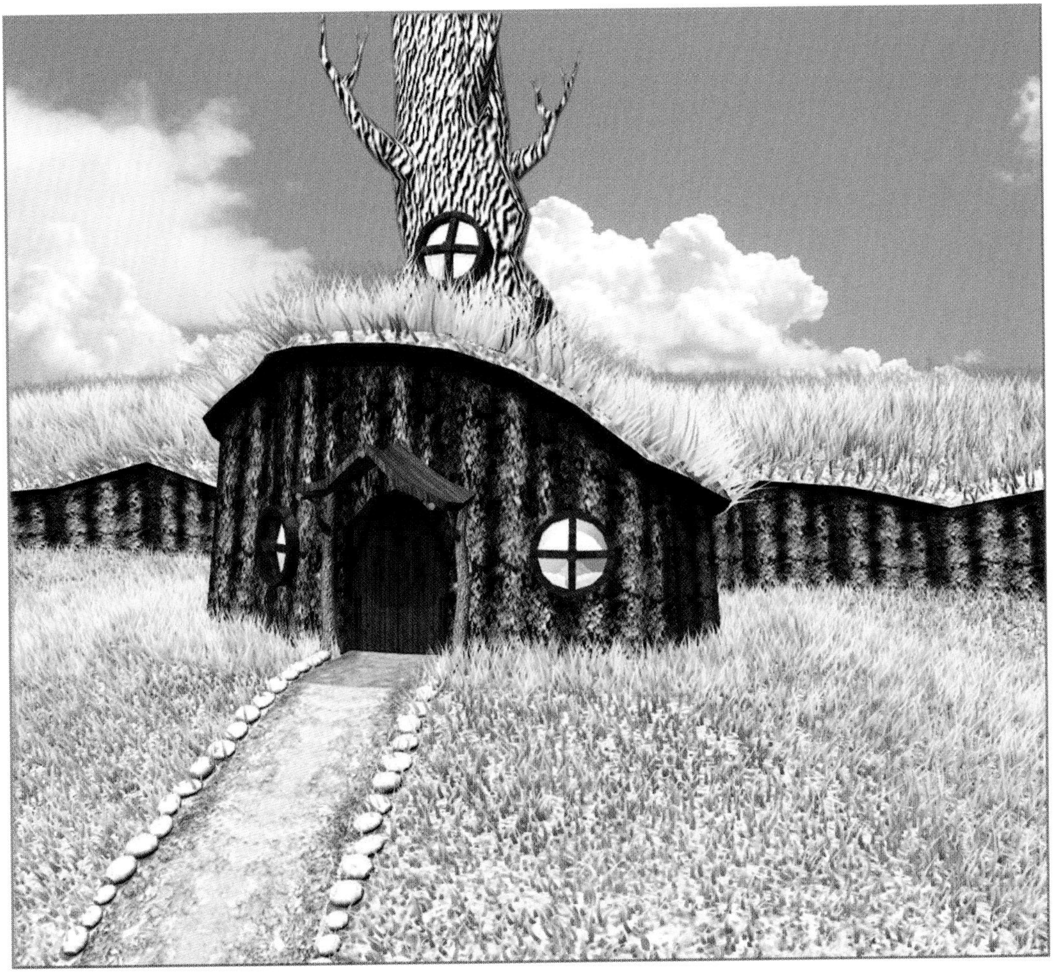

INDEX

A

acting and body language, 14
action line, 60
camera angle and, 59
for exaggerated motion, 52–53
actors, animators as, 3
adjusting skin weights, 95–113
Alt key, Maya, 201
ambient sound, 142
anger
body language showing, 24
as dramatic effect, 139
emotional state, animating, 43–45
facial expressions, 71
real life expressions, 66
Animate menu, Maya, 216
Animation configuration, Maya, 203
animation in total production, 192
Animation menu, Maya, 216
anticipation
reaction, animating, 31
surprise and, 34
arrogance, body language showing, 26–27
Attribute Editor, Maya, 210
audience
connecting with, 188–189
defining, 190–191
websites on researching, 191
audio. *See* music; sound effects
authoritarian posture, 26–27
Autodesk Maya and Autodesk 3ds Max Side-by-Side, 72

B

background artists, 136
balance composition, 54–55
ball, creating, 206–212
bashful characters, 33
binding head, 92–95
bird's eye view, 61
Blinn material, 181, 210
blue color scheme, 57
body language, 13–27
acting and, 14
anger, 24
animating, 15–16
arrogance, 26–27
fluency in, 14
happiness, 25–26
sadness, 26
surprise, 25
bones, 75–77
of head, 68–69
Brush option for skin weights, 100
building phase of reactions, 31

C

camera angle
abrupt changes in, 59
action line and, 59
different view, cutting to, 58–59
as dramatic technique, 141
exaggeration of, 49, 58–61
storyboards showing, 129
camera movement, 58–59
as dramatic technique, 141
carefree emotion, 5
Character menu, Maya, 216
character rigging. *See also* joints
facial rigging, 78–92
joints and bones, 75–77
mouth, rigging, 86–92
characters
contrast and, 135
and environment, 134–137
expressions, 142
lighting of, 137
perspective and, 134–135
placement, 56
storyboards showing, 129
style of, 136
in total production, 193
cheeks, 68–69
polygons around, 74–75
chin
exaggeration of, 49–50
skin weights for, 103, 106

Cloth configuration, Maya, 203
Cloth menu, Maya, 219
color
  and composition, 57
  contrasts in, 57, 136
  exaggeration in, 57
Color menu, Maya, 217
Component Editor, 96–99
composition
  balance in, 54–55
  character placement in, 56
  color and, 57
  contrast in, 54–55
  exaggeration in, 49, 54–57
  focal point, 57
confident pose, 16
Constraints menu, Maya, 219
continual interaction, 126–128
contrast
  characters and, 135
  in color, 57, 136
  in composition, 55–56
  of emotions, 6–7
  exaggeration of, 48, 56
  motion and, 135
  in story timing, 130
cool color schemes, 57
Corel Painter, 10
Create menu, Maya, 215
Create Render Node window, Maya, 210–211
Create UVs menu, Maya, 217
Customize configuration, Maya, 203

D

daydreaming, 5
Deform menu, Maya, 216
degrees of emotion, 2
dialog boxes, Maya, 206, 214
dialogue
  dividing scenes for, 123
  as dramatic technique, 143
Disney
  Fantasia, 14
  Pinocchio, 137
Display menu, Maya, 215
distortion
  exaggeration by, 48, 53–54
  subtle variations, 54
dividing scenes, 123–124
Dr. Seuss movies, 138
drama, creating, 143
dramatic effect, 137–140
  anger, 139
  fear, 139
  humor, 138
  interest, creating, 140
  intrigue, 140
  sentiment, 138
  surprise, 139
  suspense, 138
dramatic technique, 140–143
  camera movement, 141
  dialogue, 143
  expression, 142
  lighting as, 142
  music, 143
  sound as, 142
  timing, 141
Duplicate Joints function, Maya, 83
Dynamics configuration, Maya, 203
Dynamics menu, Maya, 217–218

E

Edit Curves menu, Maya, 217
Edit menu, Maya, 215
Edit Mesh menu, Maya, 216
Edit NURBS menu, Maya, 217
Edit UVs menu, Maya, 217
editing tools, Figure Artist, 18
Effects menu, Maya, 218
eFrontier. *See* Figure Artist; Poser
emotional body, 24–27
emotional states, 30
  anger, animation of, 43–45
  animating, 33–45
  fear, animation of, 39–42
emotional transitions, 29–45
environment, 133. *See also* textures
  background objects, creating, 157–167
  characters and, 134–137
  dramatic effect, 137–140
  exaggeration of, 49, 61–63
  3D set, creating, 144–156
  in total production, 193

exaggeration, 47–63
of camera angle, 49, 58–61
on camera movement, 60
in character placement, 56
in color, 57
in composition, 49, 54–57
of contrast, 48, 56
by distortion, 53–54
of emotion, 8
of happiness, 25
of key reaction phase, 32
of many elements, 51
methods for, 48
of motion, 52–53
multiple exaggerations, 63
of music, 49, 63
of physical traits, 49–51
purpose of, 48
of settings, 49, 61–63
of sound, 49, 63
types of, 48–49
excitement, 7
expression, 2
as dramatic technique, 142
external timing, 123–128, 130–131
continual interaction, 126–128
figure interaction, 124–128
interaction points, 124–126
scenes, dividing, 123–124
Extract feature, 167
eyebrows, joints for, 81–82
eyes
binding, 95
exaggeration of, 49–50
joints for, 81–82
polygons for, 73
skin weights for, 103–105

F

facial expressions, 65–113
anger, 71
binding and, 95
bones and, 75–77
fear, 71
influence, adding, 75–77
joints and, 75–77
muscles controlling, 69–71
polygons, working with, 72–75
in real life, 66–67
rigging, 78–92
3D animation of, 72–75
worry, 72
***Fantasia*, 14**
fear
as dramatic effect, 139
emotional state, animating, 39–42
facial expressions, 71
Fields menu, Maya, 217
Figure Artist
arm, raising, 22–23
for body language, 15–16
key frames in, 24
library, using, 20–24
parameter dials in, 20
selecting in, 19
standing pose folder, 21
tools in, 18–20
using, 17–24
File menu, Maya, 213, 215
FlipBook, 10
fluency in body language, 14
Fluid Effects menu, Maya, 217
focal point, 57
forehead, polygons for, 72–73
frames
counts, 124
dividing scenes, 123–124
frontal bone, 68–69
frontalis muscles, 69–71
polygons following, 73
frowns, muscles controlling, 71
frustration, 4
Fur menu, Maya, 218

G

***Game Character Animation All in One*, 72**
gnome house set, creating, 144–156
grass, creating, 169–171

H

Hair menu, Maya, 218
happiness, body language showing, 25–26
hard binding, 92
head. ***See also*** **facial expressions**
  binding, 92–95
  bones of, 68–69
  joints, 79
  muscles of, 69–71
  understanding of, 67–72
Help menu, Maya, 215
History buttons, Maya, 203
horizon line, 134–135
hotkeys, Maya, 213
humor, 138
Hypergraph utility, 91, 94–95

I

influence, 75–77
intensity of reactions, 31
interaction of figures, 124–128
interaction points, 124–126
interest, creating, 140
internal timing, 116–122, 130
  for personality, 122
  smooth animations, 119
  story timing compared, 130
intrigue, 140
inverse kinematics (IK) handles, 88–92

J

jaw, 68–69
  joints for, 79
  skin weights for, 103, 105
Jaws**, 63**
jerky camera movement, 59
joints, 75–77. ***See also*** **mirroring joints**
  binding, 92–95
  for eyes, 81–82
  head joints, 79
  mouth, rigging for, 86–92
  moving joints, 84–85
  naming, 82
  for sides of mouth, 79–80
  for tongue, 79–80
  views for, 83
joy, body language showing, 25–26

K

key frames
  in Figure Artist, 24
  in Poser, 34
key reactions, 32
  for surprise, 34
kicking motion, exaggeration of, 52–53

L

Lambert material, 145, 168
Lasso tool, Maya, 202
Last tool, Maya, 202
let down phase, 32
  for surprise, 34
library in Figure Artist, 20–24
lighting
  of characters, 137
  as dramatic technique, 142
Lighting control, Figure Artist, 18
Lighting/Shading menu, Maya, 218
line of action. ***See*** **action line**
linear perspective, 134–135
lips. ***See*** **mouth**

M

Main menu, Maya, 202
mandible. ***See*** **Jaw**
manipulation tools, Figure Artist, 18
marking menus, Maya, 212
masseter muscles, 70–71
  polygons following, 74–75
maxillary bond, 68
Maya, 9
  adjusting skin weights in, 95–113
  Alt key, use of, 201
  Animation menu options, 216
  animation tools, 205

ball, creating, 206–212
Cloth menu options, 219
command boxes, 205
common menu options, 215
Component Editor, 96–99
configurations in, 203
dialog boxes, 206, 214
dolly, 201
Duplicate Joints function, 83
Dynamics menu options, 217–218
for facial expressions, 72
functions in, 203
hotkeys, 213
layout of menus, 213–214
Main menu, 202
marking menus, 212
menus in, 212–219
message boxes, 205
Mirror Joint function, 83
Paint Skin Weights feature, 99–113
Panels menu, 198, 200
Polygon menu options, 216–217
Quick Layout button, 201–202
Rendering menu options, 218
screen, 197–198
shelves, 204
sidebar, 204
skinning in, 92–95
status line, 203
Surfaces menu options, 217
3D set, creating, 144–156
Toolbox, 201–202
tracking, 201
tumbling, 201
tutorial, 197–219
UV system, 167–177
Workspace, 198–201

Mesh dictionary, 167

Mesh menu, Maya, 216

middle nasal concha, 68

Mirror Joint function, Maya, 83

mirroring joints, 83–85
mouth, rigging for, 87

mirrors, 2–3

Modify menu, Maya, 215

momentum, laws of, 120–122

mood and color, 57

motion. ***See also*** **camera movement; timing**
character placement and, 56
contrast and, 135
exaggeration of, 48, 52–53
joints, 84–85
laws of, 120–122
Newton's first law of motion, 120–121
Newton's second law of motion, 121
Newton's third law of motion, 121–122
pass frames and, 117–118
physics of, 120–122

motion blur, 59

mouth
inverse kinematics (IK) handles, animation with, 88–92
polygons around, 74–75
rigging, 86–92
sides of mouth, joints for, 79–80
skin weights for, 106–109

Move tool
Figure Artist, 18
Maya, 202

muscles of head, 69–71

music
as dramatic technique, 143
exaggeration of, 49, 63
in total production, 192

N

names for joints, 82

nasal bone, 68

New Scene dialog box, Maya, 214

Newton's first law of motion, 120–121

Newton's second law of motion, 121

Newton's third law of motion, 121–122

Normals menu, Maya, 217

nose
exaggeration of, 49–50
skin weights for, 103

O

observation, 4
orbicularis oculi muscles, 69–72
orbicularis oris muscles, 74–75
Outliner, naming joints in, 82

P

pain, 5
Paint Effects menu, Maya, 218
Paint Selection tool, Maya, 202
Paint Skin Weights feature, 99–113
Panels menu, Maya, 198, 200
parietal bone, 69
Particles menu, Maya, 217
pass frames, 117–118
personality, internal timing for, 122
perspective, characters and, 134–135
physical aspect, exaggeration of, 48
physical traits, exaggeration of, 49–51
physics, laws of, 120–122
Pinocchio, 137
pirate figure, exaggeration in, 50
Pixar movies, 136
placement of characters, 56
Planar Mapping tool, Maya, 168, 181
platysma muscles, 70–71
Polygon menu, Maya, 216–217
polygon plane, creating, 145
Polygon Primitive tool, Maya, 206
Polygon Sphere Options dialog, Maya, 207
polygons
- head, animation of, 72–75
- splitting, 153

Polygons configuration, Maya, 203
Poser, 8–9
- anger, animation of, 43–45
- for body language, 15–16
- fear, animation of, 39–42
- key frames in, 34
- surprise reaction, animating, 34–38

practicing emotion, 2
production, 191–194
proud posture, 26–27
Proxy menu, Maya, 217
purpose of exaggeration, 48

Q

Quick Layout button, Maya, 201–202

R

reactions, 30
- animating, 30–32
- anticipation, 31
- building phase of, 31
- distortion of, 54
- key reaction phase, 32
- let down phase, 32
- for surprise, 34

red color scheme, 57
Render buttons, Maya, 203
Render menu, Maya, 218
Rendering configuration, Maya, 203
rigging. *See* character rigging
rigid binding, 92
risorius muscles, 70–71
rocks, adding texture to, 178
Rotate Edit tool, Figure Artist, 18–19
Rotate tool
- Figure Artist, 18–19
- Maya, 202

S

sadness, body language showing, 26
Scale tool, Maya, 202
Scene buttons, Maya, 203
scenes. *See also* composition; environment
 dividing, 123–124
 interaction points, 124–126
seeing emotion, 2
Select menu, Maya, 216
selecting in Figure Artist, 19
Selection Mask drop-down list, Maya, 203
Selection tool, Maya, 202
sentiment, 138
Set Field Entry Mode buttons, Maya, 203
settings. *See* environment
shortcut keys, Maya, 213
Show/Hide Editors buttons, Maya, 203
Show Manipulator tool, Maya, 202
sidebar, Maya, 204
Simulation menu, Maya, 219
Skeleton menu, Maya, 216
sketch template, removing, 161
Skin menu, Maya, 216
skin weights, 95–113
 Brush option, 100
 Component Editor, 96–99
 Paint Skin Weights feature, 99–113
 vertices, fixing, 110–111
sky background, 183
smooth binding, 92
Snap Mode buttons, Maya, 203
Soft Modification tool, Maya, 202
Soft/Rigid Bodies menu, Maya, 217
software, 8–10
Solvers menu, Maya, 218
sound effects. *See also* music
 as dramatic technique, 142
 exaggeration of, 49, 63
 in total production, 193
spacing
 internal timing and, 116
 timing and, 117–120
speed of action and personality, 122
Split Polygon tool, 153
staging. *See* external timing
states. *See* emotional states
story timing, 128–131
 and emotion, 128–129
 planning story, 129–130
 in total production, 192
storyboards, 129
style guides, 136
style of character, 136
Subdiv Surfaces menu, Maya, 217
subtle elements, 6–7
Surfaces configuration, Maya, 203
Surfaces menu, Maya, 217
surprise
 body language showing, 25
 as dramatic effect, 139
 emotional state, animating as, 34–38
suspense, 138

T

teeth, 68
 binding, 93–94
temporal bone, 68–69
textures
 model, adding to, 167–177
 preparation for, 167
 scene objects, texturing, 177–183
Texturing menu, Maya, 218
thoughtful pose, 16
3D animation, 8
 background objects, creating, 157–167
 of facial expressions, 72–75
 learning, 45
 set, creating, 144–156

Tidwell, Mike, 72
timing, 115–131
  continual interaction, 126–128
  as dramatic technique, 141
  external timing, 123–128
  figure interaction, 124–128
  incorrect timing, 117
  internal timing, 116–122
  Newton's first law of motion, 120–121
  Newton's second law of motion, 121
  Newton's third law of motion, 121–122
  pass frames and, 117–118
  for personality, 122
  physics, laws of, 120–122
  spacing and, 117–120
  story timing, 128–130
tongue
  joints for, 79–80
  skin weights for, 106
Toolbox, Maya, 201–202
Toon menu, Maya, 218
total production, 191–194
triangularis muscles, 70–71
turbosquid.com, 72
2D animation, 8
  learning, 45

U

Universal Manipulator tool, Maya, 202
UV system, 167–177

V

View Selected feature, 157
voice talent, 194

W

warm color schemes, 57
websites
  audience research sites, 191
  turbosquid.com, 72
weighting facial expressions, 95–113
weights. *See* skin weights
Window menu, Maya, 215
Woody, 30
Workspace, Maya, 198–201
worried facial expression, 72

X

X sheets, 33

Y

yellow color scheme, 57

Z

ztran tool, Figure Artist, 18
zygomasticus muscles, 70–71
zygomatic bone, 68–69

License Agreement/Notice of Limited Warranty

By opening the sealed disc container in this book, you agree to the following terms and conditions. If, upon reading the following license agreement and notice of limited warranty, you cannot agree to the terms and conditions set forth, return the unused book with unopened disc to the place where you purchased it for a refund.

License:
The enclosed software is copyrighted by the copyright holder(s) indicated on the software disc. You are licensed to copy the software onto a single computer for use by a single user and to a backup disc. You may not reproduce, make copies, or distribute copies or rent or lease the software in whole or in part, except with written permission of the copyright holder(s). You may transfer the enclosed disc only together with this license, and only if you destroy all other copies of the software and the transferee agrees to the terms of the license. You may not decompile, reverse assemble, or reverse engineer the software.

Notice of Limited Warranty:
The enclosed disc is warranted by Thomson Course Technology PTR to be free of physical defects in materials and workmanship for a period of sixty (60) days from end user's purchase of the book/disc combination. During the sixty-day term of the limited warranty, Thomson Course Technology PTR will provide a replacement disc upon the return of a defective disc.

Limited Liability:
THE SOLE REMEDY FOR BREACH OF THIS LIMITED WARRANTY SHALL CONSIST ENTIRELY OF REPLACEMENT OF THE DEFECTIVE DISC. IN NO EVENT SHALL THOMSON COURSE TECHNOLOGY PTR OR THE AUTHOR BE LIABLE FOR ANY OTHER DAMAGES, INCLUDING LOSS OR CORRUPTION OF DATA, CHANGES IN THE FUNCTIONAL CHARACTERISTICS OF THE HARDWARE OR OPERATING SYSTEM, DELETERIOUS INTERACTION WITH OTHER SOFTWARE, OR ANY OTHER SPECIAL, INCIDENTAL, OR CONSEQUENTIAL DAMAGES THAT MAY ARISE, EVEN IF THOMSON COURSE TECHNOLOGY PTR AND/OR THE AUTHOR HAS PREVIOUSLY BEEN NOTIFIED THAT THE POSSIBILITY OF SUCH DAMAGES EXISTS.

Disclaimer of Warranties:
THOMSON COURSE TECHNOLOGY PTR AND THE AUTHOR SPECIFICALLY DISCLAIM ANY AND ALL OTHER WARRANTIES, EITHER EXPRESS OR IMPLIED, INCLUDING WARRANTIES OF MERCHANTABILITY, SUITABILITY TO A PARTICULAR TASK OR PURPOSE, OR FREEDOM FROM ERRORS. SOME STATES DO NOT ALLOW FOR EXCLUSION OF IMPLIED WARRANTIES OR LIMITATION OF INCIDENTAL OR CONSEQUENTIAL DAMAGES, SO THESE LIMITATIONS MIGHT NOT APPLY TO YOU.

Other:
This Agreement is governed by the laws of the State of Massachusetts without regard to choice of law principles. The United Convention of Contracts for the International Sale of Goods is specifically disclaimed. This Agreement constitutes the entire agreement between you and Thomson Course Technology PTR regarding use of the software.